Quicken for Contractors

Karen Mitchell   Jim Erwin

Craig Savage   Rex Underwood

Craftsman Book Company
6058 Corte del Cedro / P.O. Box 6500
Carlsbad, CA 92018

Quicken for Contractors

© 1998 Craftsman Book Company

Editor-in-Chief:	Laurence D. Jacobs
Production Manager:	Karen Sheffield
Interior Design:	Emil Ihrig, Helios Productions
Page Composition:	Sybil Ihrig, Helios Productions
Cover Design:	John Wincek
Proofreader:	Deborah O. Stockton

Library of Congress Cataloging-in-Publication Data

Quicken for contractors / by Karen Mitchell . . . [et al.].
      p. cm.
    Includes index.
    ISBN 1-57218-043-9
    1. Building--Estimates--Data processing. 2. Quicken. I. Jones
-Mitchell, Karen.
TH437.Q53   1998
692'.5'02855369--dc21
                           97-46798
                            CIP

© 1998 Craftsman Book Company

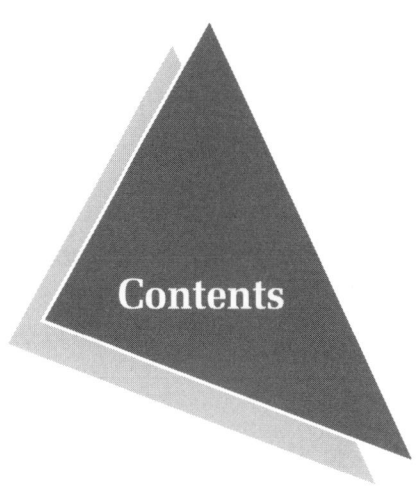

Contents

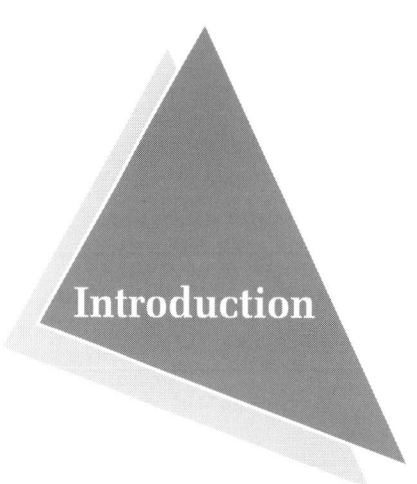

Quicken is truly a good fit for the construction office. If you are a contractor, builder, or remodeler, you have much to gain by using this software tool to help manage your business finances. But Quicken has been created for generic financial use, which means you have to customize it to reflect the business practices commonly used in the construction field. That's why we've written this book and provided the accompanying diskette—to give construction professionals like you the tools to tailor Quicken to your special needs.

Why You Should Buy This Book

Buying this book signals your ongoing commitment to improve the management and operation of your construction business.

Unless you're a contractor or builder who has the good fortune of being the only game in town, you're forced to deal with the realities of surviving and prospering in a competitive marketplace. Tougher quality standards and a smarter buying public place ever-increasing demands on builders and contractors. It is this competition that determines the price at which your product or services will sell, not you. You do, however, have a great deal of control over what it costs to produce and deliver your product or services. Controlling your costs through informed and intelligent decision-making is the key to maintaining profitability and protecting your investment.

The most important tool you can use to control your project costs is an efficient job-costing system. Job costing provides a way to track and report on the actual costs of a construction project as it progresses. It also allows you to compare your actual costs with your estimated costs. The basis of an efficient job-costing system is a well-designed, accurate, computerized estimating program coupled with financial management software that is properly fitted to your business.

This book is a working model for setting up such a system using Quicken. It is written to help you get up and running quickly, and to provide you with the vital controls that can make the difference between success and failure in your construction business. We've made every effort to present this material in a straightforward and easily understood manner, without using the usual ledgerspeak and technobabble.

You don't have to spend a great deal of time doing your bookkeeping; you just have to spend the time well. This book will show you how. You'll learn how to set up the program correctly so that you can easily get meaningful information from your reports. For example, we'll show you how to set up jobs, job divisions (the specific phases of a job, such as concrete, framing, or site wiring), and job budgets (estimates). Then we'll give you step-by-step instructions on how to print a report that gives you the estimated versus actual costs for each job, broken down by job division, if needed. With this kind of help you'll soon have control over your financial matters without spending your life at the computer.

🏠 Quicken in Construction

Why use Quicken? We believe it offers the best combination of power and simplicity available today for the small-volume builder or general contractor. The importance of simplicity cannot be overstated.

What is Quicken? It's an entry-level financial management software program for Windows and Macintosh computers. Quicken is a registered trademark of Intuit. It's a good alternative to the mystery and complexity of traditional accounting software. Instead of using technical accounting jargon, Quicken uses terms that you're familiar with. Its format is user-friendly and straightforward. It allows you to work in a way that is comfortable, familiar, and understandable. Using Quicken to capture and calculate all your daily transactions, including checks and deposits, is much faster than entering and calculating everything by hand. Quicken can summarize your transactions, presenting them in reports and graphs that give you a good idea of where you stand financially. You can record your assets (equipment, cash-in-bank, vehicles) and liabilities (truck and construction loans, payroll taxes), as well as track income, job costs, and overhead expenses. Quicken gives you quick access to critical business information that you never thought possible.

🏠 What Can I Expect to Learn from This Book?

We've written this book because we've watched builders struggle with their bookkeeping and accounting systems. Even though Quicken was written to be easy to use and understand, the complexities of construction accounting make this book necessary. If you follow the setup procedures we've laid out in this book, you can expect your bookkeeping and accounting systems to give you back information that will make your business more productive with less effort.

By following along with this book, you'll learn:

◆ How to set up easily manageable cash-basis categories and accounts in Quicken.

◆ How to create, edit, and use classes. (In Quicken, a new job or project is set up as a class.)

◆ How to set up a simple and effective job-costing system.

◆ How to create and use budgets.

◆ How to create and interpret reports that are designed to keep you in touch with the vital signs of your business.

◆ How to process payroll.

◆ How to prepare interim financial statements when required by a lender or new supplier to determine your creditworthiness.

◆ Tips and tricks for getting the most out of Quicken.

If you're willing to make a small but regular, disciplined investment of time and effort to understand and apply the techniques and methods covered in this book, you'll see measurable and continuing improvement in your accounting skills. In addition, you'll gain the personal and financial rewards that come from working not just harder, but smarter.

About the Authors

Karen Mitchell has 15 years experience as a general contractor and finance consultant. Her company, Online Accounting, helps construction companies around the world computerize their accounting using Quicken and QuickBooks. Ms. Mitchell has an extensive background in construction accounting, frequently publishes articles on computerized business management in leading construction publications, and, with Craig Savage, co-authored the popular book *Construction Forms & Contracts*.

Craig Savage has been a general building contractor for over 25 years, and now does consulting as a specialist in computer solutions for construction companies, helping builders move beyond "shoebox or dashboard" accounting to more organized and accurate systems using Quicken or QuickBooks Pro. His concepts of bookkeeping and job costing are easy to understand and implement, and his step-by-step explanations make setup and reporting simple. He has written numerous articles for construction magazines, edits two newsletters, and is associate editor for the *Journal of Light Construction*. He is a regular speaker at builder-oriented conventions and conducts seminars dealing with construction management. He is the author of *Trim Carpentry Techniques* and co-author of *Construction Forms & Contracts*.

Jim Erwin is a partner in several second-generation family-owned construction companies in upstate New York involved in land development, residential construction, and light commercial construction. He is an active member of the National Association of Home Builders and has written articles on the use of computers in construction for a variety of construction magazines. Mr. Erwin is also the creator of GC/Works, a full-featured software solution for the construction industry that uses Quicken or QuickBooks Pro as its basis.

Rex Underwood is a general contractor, designer, programmer, and journalist with 20 years experience in the construction industry. He is the owner of the Rex Underwood Design Group in Santa Barbara, California, specializing in high-end custom residential and light commercial construction. Rex is a writer and associate editor of the *Macintosh Construction Forum, Construction Business Computing,* and *Rural Builder Magazine,* whose articles have enjoyed a readership of over 400,000 people worldwide. His speaking engagements, as well as his programming efforts, focus on construction office software integration and automation.

The Right Tool for the Job

There'll come a time in your construction business when the "dashboard" system of accounting and job costing just doesn't cut it. At that stage, most contractors, remodelers, and even specialty subcontractors begin to think about adding a computer. But the computer, like any tool, needs to be operated with skill and experience, or the results can be disastrous. Every contractor has heard horror stories about difficult software that costs too much and is too difficult to learn.

This book treats your computer, running the check register software called *Quicken,* as if it were any other tool in your tool box. Turn it on, do the job, and turn it off.

Quicken Overview

Quicken is a simple-to-set-up and easy-to-learn program that works just like your checkbook. If you are currently running your business out of your checkbook, you'll be right at home using Quicken. Quicken is an electronic check register with lots of extra "bells and whistles"—categories that let you outline your job costs, memorized transactions that speed up data entry—to help you categorize and report on your spending and earnings. Pictures of checks and deposit slips that you fill out on screen turn computerized accounting into a job you already know how to do. And because your checks are in the computer, you can do much more. Just follow the simple step-by-step setup instructions in this book. You'll see how easy it is to track the costs of all your jobs, compare your estimated costs to your actual costs, know if you have money in the bank, and more. With Quicken, you'll always know exactly what financial state your company is in.

Check Register

The check register in Quicken (Figure 1–1) looks and acts very much like the paper one you're used to filling out every time you write a check. You can enter the date, the check number, the name of the payee, the amount of the payment or deposit, and details about a particular purchase. In this electronic check register, though, much of the information practically enters itself. Once Quicken becomes familiar with your typical entries, it intelligently anticipates your keystrokes, saving you time and work. Quicken also automatically calculates balances for you, so you don't have to worry about arithmetic mistakes.

An important field within Quicken's check register is the Category field, which we'll introduce briefly here and in greater detail in the "Using Categories and Supercategories" section of Chapter 2, "Getting Started with Quicken."

Categories and Classes

When you write a check or make a deposit in Quicken, you can assign the amount to a *category* and, optionally, to a *class*. Categories and classes let you track income and expenses according to the way you run your business. As you begin to use Quicken, you'll see how a category relates to a job division or phase of construction, and how a class is used to identify a job or project. For example, you can use category CS:01, Plans & Permits, to define the job division and create a class for a Johnson Kitchen Remodel job (see the Quicken data files we've provided on the diskette in the back of this book and Chapter 5, "Budgeting with Quicken: Job Costing and Estimating"). Figure 1–2 shows an example of Quicken's Category & Transfer List window, with categories that might apply to some construction-industry businesses. Figure 1–3 shows a sample Class List window, where you define, edit, and assign classes to a specific job.

When you fill in the Category and Class fields of the check register, Quicken gives you the opportunity to sort and report on the contents

Figure 1–1

Quicken's Check Register includes many automated features that let you categorize and report on income and expenses related to your business.

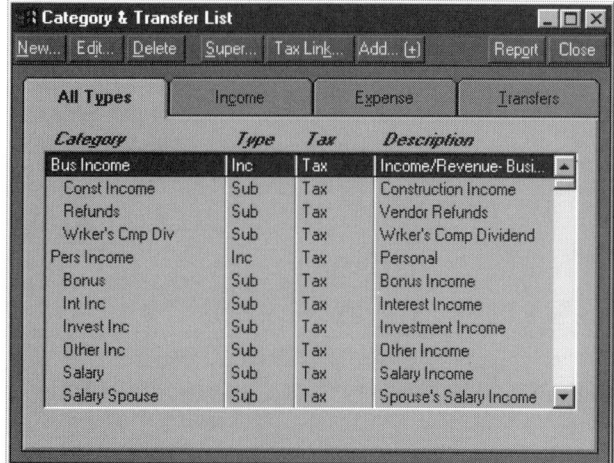

Figure 1–2

Quicken's Category & Transfer List window lets you use, edit, and define categories that help you organize business income and expenses.

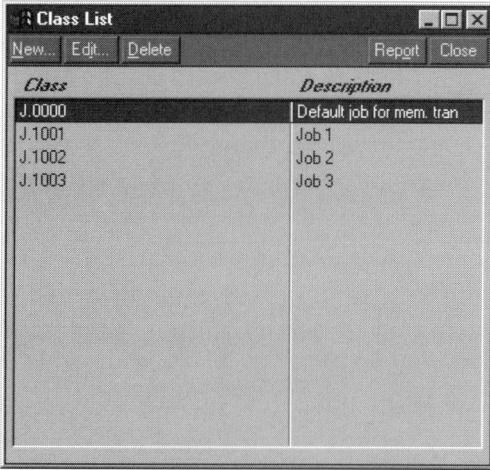

Figure 1–3

A sample Class List within Quicken. For construction businesses, classes are useful for identifying specific jobs or projects.

of those fields. These reports include the job-cost reports that every contractor lives by; you'll find more information about creating these reports in Chapter 5.

Accounting Methods

There are two recognized methods for keeping your books: the accrual method and the cash method.

Accrual Basis

In accrual-basis accounting, an expense is recognized when it happens. For example, when you charge materials at the lumberyard and are handed an invoice, that invoice is entered as a bill in your accounting program. Even though you might not pay the bill for 30 days, the expense is recognized on the day the materials were purchased. Quicken does not handle these types of transactions.

Advantages of accrual-basis accounting Accrual-basis accounting keeps you informed about how much you currently owe and how much is currently owed to you, but has not yet been paid. This gives you the advantage of knowing your cash position among other things. For example, you can

- ◆ track accounts payable
- ◆ track accounts receivable
- ◆ match income and expense for the same time period
- ◆ prepare up-to-the-minute financial and job-cost reports

Disadvantages of accrual-basis accounting Accrual-basis accounting is not for everyone. It takes more time to process and requires that you enter a greater number of transactions.

Cash Basis

In cash-basis accounting, an expense is recognized when you write a check or make a deposit. As an example, suppose you go to the lumberyard and charge a box of nails. With a cash-based system like Quicken, that expense isn't recognized until you write a check for it. Likewise, if a customer owes you money for work completed, Quicken won't show that you have earned that money until you record the deposit. So if you decide to use a cash-basis accounting system, Quicken will do the job. The information we provide in this book assumes you will be using a cash basis of accounting.

Advantages of cash-basis accounting Cash-basis accounting has advantages for the small businessperson who wants to avoid complexity. This method

◆ takes less time

◆ allows simple tax reporting at year-end

◆ is easy to understand

◆ requires that you enter fewer transactions

Disadvantages of cash-basis accounting Cash-basis accounting has its disadvantages, too.

◆ Reports are not up-to-date.

◆ There's no way to track accounts receivable.

◆ There's no way to track accounts payable.

Budgets (Estimates)

Budgeting is another Quicken function that's useful for construction-industry professionals. A *budget* is nothing more than an amount you plan to spend. From a contractor's view, each budget amount is equal to an estimate figure. Quicken lets you set up multiple budgets.

After you have entered a job budget in Quicken, you can compare that estimated amount to the actual job expenses. For example, if the CS:01 Permits & Fees category for the Johnson Kitchen Remodel job were estimated at $725.00 and the actual costs were $712.15, the job-cost report (Figure 1–4) would show Actual = $712.15, Estimate = $725.00, and Difference = $12.85.

Checkfree and Intuit's Online Banking

One of the benefits of using an electronic check register is that all your transactions are in a digital format. With the aid of a modem, your electronic checks can be "sent" to a service that makes payments for you. This service, called Checkfree, is built right into Quicken.

If you sign up with one of the many banks that have joined forces with Intuit, the makers of Quicken, you can also participate in electronic banking. With more banks and services going online every day, you'll find that electronic banking will speed up your work, with fewer opportunities for making mistakes. Whereas Checkfree only allows you to pay bills from Quicken, Intuit's Online Banking service

Figure 1–4

Use Quicken's Budget Reports to track the differences between estimated and actual job costs.

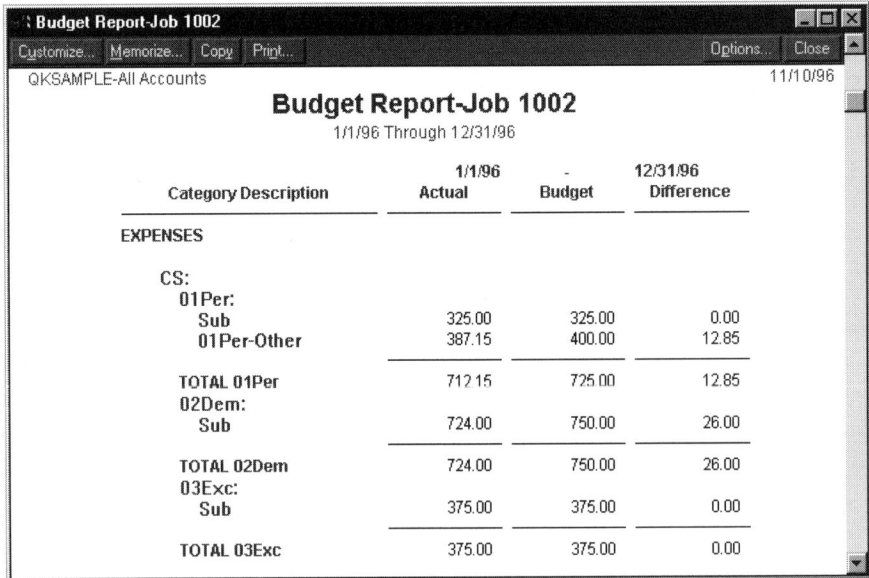

offers additional services—like money transfers between accounts, credit card reconciliations, and much more.

Investments

When your business begins to show a profit (or if it's already profitable), you'll need to consider investing. One of Quicken's real strengths is its ability to track investments, whether they are stocks, bonds, mutual funds, money market funds, or some of each. You can even make trades online.

Links to Tax Software

Quicken's tax form links allow you to streamline and simplify your annual tax return preparation. You can directly export your year-end information into Intuit's tax programs (TurboTax for PC users and MacInTax for Macintosh users) or prepare year-end tax reports for your accountant. While you are paying bills all year long, Quicken is quietly working in the background, organizing your accounting data for income tax time.

One way Quicken accomplishes this is by putting a special "tax-related" tag on each category. Take, for example, the OH:Tel category, described as a Telephone Expense in the Category & Transfer List window in the Company file (included on the diskette that accompanies this book). If you're a sole proprietor, you can link this tax-related telephone category to the IRS's Utilities expense line in Part II of your Schedule C tax form. Then every time you write a check to the telephone company and assign the OH:Tel category to the transaction, Quicken tags the expense. When you calculate your expenses at the end of the year, all the telephone expenses will be lumped together, ready to flow into the Schedule C form. This will save you a lot of time at year-end.

 NOTE: *Intuit has released three editions of Quicken 98: Quicken Basic, Quicken Deluxe, and Quicken Home & Business. We used Quicken Deluxe when writing this book, but you can use the techniques we describe with any of the three Quicken editions. If you use Quicken Basic, your only limitation is that you won't be able to use the software to set up an IRA account or 401(k) account. Quicken Home & Business edition includes additional features (such as invoicing) that aren't covered in this book.*

🏠 Hardware and Software Considerations

Once you've chosen the best accounting package for your business needs, you'll want to make sure your system is set up to run the software efficiently. After all, you want the process of keeping your books to run as smoothly as possible. Review the following suggestions for hardware and software to make sure you have the correct configuration for running your accounting application.

Hardware

Computer hardware is getting less expensive and more powerful every day. Although most users now understand the meaning of basic industry terms such as hard drive and RAM (Random Access Memory), not everyone has a state-of-the-art system. This section presents information about the components you should have to run your accounting package efficiently. In order to take full advantage of all the ideas in this book, you will need to have a PC system that runs Windows 3.1 or higher.

CPU and Memory

Windows will run on a computer with a 486 processor and 8 megabytes (MB) of RAM. We don't recommend that configuration because it will run frustratingly slowly. A much more realistic system would be a Pentium-processor machine running at a speed of at least 100 megahertz (MHz), with 16 MB of RAM, and a 1-gigabyte (GB) hard drive. Of course, more is better; those of you with a faster Pentium system and more RAM will see a tremendous increase in performance.

Monitor

With monitors, bigger is better but not necessary. Let your budget decide. Having a 15-inch diagonal or larger screen increases your productivity by allowing you to display more than one program (or more than one window of the same program) at a time. A larger screen also reduces the amount of scrolling you need to do to see the information you want.

Modem

Modems let you connect your computer to a telephone line and begin to exchange information with other computer users. Today that's truer than ever, now that access to the Internet has become easy and affordable. Craftsman Book Company has a Web site:

http://www.craftsman-book.com

where you can ask questions and download programs useful to people in the building and construction industries. Intuit, the publisher of Quicken and QuickBooks Pro, also has a very informative Internet site at http://www.intuit.com, where loads of small-business tips and other information are available. Many of the companies that are now successfully marketing construction-specific software and construction consulting services have informative sites on the Internet, too.

Most computer systems come with a modem these days. But if you're buying a modem, the slowest speed you'll want to consider is 28.8 kilobytes per second (Kbps). Because the graphic portion of the Internet — the World Wide Web — is becoming increasingly popular, we strongly recommend that you purchase a faster modem, such as a 33.6-Kbps modem.

Software

To help you get more out of Quicken, we've provided software and custom Quicken data files (Sample and Company files) on the disk that accompanies this book. For best results, you might want to consider adding the software packages mentioned on the next page to your system. Since most new computer systems come with "Works" (combination software) packages, you'll probably already have them.

Spreadsheet Software

Spreadsheets are electronic "columnar pads" that you can set up to look like any paper form, such as an invoice. Because Quicken is designed to meet the needs of a broad group of businesses, some of the available reports are not as useful to construction professionals as we would like them to be. To make these reports more construction specific, you might occasionally want to export the report numbers to a spreadsheet, where you can "massage" them into reports that make more sense to a builder.

Any spreadsheet software you may already own will work for this purpose. Lotus 123 and Excel, for example, will accept data from Quicken. The spreadsheets in Microsoft Works or Claris Works will also accept data from Quicken.

Word Processor

Almost every computer has some form of word processor on it, so we won't dwell on this point. With a word processor, you can open files exported from Quicken and mold them into useful reports such as invoices, job-cost reports, and change orders.

Databases

Databases allow the user to store and sort information in many ways. If you could look at the foundation of Quicken, you would find a complex and powerful database. This database is not, however, meant to be modified — at least, not by builders. If you are compelled to do some "remodeling" of the data, we recommend that you export the Quicken data into a stand-alone database program for further analysis.

The Role of Your Accountant

This book isn't meant to take the place of your accountant. Our intention is to assist you in setting up Quicken, entering transactions, and printing and understanding reports that will help you manage your construction business. You should call in your accountant, or at least print and send out reports to your accountant, on a quarterly basis.

⬚ What You Get in This Book and the Companion Diskette

We like to think of this book as a "construction office in a box." We say that because, if you use all the components we've provided on the diskette that accompanies this book, you will be able to estimate a job, turn the estimate into a budget, and then track and compare the budget and actual costs. You'll also be able to invoice your customers and ultimately take all the job cost and customer information and analyze it in ways that will help your business stay profitable and grow.

In writing this book, we have made an attempt to cover the major types of construction businesses. In other words, if you are a developer, custom or semi-custom homebuilder, specialty builder, remodeler, or specialty subcontractor, you will find specific answers to your accounting and job-costing needs. If you follow the examples we have provided, and use the pre-set chart of accounts and memorized reports that fit your business, you will have the basis of an accounting system that will return all the information needed to run a successful business.

Quicken is an extremely powerful financial tool, especially if you consider its low cost. But it's important to realize that no accounting or job-costing software, whether you pay $180 or $18,000, is going to give you everything you want right out of the box. The key is to customize the software so it works for your unique needs, which we've done by providing the Sample and Company files on the companion diskette. Once you do that, you can create a few necessary workarounds by, for example, exporting data to a spreadsheet program where you can present the information any way you want it.

Custom Quicken Data Files

To simplify your startup process, you can use the custom Quicken data files located on the diskette that accompanies this book. The sample Quicken files are found in the Sample and Company folders on the diskette. The files in the Sample folder contain actual data and examples for your reference. The customized files in the Company folder are blank and are intended as starter files for your own company's accounting data. The accounting files in these two folders are the collaborative product of many years of collective experience that the authors have gained as builders, contractors, and consultants.

The construction industry is made up of a large number of diverse businesses that have very specific needs when it comes to accounting. For instance, the builder who builds 25 houses a year and gets construction money through vouchers from a bank has different job-costing requirements than the remodeler who runs 11 jobs at a time and bills his clients every Friday night. Because of these differences, we explain how to set up different systems for each type of business.

Sample Forms and Templates

We've also included construction-specific forms and software templates on the companion diskette. Following are brief descriptions of what you'll find.

Forms

A sample set of spreadsheet forms from the book *Construction Forms & Contracts* by Craig Savage and Karen Mitchell (Craftsman Book Company, 1994) has been included for your use. The files we've included that are pertinent to this book are as follows (all files are in Microsoft Excel format and have the .xls extension):

Form name	Filename	Description
CSI estimator	CSI-EST	Provides a checklist of more than 400 items (fees, permits, and tasks) encountered on most construction jobs, organized according to CSI categories
Change order	CHANGEOR	Documents changes made to an original construction contract
Employee time card	EMPLOYTC	Tracks employees' labor on a daily basis by date, client, job, and task
Estimate checklist	ESTCHECK	Provides a checklist of hundreds of construction tasks, organized by category (for example, site work, rough lumber, HVAC), to ensure an accurate job estimate

Final project punch list	FINALPRO	Lets you document and get approval for any remaining changes that need to be made after the final walk-through
Job invoice	JOBINV	Job invoice form broken down by materials, labor, and subcontractor categories
Proposal	PROPOSE	A proposal form that's perfect for small jobs involving few tasks and a small number of subcontractors
Timecard (categorized)	TIMECARD and TIMECAT	Use this timecard to track employee time spent on jobs by category

The book is available from Craftsman Book Company (see the order form in the back of this book) if you'd like to obtain the full set of files.

Using Quicken Categories, Accounts, and Classes

I f you've chosen to use Quicken for your construction business, this chapter is the place to start. We'll guide you through the process of installing Quicken and show you how to use the sample files provided on the companion diskette. Then, we'll take you on a brief tour of categories, accounts, and classes—important Quicken concepts that can help you organize your jobs and your business accounting or bookkeeping.

▣ Installing Quicken

If you haven't already installed Quicken to your computer's hard drive, do so now. The instructions in the Quicken documentation are easy to follow. If you experience any problems, you can call Intuit's support line for help with the installation process. The product support number is (520) 618-7228.

▣ Using the Quicken Data Files

All the information you enter into Quicken is stored in a set of Quicken data files. The Sample folder on the diskette that accompanies this book contains sample data files for a hypothetical company, with data already set up for the needs of general contractors. The path to the sample files, assuming that your floppy drive is drive A, is

A:\Quicken\Sample

and the Sample folder contains the following five files:

Q3.dir
Qksample.abd
Qksample.qdf
Qksample.qel
Qksample.qsd

The Qksample files contain preconfigured categories, classes, sample vendors, sample transactions, and examples of memorized transactions and memorized reports. We have provided the Qksample files as a reference tool so that you can follow along with the book and see actual examples of how Quicken performs common financial tasks; however, these files aren't meant to be used for your own company's accounting data.

Also on the diskette are Company data files that you can use as a basis for entering your own company's accounting data. The path to the Company files is

A:\Quicken\Company

and the folder contains the following five files:

Q3.dir
Company.abd
Company.qdf
Company.qel
Company.qsd

The Company files use the same categories, classes, accounts, and memorized transaction and report setups as the Qksample files, with the exception that the Company files contain no sample data. Use these files to start setting up the books for your own company.

 NOTE: *You'll learn more about Quicken's ability to "memorize" transactions and reports in Chapters 6 ("Using Memorized Transactions") and 7 ("Using Memorized Reports"). For now, it's enough to know that Quicken can store and instantly recall data from all your transactions, thereby helping you to enter repeated transactions speedily and automatically. Quicken also can store and recall information for customized business reports.*

Copying the Quicken Data Files

To copy the Qksample and Company files (and their folders) to your hard drive:

1. Insert the companion diskette from the back of this book into the floppy drive on your computer.

2. Using Windows Explorer in Windows 95 or the File Manager in Windows 3.1, copy the Sample and Company folders on the companion diskette to the folder on your hard drive where you installed Quicken.

3. Open the Quicken application. Then select the File | Open command.

4. Open the Sample or Company folder and highlight the data files you want to open (they're named Qksample for the Sample files and Company for your own company data). Click OK to open the file. If the Account List window doesn't appear, display it by selecting Lists | Account from the menu.

The Qksample files describe a generic company and were created for a typical general contracting business. In order to customize Quicken for your specific business, you'll want to start with the Company files and add, delete, or modify many of the accounts, categories, and classes that you find there. Step-by-step instructions in the following sections make this an easy task.

Using Categories and Supercategories

Categories are at the heart of Quicken. Similar to what accountants refer to as charts of accounts, categories make it possible to organize all your finances. In this section, we'll introduce the basic types of categories and give examples of construction-related categories. You can use the Qksample and Company files as models for understanding how categories work. In this section we've also included three sample category lists for your reference.

Types of Categories

Categories are used in Quicken to classify, or *categorize*, a transaction. For example, when you write a check to the local building department for a permit, you might categorize that transaction as a

Permit Expense. Quicken allows you to assign transactions to five different types of categories:

- ◆ Assets
- ◆ Liabilities
- ◆ Equity
- ◆ Income
- ◆ Expense

Let's take a closer look at each type.

Assets

Assets are categories that describe what your company *owns*. For example, Checking Account, Trucks, and Machinery are all assets.

Liabilities

Liabilities are categories that describe what your company *owes*. Credit Cards, Bank Loans, and Construction Loans are all liabilities.

Equity

In Quicken, equity is the difference between your assets and liabilities. When you display a balance sheet in Quicken (see Chapter 7), you see the total value of your assets, the total value of your liabilities, and the difference—your equity. When equity is a positive value, you own more than you owe. When it's negative, the opposite is true.

Income

These are categories that describe how income is generated. Examples include Construction/Job Revenue, Vendor Refunds, and Workers' Comp Dividends.

Expense

These are categories that describe how money was spent. Examples of expenses are Plans & Permit costs, Framing Materials, and Office Expenses. Figure 2–1 shows the list of expense-related categories from the sample files on the companion diskette.

Category Lists for Quicken

The Company file that we've provided on the companion diskette contains a complete category list made up of 31 categories and many more subcategories (see Figure 2–2). This file, designed for use by a

Figure 2–1

The expense-related categories from the Qksample and Company files can be modified to suit your needs.

Category	Description
CS Expns	*Costs of goods sold*
01Per	Plans & Permits
Lab	Labor
Mat	Materials
Sub	Subcontract
02Dem	Demolition
Lab	Labor
Mat	Materials
Sub	Subcontract
03Exc	Excavation
Lab	Labor
Mat	Materials
Sub	Subcontract
04Con	Concrete
Lab	Labor
Mat	Materials
Sub	Subcontract
05Mas	Masonry
Lab	Labor
Mat	Materials
Sub	Subcontract
06Flo	Floor Framing
Lab	Labor
Mat	Materials
Sub	Subcontract
07Wal	Wall Framing
Lab	Labor
Mat	Materials
Sub	Subcontract
08Rof	Roof Framing
Lab	Labor
Mat	Materials
Sub	Subcontract
09R&F	Roofing, Flashing
Lab	Labor
Mat	Materials
Sub	Subcontract
10Trm	Ext. Trim, Decks
Lab	Labor
Mat	Materials
Sub	Subcontract

Figure 2–1
(continued)

Category	Description
11Sid	Siding
Lab	Labor
Mat	Materials
Sub	Subcontract
12Dor	Doors & Trim
Lab	Labor
Mat	Materials
Sub	Subcontract
13Win	Windows & Trim
Lab	Labor
Mat	Materials
Sub	Subcontract
14Plu	Plumbing
Lab	Labor
Mat	Materials
Sub	Subcontract
15HVC	Heating & Cooling
Lab	Labor
Mat	Materials
Sub	Subcontract
16Ele	Electrical
Lab	Labor
Mat	Materials
Sub	Subcontract
17Ins	Insulation
Lab	Labor
Mat	Materials
Sub	Subcontract
18Int	Interior Walls
Lab	Labor
Mat	Materials
Sub	Subcontract
19Cei	Ceiling Covering
Lab	Labor
Mat	Materials
Sub	Subcontract

Figure 2–1
(continued)

Category	Description
20Mil	Millwork & Trim
Lab	Labor
Mat	Materials
Sub	Subcontract
21Cab	Cabinets
Lab	Labor
Mat	Materials
Sub	Subcontract
22Spe	Specialties
Lab	Labor
Mat	Materials
Sub	Subcontract
23Flr	Floor Covering
Lab	Labor
Mat	Materials
Sub	Subcontract
24Pnt	Painting
Lab	Labor
Mat	Materials
Sub	Subcontract
25Cln	Cleanup
Lab	Labor
Mat	Materials
Sub	Subcontract
26Lnd	Landscape-paving
Lab	Labor
Mat	Materials
Sub	Subcontract
27Ctg	Contingency
Lab	Labor
Mat	Materials
Sub	Subcontract
28Sls	Sales commissions
29Spv	Supervision
30Int	Job loan costs
31Bdn	Labor burden cost

Figure 2-2

The categories supplied in the Qksample and Company files are designed for general contracting use.

Category/ Subcategory	Type	Tax applic.	Description
Bus Income	Inc	Tax	Income/Revenue- Business
Const Income	Sub	Tax	Construction Income
Refunds	Sub	Tax	Vendor Refunds
Wrker's Cmp Div	Sub	Tax	Wrker's Comp Dividend
Pers Income	Inc	Tax	Income/Revenue- Personal
Bonus	Sub	Tax	Bonus Income
Int Inc	Sub	Tax	Interest Income
Invest Inc	Sub	Tax	Investment Income
Other Inc	Sub	Tax	Other Income
Salary	Sub	Tax	Salary Income
Salary Spouse	Sub	Tax	Spouse's Salary Income
_DivInc	Inc	Tax	Dividend
_IntInc	Inc	Tax	Investment Interest Inc
_LT CapGnDst	Inc	Tax	Long Term Cap Gain Dist
_RlzdGain	Inc	Tax	Realized Gain/Loss
_ST CapGnDst	Inc	Tax	Short Term Cap Gain Dist
_UnrlzdGain	Inc		Unrealized Gain/Loss
CS	Expns	Tax	Construction/Job Costs
01Per	Sub	Tax	Plans & Permits
Lab	Sub	Tax	Labor
Mat	Sub	Tax	Materials
Sub	Sub	Tax	Subcontract
02Dem	Sub	Tax	Demolition
Lab	Sub	Tax	Labor
Mat	Sub	Tax	Materials
Sub	Sub	Tax	Subcontract
03Exc	Sub	Tax	Excavation
Lab	Sub	Tax	Labor
Mat	Sub	Tax	Materials
Sub	Sub	Tax	Subcontract
04Con	Sub	Tax	Concrete
Lab	Sub	Tax	Labor
Mat	Sub	Tax	Materials
Sub	Sub	Tax	Subcontract
05Mas	Sub	Tax	Masonry
Lab	Sub	Tax	Labor
Mat	Sub	Tax	Materials
Sub	Sub	Tax	Subcontract

**Figure 2–2
(continued)**

Category/ Subcategory	Type	Tax applic.	Description
06Flo	Sub	Tax	Floor Framing
Lab	Sub	Tax	Labor
Mat	Sub	Tax	Materials
Sub	Sub	Tax	Subcontract
07Wal	Sub	Tax	Wall Framing
Lab	Sub	Tax	Labor
Mat	Sub	Tax	Materials
Sub	Sub	Tax	Subcontract
08Rof	Sub	Tax	Roof Framing
Lab	Sub	Tax	Labor
Mat	Sub	Tax	Materials
Sub	Sub	Tax	Subcontract
09R&F	Sub	Tax	Roofing & Flashing
Lab	Sub	Tax	Labor
Mat	Sub	Tax	Materials
Sub	Sub	Tax	Subcontract
10Trm	Sub	Tax	Ext. Trim & Decks
Lab	Sub	Tax	Labor
Mat	Sub	Tax	Materials
Sub	Sub	Tax	Subcontract
11Sid	Sub	Tax	Siding
Lab	Sub	Tax	Labor
Mat	Sub	Tax	Materials
Sub	Sub	Tax	Subcontract
12Dor	Sub	Tax	Doors & Trim
Lab	Sub	Tax	Labor
Mat	Sub	Tax	Materials
Sub	Sub	Tax	Subcontract
13Win	Sub	Tax	Windows & Trim
Lab	Sub	Tax	Labor
Mat	Sub	Tax	Materials
Sub	Sub	Tax	Subcontract
14Plu	Sub	Tax	Plumbing
Lab	Sub	Tax	Labor
Mat	Sub	Tax	Materials
Sub	Sub	Tax	Subcontract
15HVC	Sub	Tax	Heating & Cooling
Lab	Sub	Tax	Labor
Mat	Sub	Tax	Materials
Sub	Sub	Tax	Subcontract

Figure 2–2 (continued)

Category/ Subcategory	Type	Tax applic.	Description
16Ele	Sub	Tax	Electrical
Lab	Sub	Tax	Labor
Mat	Sub	Tax	Materials
Sub	Sub	Tax	Subcontract
17Ins	Sub	Tax	Insulation
Lab	Sub	Tax	Labor
Mat	Sub	Tax	Materials
Sub	Sub	Tax	Subcontract
18Int	Sub	Tax	Interior Walls
Lab	Sub	Tax	Labor
Mat	Sub	Tax	Materials
Sub	Sub	Tax	Subcontract
19Cei	Sub	Tax	Ceiling Covering
Lab	Sub	Tax	Labor
Mat	Sub	Tax	Materials
Sub	Sub	Tax	Subcontract
20Mil	Sub	Tax	Millwork & Trim
Lab	Sub	Tax	Labor
Mat	Sub	Tax	Materials
Sub	Sub	Tax	Subcontract
21Cab	Sub	Tax	Cabinets
Lab	Sub	Tax	Labor
Mat	Sub	Tax	Materials
Sub	Sub	Tax	Subcontract
22Spe	Sub	Tax	Specialties
Lab	Sub	Tax	Labor
Mat	Sub	Tax	Materials
Sub	Sub	Tax	Subcontract
23Flr	Sub	Tax	Floor Covering
Lab	Sub	Tax	Labor
Mat	Sub	Tax	Materials
Sub	Sub	Tax	Subcontract
24Pnt	Sub	Tax	Painting
Lab	Sub	Tax	Labor
Mat	Sub	Tax	Materials
Sub	Sub	Tax	Subcontract
25Cln	Sub	Tax	Cleanup
Lab	Sub	Tax	Labor
Mat	Sub	Tax	Materials
Sub	Sub	Tax	Subcontract

Figure 2–2 (continued)

Category/ Subcategory	Type	Tax applic.	Description
26Lnd	Sub	Tax	Landscape & paving
Lab	Sub	Tax	Labor
Mat	Sub	Tax	Materials
Sub	Sub	Tax	Subcontract
27Ctg	Sub	Tax	Contingency
Lab	Sub	Tax	Labor
Mat	Sub	Tax	Materials
Sub	Sub	Tax	Subcontract
28Sls	Sub	Tax	Sales commissions
29Spv	Sub	Tax	Supervision
30Int	Sub	Tax	Job loan costs
OH	Expns	Tax	Overhead Expenses
Ads	Sub	Tax	Advertising
Bank Chrg	Sub	Tax	Bank Charge
Bid Expense	Sub	Tax	Bid Expense
Bond Expense	Sub	Tax	Bond Expense
Bus. License	Sub	Tax	Business License & Fees
Contributions	Sub	Tax	Charitable Contributions
Depreciation	Sub	Tax	Depreciation Expense
Ins	Sub	Tax	Insurance (not health)
Burden allocate	Sub	Tax	Wage burden allocated
Disability	Sub	Tax	Disability Insurance
Liability	Sub	Tax	General Liability
Workers Comp	Sub	Tax	Workers Comp
Int Paid	Sub	Tax	Interest Paid
Misc	Sub	Tax	Miscellaneous
Mort Int	Sub	Tax	Mortgage Interest Exp
Office Supplies	Sub	Tax	Office Expenses
Postage	Sub	Tax	Postage & Delivery
Prof Fees	Sub	Tax	Legal & Prof. Fees
Accounting	Sub	Tax	Accounting
Legal Fees	Sub	Tax	Legal Fees
Rent	Sub	Tax	Rent
Rent-Equip	Sub	Tax	Rent-vehicle,mach,equip
Rent-Office	Sub	Tax	Rent-office, storage
Repairs	Sub	Tax	Repairs
Building	Sub	Tax	Building Repairs
Equipment	Sub	Tax	Equipment
Office Equip	Sub	Tax	Office Equipment
Subscriptions	Sub	Tax	Subscriptions
Tax, Bus	Sub	Tax	Taxes & Licenses

**Figure 2–2
(continued)**

Category/Subcategory	Type	Tax applic.	Description
Fed	Sub	Tax	Federal Tax
Local	Sub	Tax	Local Tax
Property	Sub	Tax	Property Tax
State	Sub	Tax	State Tax
Tel	Sub	Tax	Telephone Expense
Fax Line	Sub	Tax	Fax Line
Main Line	Sub	Tax	Main Office Phone Line
Mobile Phone	Sub	Tax	Mobile Phone
Pager	Sub	Tax	Pager
Tools	Sub	Tax	Tools & Machinery
Trav & Ent	Sub	Tax	Travel & Entertainment
Entertain	Sub	Tax	Entertainment Expense
Meals	Sub	Tax	Meals Expenses
Travel	Sub	Tax	Travel Expenses
Utilities	Sub	Tax	Water, Gas, Electric
Gas & Electric	Sub	Tax	Gas & Electricity
Water	Sub	Tax	Water
Vehicle	Sub	Tax	Auto & Truck Expenses
Fuel	Sub	Tax	Auto Fuel
Insurance	Sub	Tax	Auto Insurance
Loan	Sub	Tax	Auto Loan Payment
Service	Sub	Tax	Auto Service
Wages	Sub	Tax	Wages
Office Wages	Sub	Tax	Wages- Office Staff
Payroll Tax	Sub	Tax	Payroll Tax- Office Staff
Pers Exp	Expns	Tax	Personal Expense
Charity	Sub	Tax	Charitable Donations
Cash Contrib.	Sub	Tax	Cash Contributions
Non-Cash	Sub	Tax	Non-Cash Contributions
Childcare	Sub	Tax	Childcare Expense
Home Repair	Sub		Home Repair & Maint.
Invest Exp	Sub	Tax	Investment Expense
IRA Contrib	Sub	Tax	IRA Contribution
IRA Contrib Spo	Sub	Tax	IRA Contribution Spouse
Medical	Sub	Tax	Medical Expense
Doctor	Sub	Tax	Doctor & Dental Visits
Medicine	Sub	Tax	Medicine & Drugs
Mort Int	Sub	Tax	Mortgage Interest Exp
Tax	Sub	Tax	Taxes

Figure 2–2
(continued)

Category/ Subcategory	Type	Tax applic.	Description
Fed	Sub	Tax	Federal Tax
Medicare	Sub	Tax	Medicare Tax
Other	Sub	Tax	Misc. Taxes
Property	Sub	Tax	Property Tax
Soc Sec	Sub	Tax	Soc Sec Tax
State	Sub	Tax	State Tax
Tax Spouse	Sub	Tax	Spouse's Taxes
Fed	Sub	Tax	Federal Tax
Medicare	Sub	Tax	Medicare Tax
Soc Sec	Sub	Tax	Soc Sec Tax
State	Sub	Tax	State Tax
_Accrued Int	Expns	Tax	Accrued Interest
_IntExp	Expns	Tax	Investment Interest Exp
[Checking]	Bank		Company Checking Acct
[Savings]	Bank		Company Savings Acct
[Mastercard]	CCard		Credit Card- Master
[Visa]	CCard		Credit Card- Visa
[Petty Cash]	Cash		Company Cash Acct
[Adjustments]	Oth A		Adjustments
[Asset-Auto]	Oth A		Automobiles & Trucks
[Asset-Comp Dep]	Oth A		Wrker's Comp Deposit
[Asset-Depr]	Oth A		Accum. Depreciation
[Asset-Machinery]	Oth A		Machinery & Equipment
[Asset-Off Equip]	Oth A		Office Equipment
[Asset-Sec Dep]	Oth A		Security Deposit
[Cust. deposits]	Oth L		Customer deposit held
[Loan-Construct]	Oth L		Liability- Const Loan
[Loan-Truck]	Oth L		Liability- Truck Loan
[Mortgage]	Oth L		Mortgage payable
[Payroll-FICA]	Oth L		P/R tax due FICA
[Payroll-FUTA]	Oth L		P/R tax due FUTA
[Payroll-FWH]	Oth L		P/R tax due FWH
[Payroll-MEDI]	Oth L		P/R tax due Medicare
[Payroll-SDI]	Oth L		P/R tax due state dbl
[Payroll-SUI]	Oth L		P/R tax due state unp
[Payroll-SWH]	Oth L		P/R tax due state w/h
[Sales tax]	Oth L		Sales tax payable
[Investment]	Invst		

general contractor, assumes that you're doing new construction. As such, we've added accounts for tracking construction loans and a simple payroll account. We've also modified the categories to reflect the use of subcontractors on projects. The list of categories shown in Figure 2–2 reflects what you'll find in the Company file.

If you're currently estimating or job costing based on the standards used by the National Association of Home Builders (NAHB) or the Construction Specifications Institute (CSI), we've included a standardized category list for each organization for your reference (Figures 2–3 and 2–4). The NAHB categories are designed more with home builders in mind, while the CSI categories fit an industrial or commercial builder better.

Working with Categories

You can use the sample category list we've provided as is, or modify it for your company's specific needs. Your category list should reflect your job-cost divisions.

Viewing the Category & Transfer List Window

You do the work of creating and assigning categories in Quicken's Category & Transfer List window. To access this window, make sure the Qksample or Company file is open, then select Category & Transfer from the Lists menu. The window shown in Figure 2–5 appears.

The beauty of Quicken's categories is that you can customize them to suit your needs. You can add new categories, rename categories, or delete categories—with some exceptions. If you scroll all the way down the Category & Transfer List window, you'll notice that some account categories at the bottom of the list are enclosed in brackets—for example, [Checking], [Savings], and [Mastercard]. The brackets indicate that Quicken has generated these categories automatically. They aid in the reconciliation process when you transfer assets and liabilities between accounts. Quicken does not allow you to delete them.

 NOTE: *We've set up a number of memorized transactions in the Qksample and Company files (see Chapter 6 to learn more about using memorized transactions). If you delete categories used in those transactions, the memorized transactions won't work correctly. So be careful when you're deleting a category.*

Figure 2–3

The NAHB Category List is designed with home builders in mind.

1000-1999 Preparation Preliminaries
1000 Permits and Fees
1100 Architectural Engineering
1200 Site Work
1300 Demolition
1400 Utility Connections
1500 Construction Period Financing Costs
2000-2999 Excavation and Foundation
2000 Excavation and backfill
2200 Waterproofing
2300 Termite Protection
3000-3999 Rough Structure
3000 Structural Steel
3100 Framing
3105 Framing Material
3400 Concrete
3500 Rough Sheet Metal
3600 Plumbing Total Contract
3700 Electrical Total Contract
3800 HVAC Total Contract
4000-4999 Full Enclosures
4000 Roofing
4100 Masonry
4105 Masonry Materials
4500 Windows and Doors
4700 Insulation
4800 Exterior Trim
4900 Exterior Painting
5000-5999 Finishing Trades
5000 Drywall
5100 Flooring
5200 Trim Carpentry
5300 Ceramic Tile
5400 Cabinets and Vanities
5600 Finish Plumbing
5700 Finish Electrical
5800 Finish HVAC
5900 Interior Decoration
6000-6999 Completion and Inspection
6000 Building Clean-Up
6100 Landscaping
6200 Driveway Contract Total
6300 Exterior Structures
6400 Walk-Through Inspection Checklist Costs

Figure 2–4

The CSI Category List applies more to industrial and commercial builders.

01000 General Requirements
01010 Summary of Work
01020 Allowances
01030 Measurement and Payment
02000 Site work
02010 Subsurface investigation
02050 Demolition
02100 Site preparation
03000 Concrete
03100 Concrete form work
04000 Masonry
05000 Metals
06000 Wood & Plastics
06100 Rough carpentry
06200 Finished carpentry
07000 Thermal & Moisture Protection
07100 Waterproofing
07200 Insulation
08000 Door & Windows
08200 Wood and plastic doors
08600 Wood and plastic windows
09000 Finishes
10000 Specialties
11000 Equipment
12000 Furnishing
12500 Window treatment
13000 Special Construction
14000 Conveying Systems
15000 Mechanical
16000 Electrical
*This table offers only an example of the CSI category format. Consult the CSI Masterformat for the complete CSI listing.

Figure 2–5

The Category & Transfer List window for the Company files is available from the List menu.

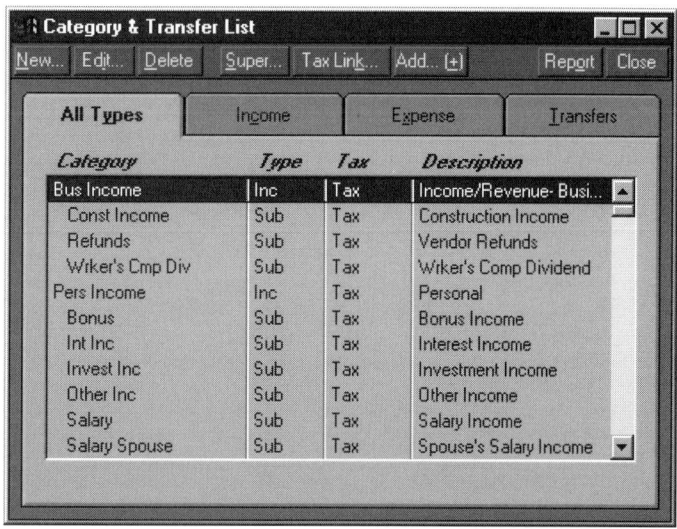

Figure 2–6

You can create a new account in the Set Up Category dialog box.

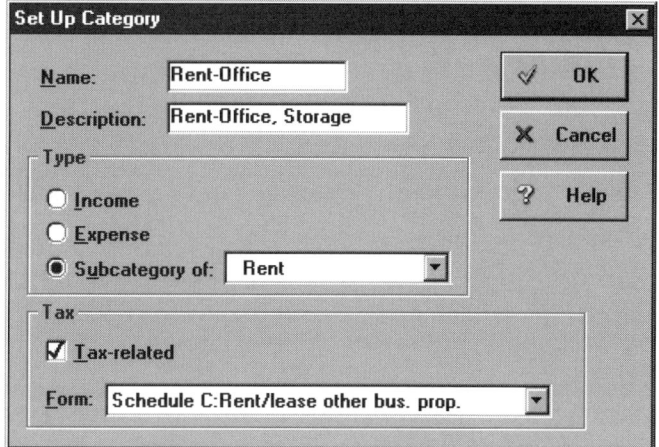

Creating New Categories

To access the Category & Transfer List window and create a new account category:

1. Click the Lists menu and select Category/Transfer. The Category & Transfer List window opens as in Figure 2–5.

2. Click the New button at the upper-left corner of the window. The Set Up Category dialog box appears, as shown in Figure 2–6.

3. In the Name text box, enter a name for the new category.

4. In the Description text box, enter a brief description (up to 25 characters) that will help you remember what the category is for.

5. In the Type field, click the option button that indicates whether the new category is to track income or expenses. If you want the new category to be a subcategory of an existing category (for instance, Lab, Mat, and Sub are all subcategories of CS:01Per, Plans & Permits), click the Subcategory of: option. Then use the scroll list to the right of the button to locate and select the appropriate parent category.

6. If the new category should be tracked for tax-related transactions, such as a material expense, click the Tax-related check box in the dialog box. Then, from the Form drop-down list, select the tax schedule line item to which you want to assign the new category. For example, if you're a sole proprietor, you might want to connect information for the new category to a specific line item in Schedule C.

7. Click OK to create the new category.

Modifying Existing Categories

Our Quicken data files provide a ready-made set of categories for you, but you can change details related to existing categories at any time. You can change the name, description, type, and tax-related information for any category you choose. For example, if you use our Company file as a basis for your own business records, you might want to change the name of one or more of those categories.

To modify details for an existing category, follow these steps:

1. Select the Lists I Category/Transfer command to display the Category & Transfer List window.

2. Locate the category you want to edit and click once to highlight it. Then click the Edit button (next to the New button at the upper-left corner of the window) to display the Edit Category dialog box shown in Figure 2–7.

3. Edit the details you want to change. For example, enter a different name for the category in the Name field, revise the Description field, or assign the category to a different tax form.

4. Click the OK button when you've made the changes you want.

 NOTE: *Whenever you edit a category, Quicken automatically updates the information for* all *memorized transactions that use that category. See Chapter 6 for more information about working with memorized transactions.*

Figure 2-7

You can change the name, description, type, or tax-related information for any existing category in the Edit Category dialog box.

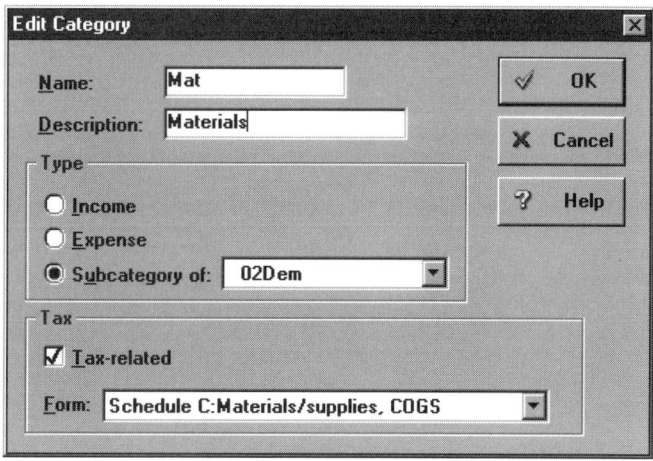

Deleting Existing Categories

As you work with the Company file and customize it to the needs of your business, you may decide to delete some categories that you don't ever use. For example, we've included a subcategory called 01Per (Plans & Permits). If you always require the owner of a building you're working on to purchase the permits, you may want to delete that category.

To delete a category:

1.   From the Lists menu, select Category/Transfer to open the Category & Transfer List window.

2.   Locate the category you wish to delete and click on it once to highlight it. Keep in mind that if this category has any subcategories, you must delete them before you can delete the parent category.

3.   Click the Delete button (next to the Edit button near the upper-left corner of the window). Quicken deletes the category automatically if it is neither a parent category nor a subcategory. If you're trying to delete a parent category or a subcategory, see the Note that follows.

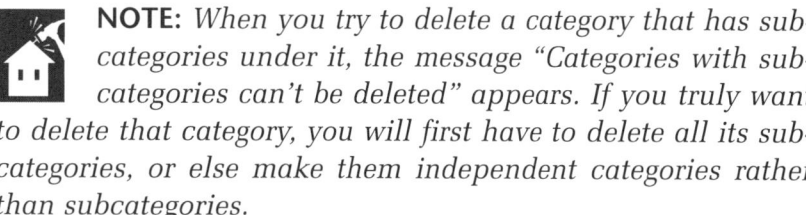 **NOTE:** *When you try to delete a category that has subcategories under it, the message "Categories with subcategories can't be deleted" appears. If you truly want to delete that category, you will first have to delete all its subcategories, or else make them independent categories rather than subcategories.*

When you try to delete a subcategory, the message "Deleting subcategory. Merge subcategory with parent?" appears. If any

> *memorized transactions use that subcategory and you delete it, Quicken automatically updates the memorized transactions to use the parent category instead.*
>
> *When you delete a category that doesn't have subcategories, all memorized transactions that use that category will be modified to show no entry in the category field. All recorded register transactions will become uncategorized. Any time you delete a category, you should examine and possibly reconfigure any of your memorized reports which use that category.*

Supercategories

In Quicken, supercategories allow you to combine categories into useful groups such as Overhead, Labor Burden, or Non-Job-Related Expenses. A supercategory consists of a group of related categories (and their subcategories, if they exist). Use supercategories when you want to associate multiple categories under one general "umbrella" heading. For example, if you are a contractor, you might want to group all non-job-related expenses into a supercategory called Overhead. Rent, Telephone, and Utilities are categories that you might choose to associate with an Overhead category. Follow along to learn how to create, modify, and delete supercategories according to your needs.

Adding New Supercategories

To add a new supercategory:

1. From the Lists menu, select Category/Transfer to display the Category & Transfer List window.

2. Click the Super button in the central upper portion of the window. The Manage Supercategories dialog box shown in Figure 2–8 appears.

3. Click the New button located under the Supercategory Name column of the dialog box. The Create New Supercategory dialog box appears as shown in Figure 2–9.

4. In the Supercategory Name field, enter the name you want to use for the new category. The example in Figure 2–9 shows "Construction Costs," which is a supercategory that we previously added to the Company file.

5. Click the OK button to return to the Manage Supercategories dialog box. The new supercategory name now appears in the Supercategory Name column.

Figure 2–8

From the Manage Supercategories dialog box, you can add, modify, and delete supercategories.

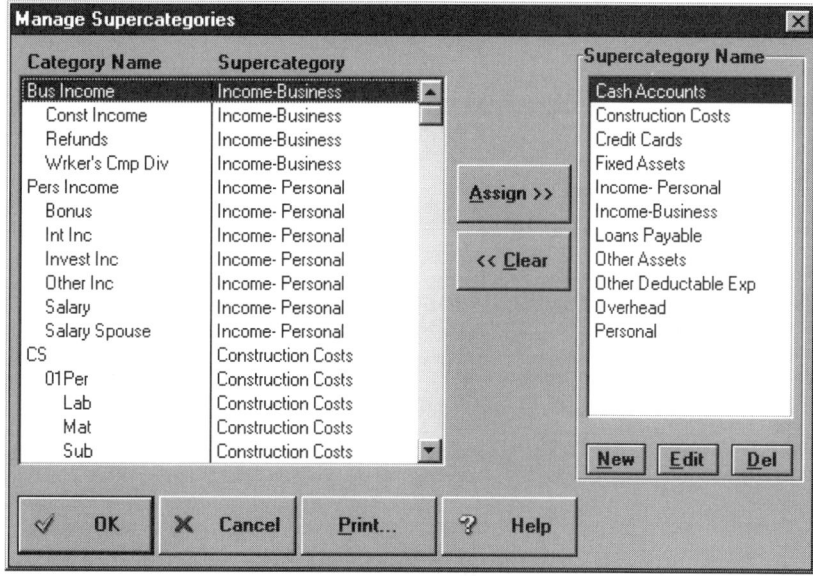

Figure 2–9

You enter a new supercategory name in the Create New Supercategory dialog box.

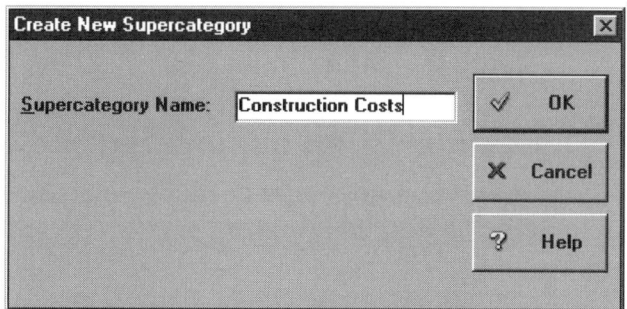

Assigning Categories to a Supercategory

Once you've created a supercategory, you need to assign existing categories to it. Here's how:

1. From the Lists menu, select Category/Transfer to display the Category & Transfer List window.

2. Click the Super button in the upper central area of the window to display the Manage Supercategories dialog box.

3. In the Supercategory Name field, highlight the supercategory to use by clicking on its name once.

4. In the Category Name field, highlight the category to assign to the supercategory.

5. Click the Assign button. You'll see the supercategory name you chose listed next to the category name in the Supercategory field.

6. Repeat this step for each category you want to include in the supercategory.

7. Click the OK button when you're finished to exit the Manage Supercategories dialog box.

Modifying Existing Supercategories

From time to time, you may wish to change the name of an existing supercategory. Here's how:

1. From the Lists menu, select Category/Transfer to display the Category & Transfer List window.

2. Click the Super button to display the Manage Supercategories window.

3. Highlight the supercategory you wish to change and click the Edit button.

4. Your only option is to change the name. In the Supercategory Name field, make the desired name change and click the OK button to return to the Manage Supercategories window.

Deleting Existing Supercategories

If you find you no longer need a given supercategory, you can delete it using the following steps:

1. From the Lists menu, select Category/Transfer to display the Category & Transfer List window.

2. Click the Super button in the upper central portion of the window.

3. Highlight the supercategory you wish to delete. Be very certain that you want to delete this category—Quicken deletes it automatically, without any warning messages. If you're sure you want to delete the supercategory, click the Del button.

 NOTE: *The only way you can undo deletion of a supercategory is to click the Cancel button immediately after you delete the supercategory.*

🏠 Accounts

Accounts are used to track the value of things you own, such as your checking or savings account. You can also use them to track the value of things you owe, such as a loan. Quicken allows you to create nine different types of accounts:

♦ Checking—A checking account is any account from which you write checks.

♦ Credit Card—A credit card account is any account for which you use your credit card to make purchases.

♦ Money Market—A money market account is similar to a checking account in many ways. The funds you place in a money market account are invested in the international money market and draw interest. Many money market accounts also let you write checks.

♦ Asset—An asset account tracks the value of things you own, such as automobiles, real estate, and so on.

♦ 401(k)—A 401(k) account is a specialized type of retirement account set up by an employer.

♦ Savings—A savings account is any account where you store savings. Typically, savings accounts don't offer much interest and are less popular than money market accounts.

♦ Cash—A cash account is used for transactions you make when you pay and receive cash.

♦ Investment—An investment account is used for transactions related to stocks, bonds, and mutual funds.

♦ Liability—A liability account shows the value of things you owe. Examples include loan balances, accounts payable, and payroll taxes.

In the next few sections, we'll show you how to create new accounts, make changes to information about existing accounts, and delete accounts. First, though, we'll provide an introduction to Quicken's online banking features, which you can use to help manage all of your accounts electronically.

Using Quicken's Online Banking Features

Quicken offers a rich variety of online banking features, which will continue to expand to make electronic banking easier and quicker for business people. No longer do you have to trudge down to your local bank branch for every transaction. Today, without ever leaving your business or home office, you can pay bills through a check-writing service, check your current balances, and conduct other transactions such as transferring money between accounts. Contractors should use every productivity tool they can find, and electronic banking is one of them. Once you are comfortable with Quicken, we suggest that you look into online banking. It will save you time and money and make your accounting more accurate.

To use the online banking services provided by Quicken, you need a modem and a way to connect your computer to the Internet. Companies that can connect you to the Internet are called Internet Service Providers (ISPs). Both locally based ISPs and national ones (such as America Online or AT&T Worldnet) are available; most offer unlimited Internet access for a competitive monthly fee. If you don't already have an ISP, Intuit will provide you with one for an hourly fee.

The process of setting up Quicken for online banking involves selecting a financial institution, specifying an ISP and a browser, and making a test connection to the Internet. Here's how to do it:

1. First, select the Online | Financial Institutions command to display the EasyStep window shown in Figure 2–10. Click the Add Financial Institution button.

2. When a message box appears asking whether you have an Internet Service Provider (Figure 2–11), click the Yes button if you have an ISP or the No button if you have none.

3. The next EasyStep window (Figure 2–12) simply describes what Quicken is going to do as it tries to locate your computer's Internet dial-up method and modem. Click the Next button to continue.

4. Next, EasyStep asks you how you presently connect to the Internet (Figure 2–13). Click the option button that applies to you and then click the Next button.

    ◆ If you have a current Internet connection through a local ISP or a national service such as America Online, choose the first option, "I use an Existing dial-up Internet Connection."

Figure 2–10

This EasyStep window is the first step in setting up for online banking.

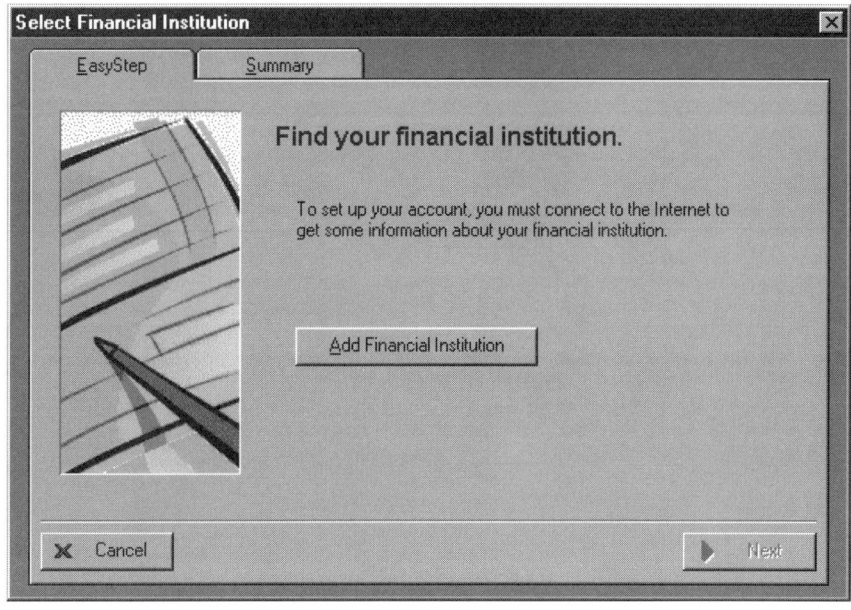

Figure 2–11

Use this message box to specify whether you currently have an ISP.

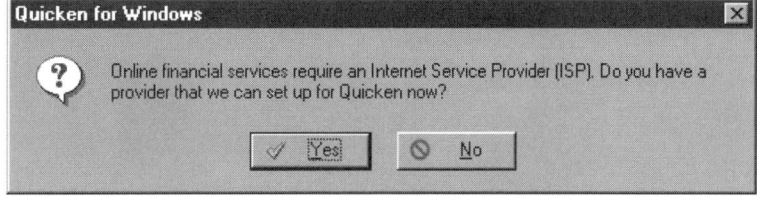

Figure 2–12

This EasyStep window describes how Quicken will attempt to look for any ISP connections you may have on your system.

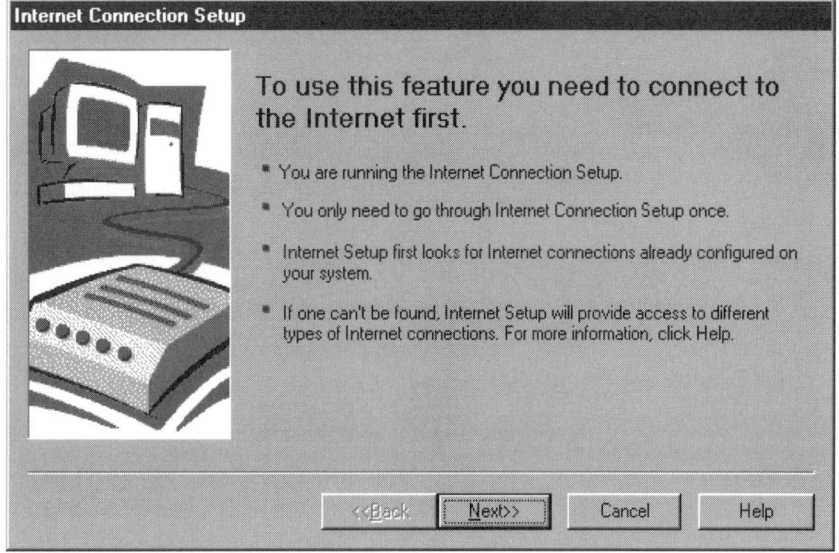

Figure 2–13

*Choose your current
Internet connection setup
in this EasyStep window.*

Figure 2–13

*Choose your current
Internet connection setup
in this EasyStep window.*

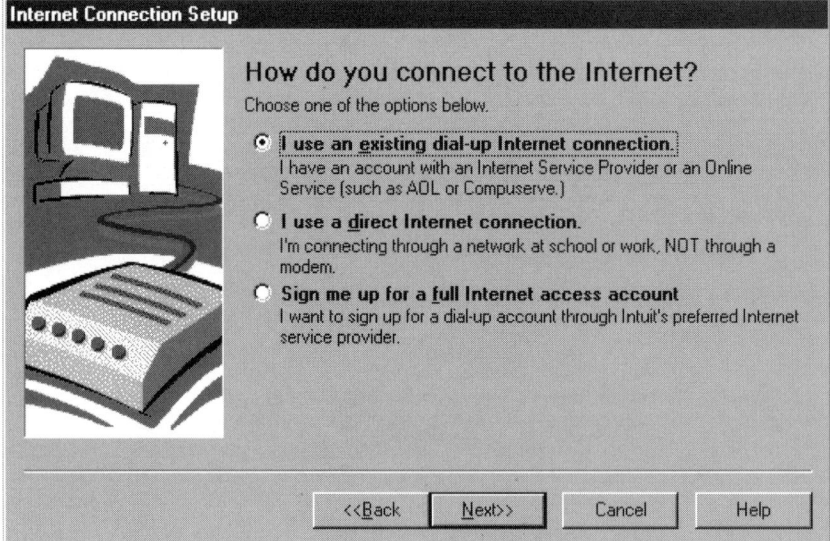

Figure 2–14

*Select the ISP you prefer
to use to connect to
the Internet in this
EasyStep window.*

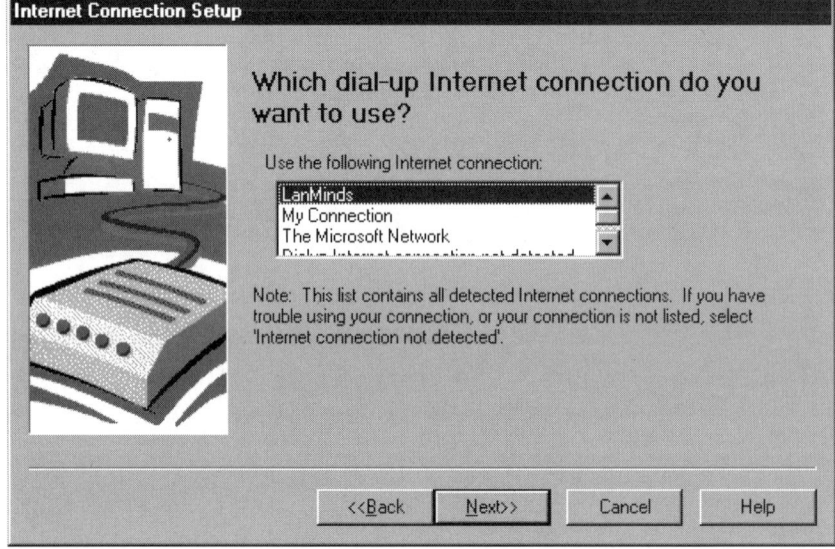

♦ If you work on a network that is connected to the Internet, choose the second option, "I use a direct Internet connection."

♦ If you currently don't have any Internet connection at all but want to sign up with a service, select the last option, "Sign me up for a full Internet access account." This is an easy (although not necessarily cheap) way to get Internet access.

5. Quicken now looks for existing Internet connection setups and then displays a window describing which dial-up functions have been found on your computer (Figure 2–14). Depending

Figure 2–15

Quicken recommends the use of Microsoft Internet Explorer as the browser.

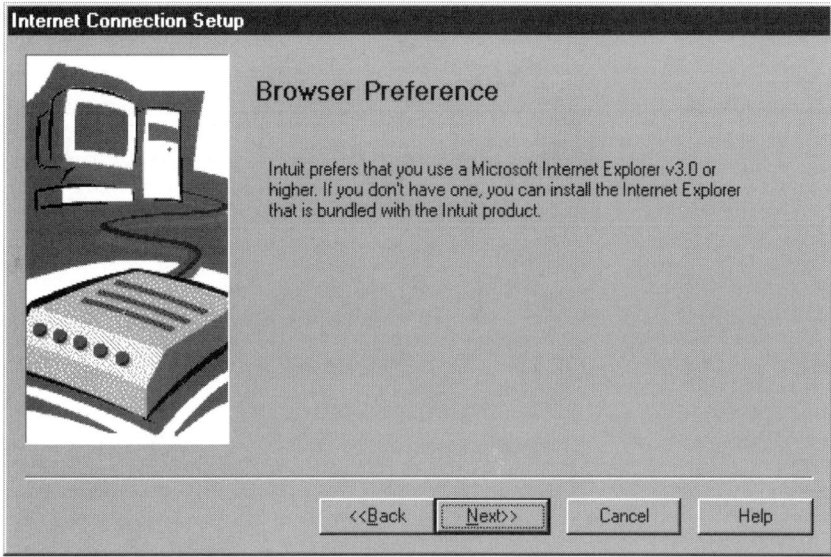

Figure 2–16

Choose an Internet browser from among the ones installed on your system.

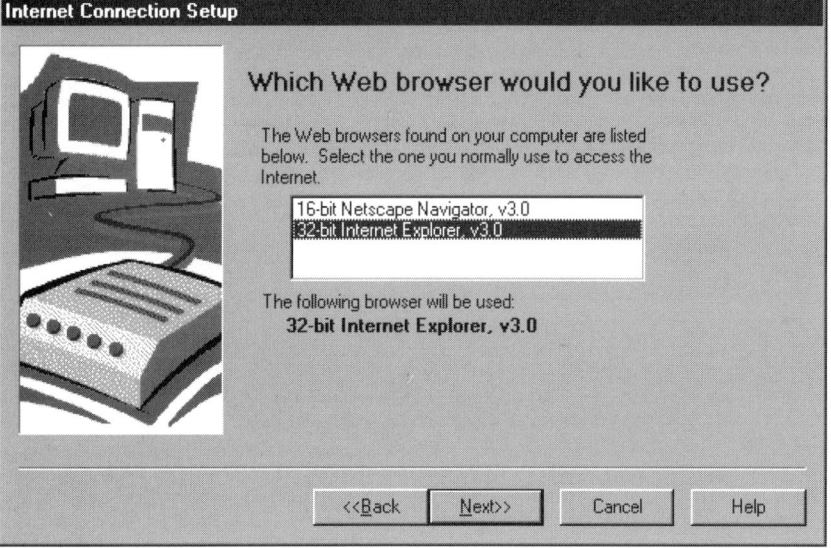

on your system, there may be more than one setup. Use the scroll list to select the service you want to use to connect to the Internet, and then click the Next button.

6. The next two windows that EasyStep presents (Figures 2–15 and 2–16) direct you to choose an Internet browser. *Browsers* are programs that let you cruise the World Wide Web, where you'll find Web sites such as Intuit's. Intuit recommends that you use Microsoft's Internet Explorer version 3 or higher as your browser, but you can also use Netscape's browser as long as it's version 3 or later. Click the desired browser as in the example in Figure 2–16 and then click Next.

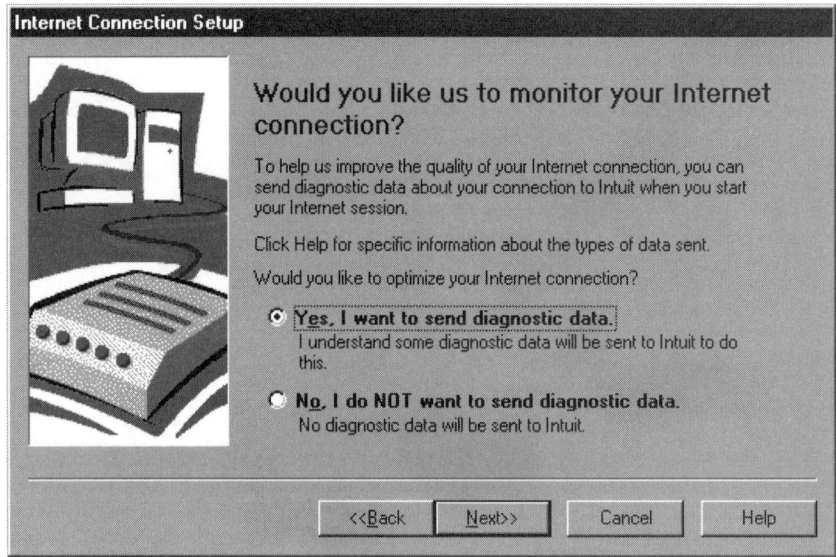

Figure 2–17

Choose whether to allow Intuit to monitor your Internet connection process, which can be helpful for technical support purposes.

7. The next window (Figure 2–17) asks whether you would like Intuit to "monitor" your Internet connection. This is a way for Intuit to download information about your computer and test your computer system while you are online. Click "Yes, I want to send diagnostic data" if you want Intuit to monitor your connection, which can be helpful if you need technical support in the future. If you have any reservations about privacy on the Internet, you can click the second option. Rejecting monitoring by Intuit will have no effect on your ability to do online banking or to do other Internet "surfing."

8. Now, a summary screen appears that shows you the ISP, modem, and browser you have chosen (Figure 2–18). If they are correct, click the Finish button, and Quicken will attempt to log you on to the Internet (Figure 2–19). If they are wrong, click the Back button and change the settings shown.

9. Once you have connected to your (or Intuit's) ISP, you will be shown a Financial Institutions List (Figure 2–20). These are the banks that currently support the use of Quicken for online banking. Click on the name of the bank to which you have applied for online banking services; it will appear in a drop-down list in the next EasyStep window (Figure 2–21)

10. In the next window (Figure 2–22), enter your bank's routing number. This should be available on an account information sheet that your bank has provided. Then click the Next button.

11. In the next window that appears (Figure 2–23), enter your customer ID number, which is typically either your Social Security number or a Tax Identification number (TIN).

Figure 2–18

This summary screen shows the Internet Service Provider, modem model, and Internet browser you have specified.

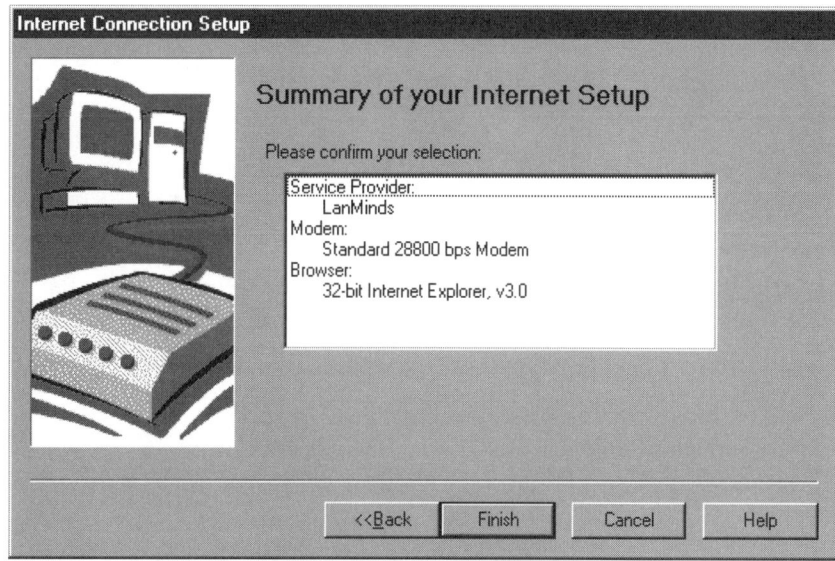

Figure 2–19

Quicken attempts to log you on to the Internet using your system's setup.

Figure 2–20

If your Internet connection is successful, you can choose a bank from a list of banks that support online banking with Quicken.

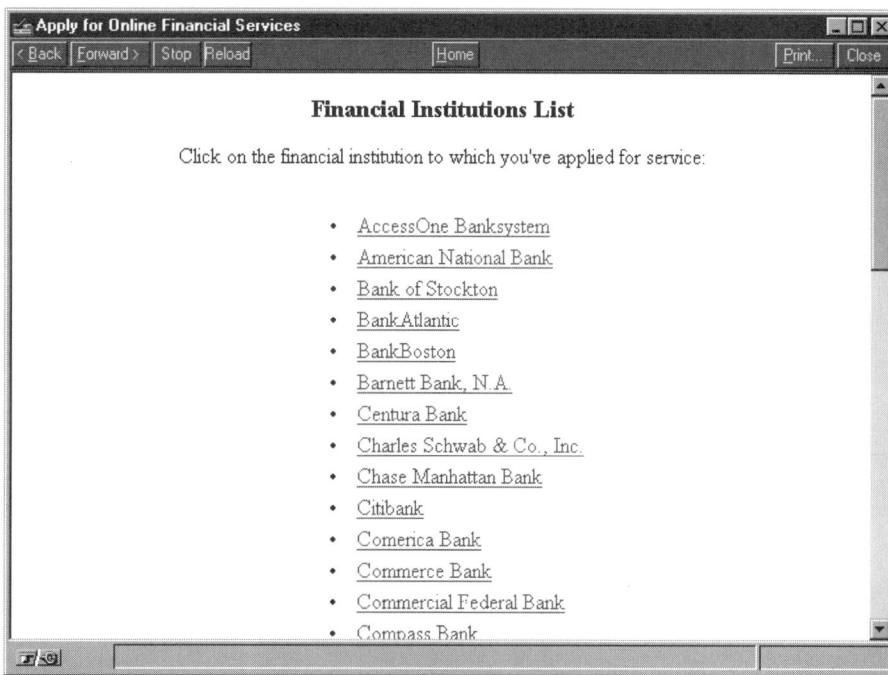

Figure 2–21

Specify your financial institution before logging on.

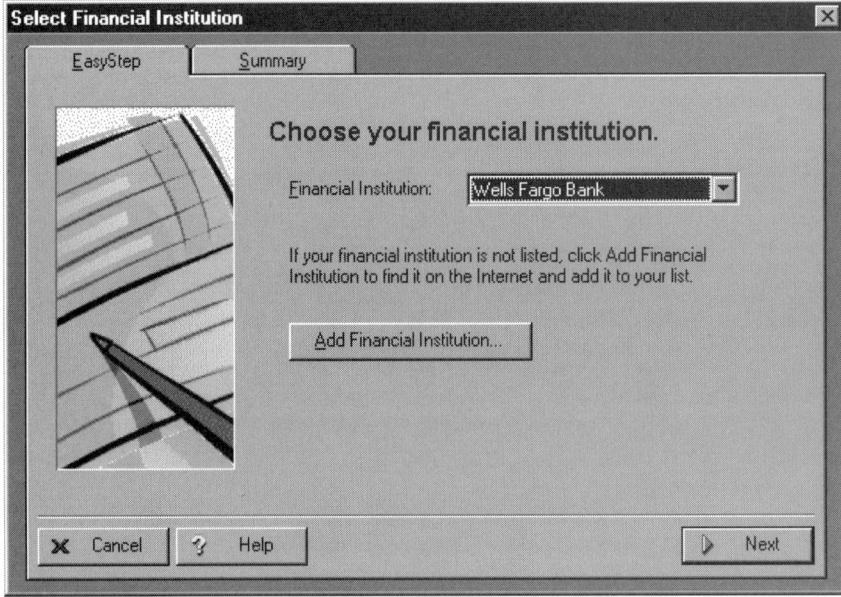

Figure 2–22

Specify your bank's routing number as it appears on your account information sheet.

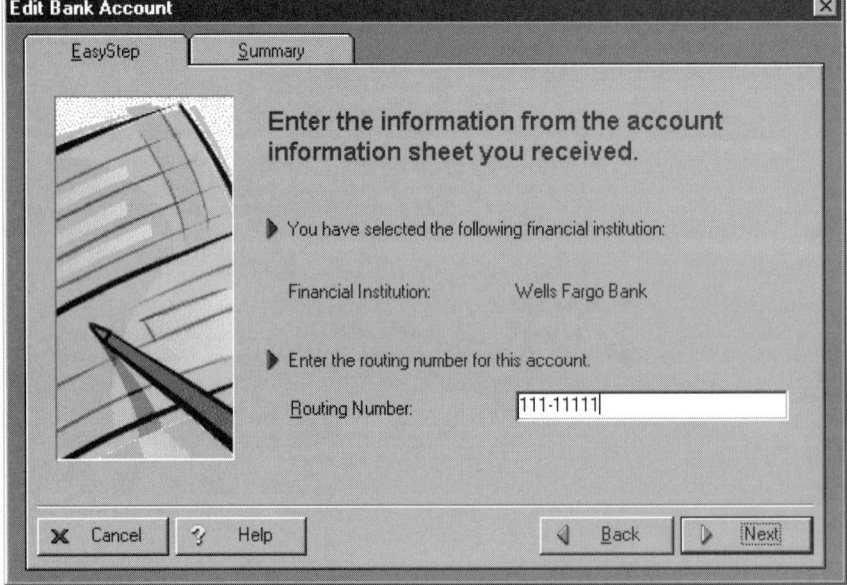

12. Finally, Quicken displays a Summary window (Figure 2–24) that lets you review previous information. Click the Enable Online Account Access check box to make a check mark appear there. If you want to make electronic payments, you must also click the Enable Online Payment check box.

Now, you're set up for online banking with Quicken. For further information, you might also want to review the Internet connection options described in Chapter 3, "Customizing Quicken."

Figure 2–23

Enter your customer identification number in the EasyStep window.

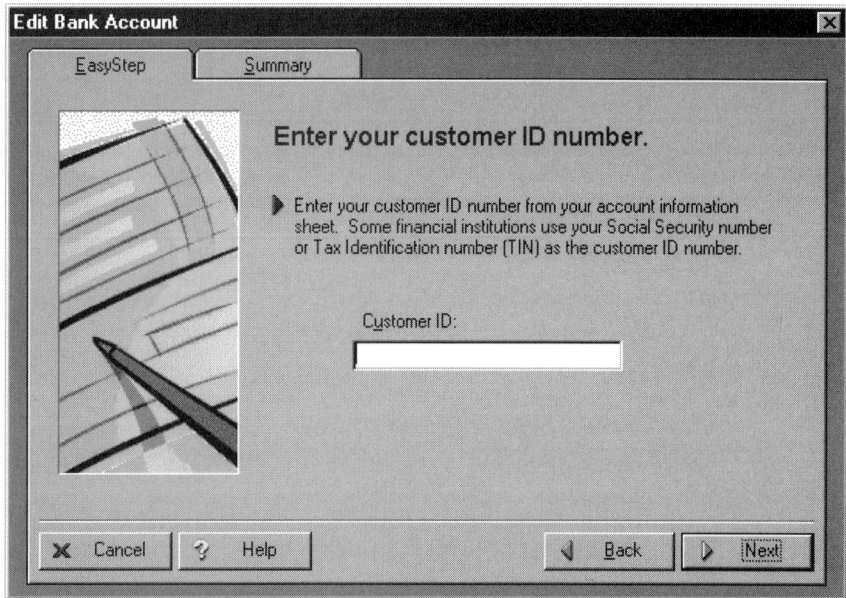

Figure 2–24

Use the Summary screen to review your information about the financial institution you've chosen.

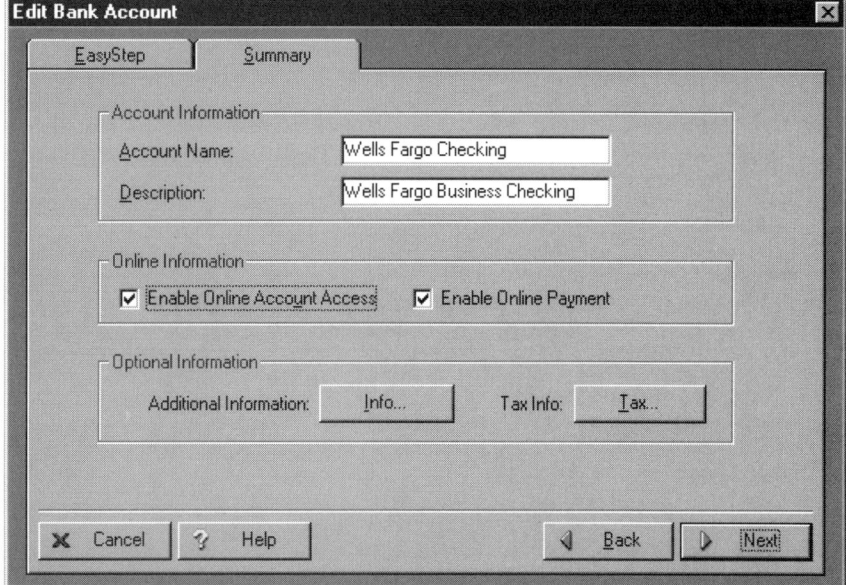

Creating New Accounts

The Qksample and Company files on the companion diskette contain all the typical accounts that a construction professional might need. But if you need to create a new account for your data file at some future point, the EasyStep feature of Quicken walks you through the process of setting one up. If you're new to Quicken, it's a good idea to follow along with the entire EasyStep process. Later, when you've gained more experience, you can skip EasyStep and go directly to the Summary window (which we'll explain shortly), where you can enter all the information on a single screen.

 NOTE: *If you prefer to bypass the EasyStep process, you still start by opening a new account as described in the following sections. When the EasyStep window opens, click the Next button and you will be presented with two tabs: EasyStep and Summary. Simply click on the Summary tab and fill out the fields to create a new account.*

You can have many accounts in a single Quicken file. For example, accounts in the Qksample and Company files include Company Checking, Company Savings, Petty Cash, MasterCard and Visa accounts, several asset-related accounts, several payroll accounts, and mortgage and sales tax accounts.

To begin creating a new account, go to the Features menu and select the Banking | Create New Account command. The Create New Account window of EasyStep appears, as shown in Figure 2–25.

In Quicken, the steps you need to follow to create an account vary, depending on the type of account. Refer to the section that applies to the kind of account you want to create.

Checking Accounts

To create a new checking account once you're in the Create New Account window of EasyStep, follow these steps:

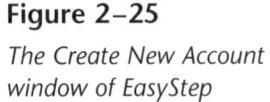

Figure 2–25

The Create New Account window of EasyStep

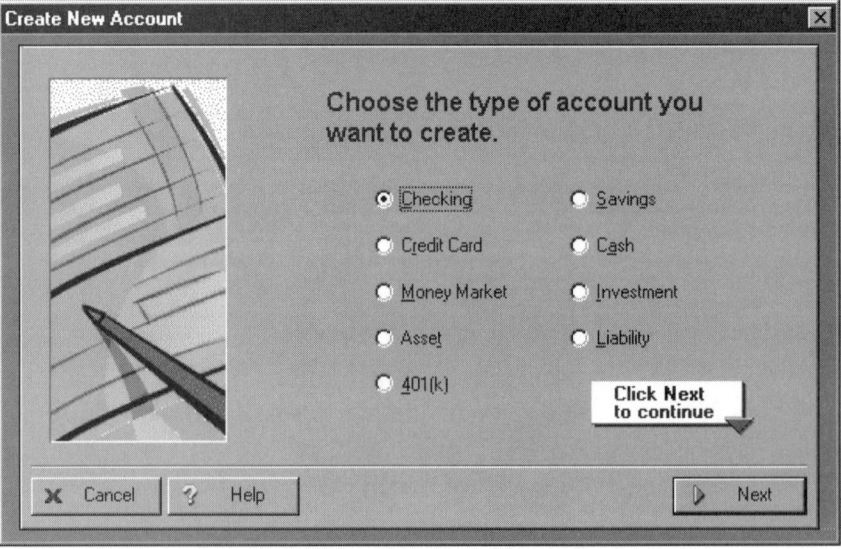

Figure 2–26

The first Checking Account Setup screen in EasyStep is where you name your new account.

1. Click the Checking option button to create a checking account. Then click the Next button at the lower-right corner of the window to display the first screen in EasyStep's Checking Account Setup process. Each successive screen prompts you to enter different types of information regarding the checking account you're creating.

2. The first screen that appears asks you to name the new account (Figure 2–26). In the Account Name field, enter a name specific to this account—for example, Bank of America Checking or Citicorp Business Account. You can enter up to 50 characters.

3. Next, create a description of the new account that will help you remember what it's for. The Description field is optional, but it's a good idea to enter your checking account number here for easy future reference. If you have multiple accounts with the same bank, entering the account number here also helps you keep your accounts straight.

4. Click the Next button to continue the account setup process.

5. The screen asks you whether you have your last bank statement for this checking account (Figure 2–27). Select Yes if this is a checking account that you were using prior to setting up Quicken for your accounting. Select No if this is a new account.

6. When you click Next to continue your account setup, the screen you see depends on whether you selected Yes or No in answer to the previous question.

Figure 2–27

*Preparing to enter an
opening balance for the
new checking account
in EasyStep*

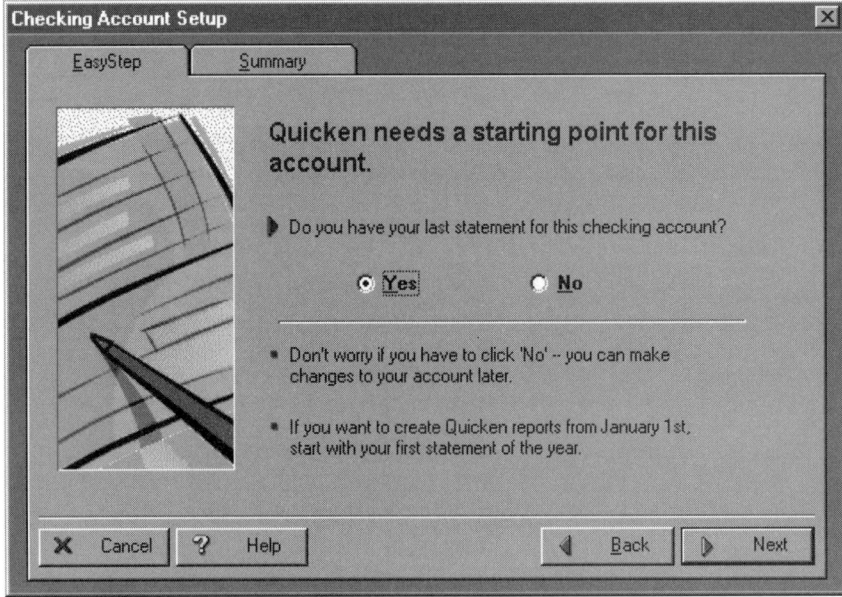

Figure 2–27

*Preparing to enter an
opening balance for the
new checking account
in EasyStep*

If you answered Yes:

◆ A screen containing the message "Enter the starting point information" appears, as shown in Figure 2–28. Enter the *ending* statement date from your most recent bank statement. For instance, if your bank statement covers the dates 1/1/98 through 1/31/98, your ending statement date would be 1/31/98.

◆ In the Ending Balance field, enter the ending balance from your bank statement.

If you answered No:

◆ The screen shown in Figure 2–29 appears. Quicken sets up the account with an initial value of $0.00, and with an opening date that is the same as the current date.

7. Click the Next button to continue the account setup process.

8. Now, it's time to enter information about any online banking and online payment options related to this account (Figure 2–30). If you click No for both options, indicating that you plan to use neither online banking nor online payment for this account, click the Next button to go directly to the Summary screen (see step 9). If you select Yes for either option, click the Next button to enter the online banking information. You will be presented with a series of three screens: one for entering information about the financial institution and its routing number, one for entering account number and account type, and one for

Figure 2–28

Entering starting point information for a new checking account in EasyStep

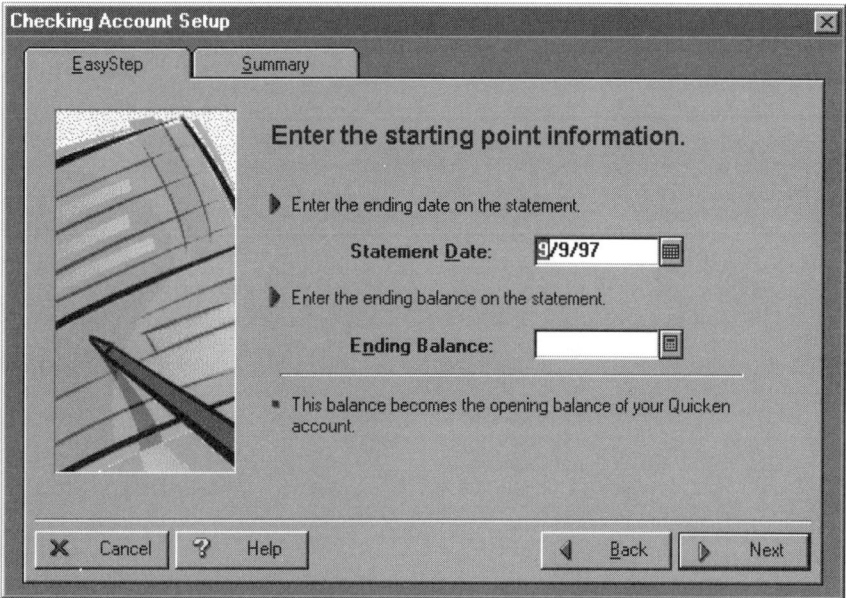

Figure 2–29

Establishing an opening balance for a checking account for which no bank statements are available

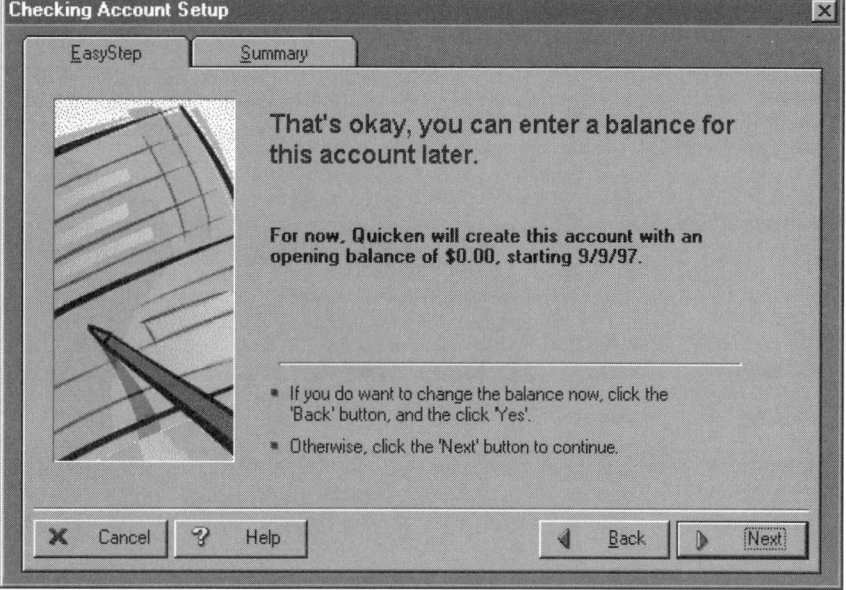

entering the Social Security number or Taxpayer Identification number associated with the new account.

 NOTE: *If you haven't signed up for online banking yet, but think you may want to use it in the future, click No and continue setting up the account. Quicken lets you edit the account to add online banking later.*

Figure 2–30

Choosing options for online banking for a new checking account in EasyStep

Figure 2–31

Entering information about the financial institution's name and routing number in EasyStep

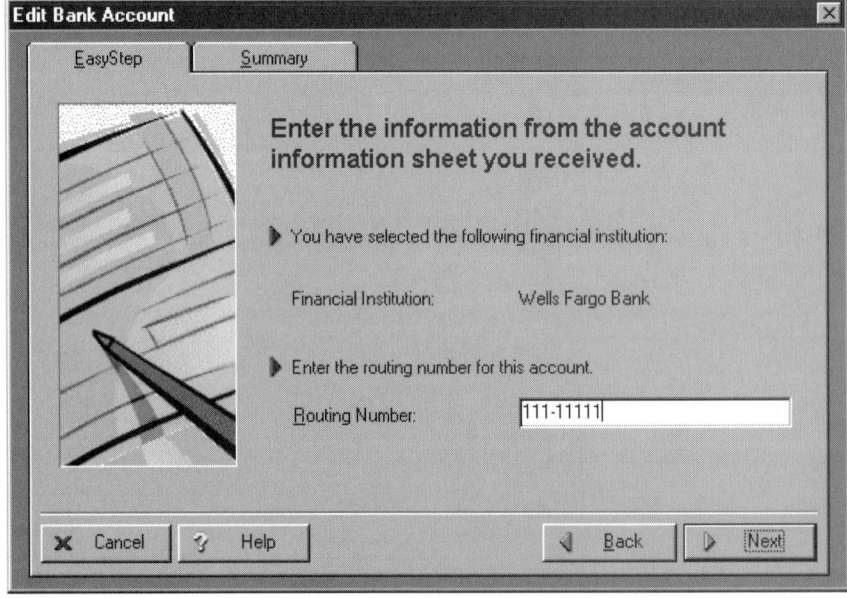

◆ The first screen contains the message, "Enter the information from the account information sheet you received" (Figure 2–31). It is here that you specify the name of your financial institution and the bank's routing number. Select your bank from the drop-down list. If your bank isn't listed, select Other, which is at the very bottom of the drop-down list. The routing number is a nine-digit number that you should have received from your bank when you filled out the paperwork for online banking.

Figure 2–32

Entering account number and type information for a new checking account in EasyStep

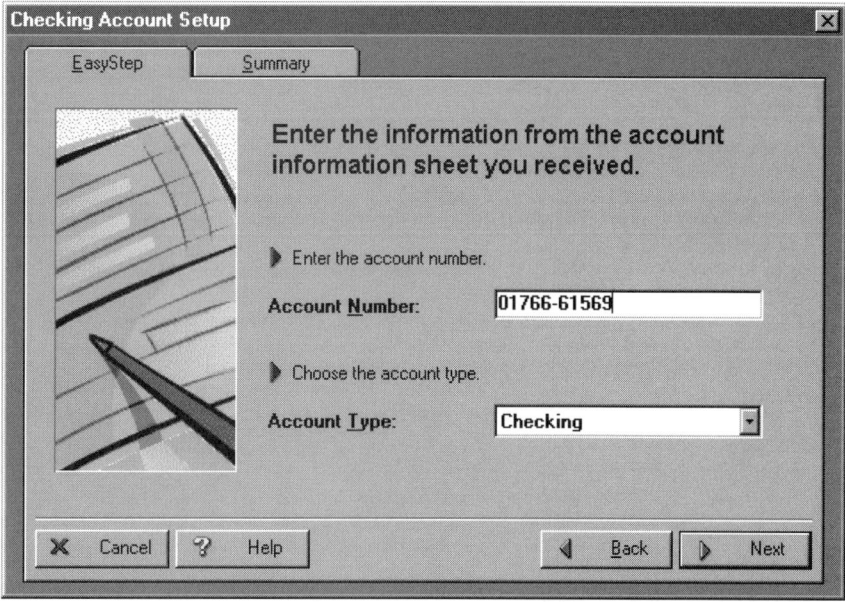

Figure 2–33

Entering the customer ID number (Taxpayer Identification number or Social Security number) for a new checking account in EasyStep

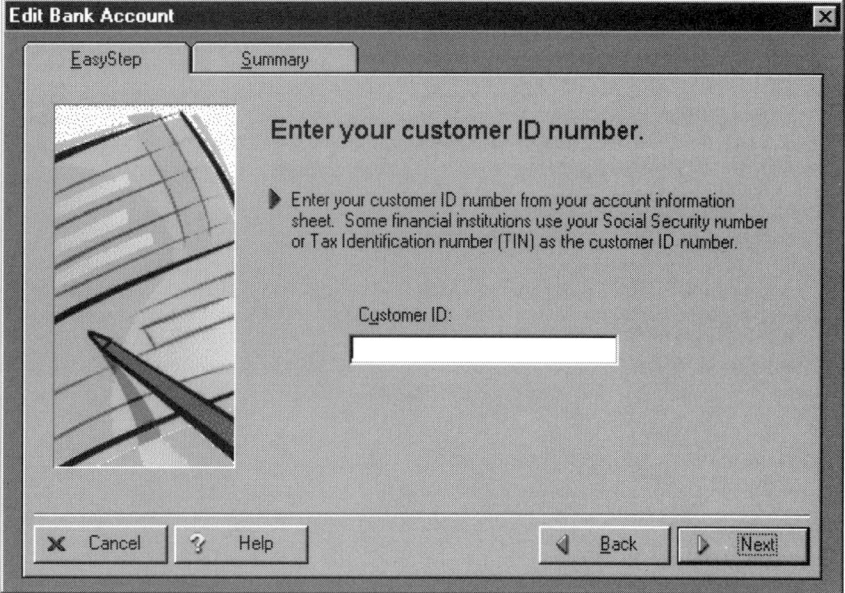

◆ Click Next to continue your account setup.

◆ The next screen (Figure 2–32) prompts you to enter the account number and account type. Enter the checking account number in the Account Number field. From the Account Type drop-down list, choose Checking and then click the Next button.

◆ In this screen (Figure 2–33), enter your Social Security number or your Taxpayer Identification number. Then click the Next button to go to the Summary screen.

Figure 2–34

The Edit Bank Account Summary screen gives you an overview of all the information you have entered concerning the new account.

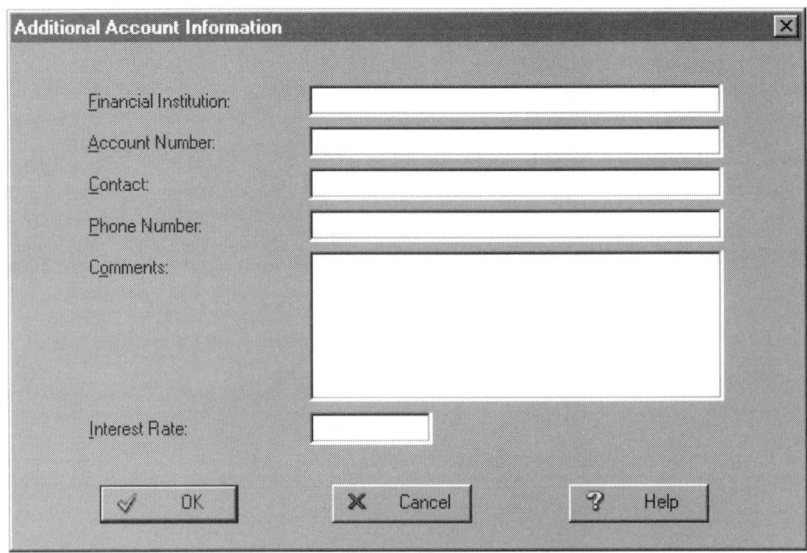

Figure 2–35

You can enter reference information for a new checking account in the Additional Account Information window.

9. The Summary screen (Figure 2–34) gives you access to all the information you've entered for the account. If you previously entered any incorrect information, you can correct it here. You also have the option of entering additional reference or tax-related information. If you wish to do so, go on to steps 10 and 11. If you don't want to enter additional information at this time, go on to step 12.

10. If you'd like to enter reference information for the new account, click the Info button in the Summary screen. In the Additional Account Information dialog box (Figure 2–35), you can enter the name of the financial institution, the account number, the

Figure 2–36

Use the Tax Schedule Information dialog box to specify tax-deferred status for a new account, or to link transfers to specific forms on your tax return.

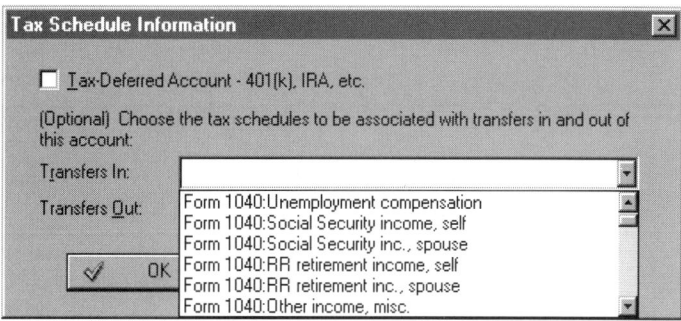

name of a contact person, the bank's phone number, miscella-neous comments, and the current interest rate. When you're done entering this optional information, click the OK button to return to the Summary screen.

11. Click the Tax button if you'd like to enter additional informa-tion about tax matters for this account. The Tax Schedule Infor-mation dialog box that appears (Figure 2–36) lets you change the tax-deferred status of the account. You can also use this window to assign transfers in and out of the account to specific tax schedules. When you're done entering this information, click OK to return to the Summary screen.

12. Click the Done button, and you've created a new account.

If you need to edit the account later, you can access the Summary tab by selecting Lists│Account from the menu, highlighting the account you want to edit, and then clicking the Edit button in the Account List window. Quicken will then open the Summary screen for that account.

Savings Accounts

Since there are no significant differences between setting up a check-ing account and a savings account, use the steps in the "Checking Accounts" section to set up your new savings account.

 NOTE: *Remember, Quicken references savings accounts as well as checking accounts in the Bank tab of the Account List window.*

Credit Card Accounts

The only significant difference between setting up a checking account and a credit card account is that for a credit card account, Quicken will ask you to provide the balance due and credit limit that

Figure 2–37

Specifying an opening balance due for a new credit card account

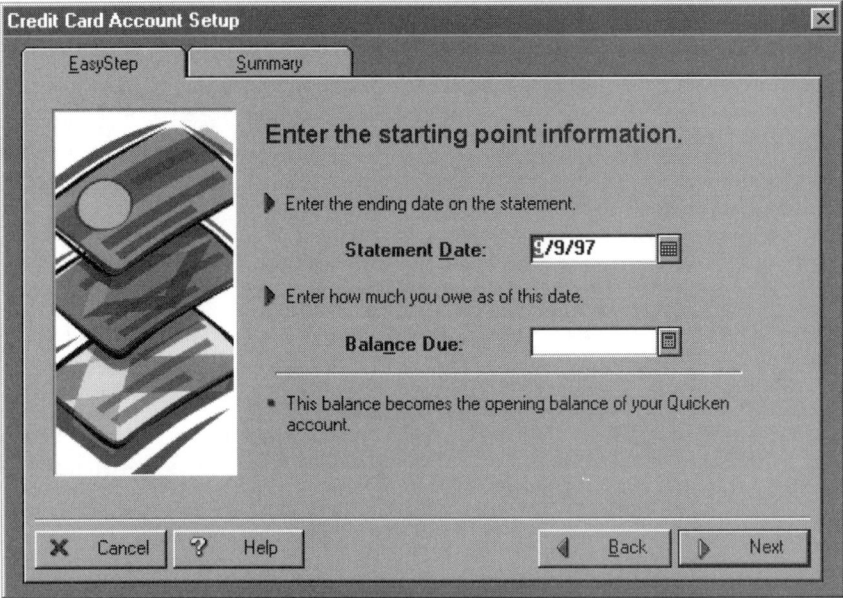

Figure 2–38

Specifying a credit limit for a new credit card account

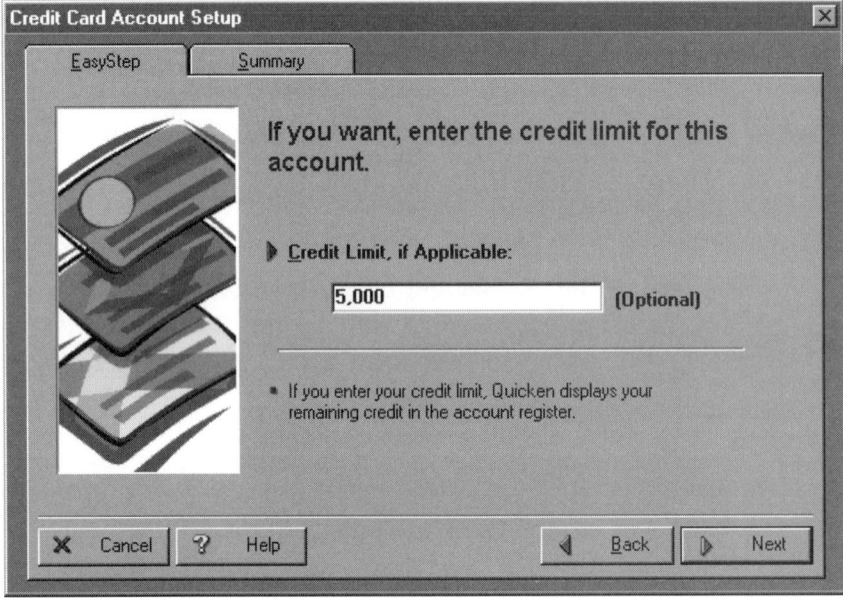

applies to the account. Use the steps in the "Checking Accounts" section to set up your new credit card account. The screens shown in Figures 2–37 and 2–38 appear at the equivalent of step 6 and after step 8, respectively.

Cash Accounts

A cash account is similar to a savings or checking account, so you can refer to the steps in the "Checking Accounts" section to set one up. There are two differences in the setup process:

◆ You'll be asked to provide the beginning amount of cash that you have on hand. If you don't know, you can edit the account later by using the Spend/Receive columns in the Register window for this account.

◆ There is no online banking screen for a cash account.

Asset Accounts

Assets are the things of value that you or your company own. To set up an asset account, follow the instructions for a checking account. You'll be asked to provide the value of the asset as of the date you're creating the account (Figure 2–39). If you're unsure of the value of the asset, you can edit the account later.

In Quicken, asset accounts include Cash, Petty Cash, Money Market, Investment, and Other Assets. In general accounting terms, checking and savings accounts are usually referred to as assets, but Quicken displays them in the Bank tab of the Accounts List window. This is an important distinction to remember, as you'll be using your checking and savings accounts frequently.

In the Qksample and Company files, the asset accounts shown in the Other tab of the Account List window include Automobiles & Trucks, Office Equipment, and Machinery & Equipment. In general accounting terms, these types of accounts are sometimes referred to as "fixed" or "capital" assets. We've configured some additional asset accounts for you in the Qksample and Company files, including

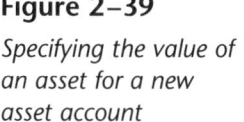

Figure 2–39

Specifying the value of an asset for a new asset account

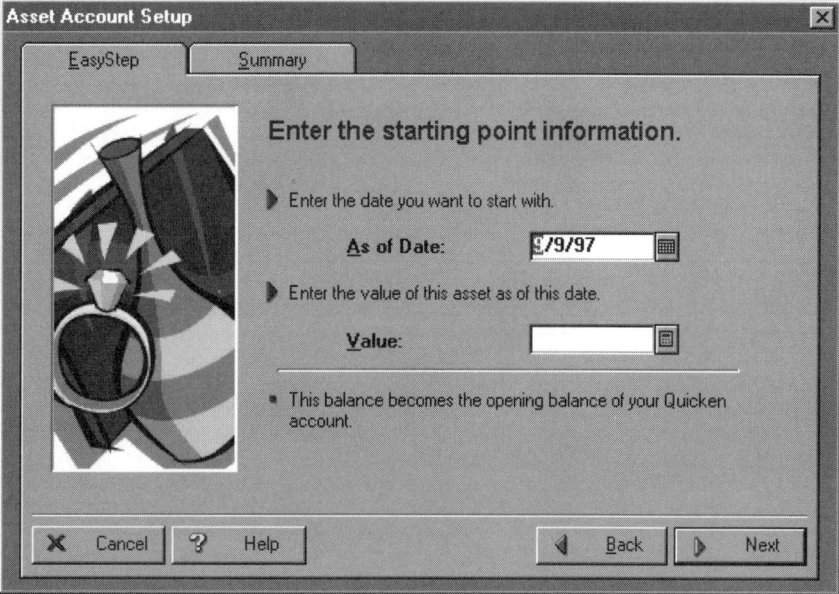

Security Deposits, Wrkrs Comp Deposits, Accum. Depreciation, and Adjustments.

Liability Accounts

Liabilities are financial obligations you or your company have to other people or companies. In the Qksample and Company files, some of the liability accounts shown are Cust. deposits, Loan-Construct, Loan-Truck, and Mortgage. To set up a liability account, follow the instructions for a checking account. You'll be asked to provide the balance due on the account (Figure 2–40). If you're unsure of the balance due, you can edit the account later.

Investment Accounts

As your construction company accumulates cash, you'll want to put your money in an account that bears more interest, or that earns more dividends than a normal checking account. You can make your dollars work for you if you keep a substantial portion of your earnings in an interest-bearing account, then transfer to your checking account just the amount needed to cover the checks you have to write. Of course, if you already operate this way and have been a little sloppy with your accounting, you know you can expect some bounced checks and irate suppliers who won't want to do business with you any more. That's why Quicken is so useful to those of us who fall into the "sloppy accounting" category.

Figure 2–40

Specifying the opening balance due for a new liability account

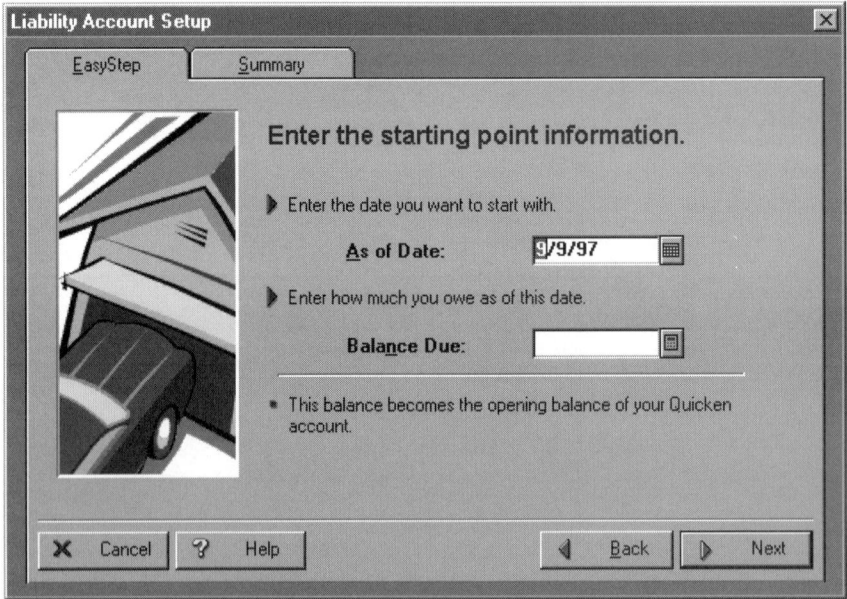

The setup process for an investment account differs significantly from other accounts, so we'll walk you through this process step-by-step. Remember, when you view your Account List window, Quicken displays investment accounts in the Invest tab.

 NOTE: *The Quicken Basic edition of Quicken 98 does not support 401(k) accounts. You'll need to upgrade to either the Quicken Deluxe or the Quicken Home & Business edition if you want to set up such an account with Quicken.*

To set up an investment account:

1. If you're not already in the Create New Account window, select Features | Banking | Create New Account. Or, if you're in the Account List window, click the New button in the upper-left corner. The Create New Account window appears (refer to Figure 2–25).

2. Click on the Investment option button to begin creating an investment account. Then click the Next button to start entering the account information. Each successive screen prompts you to enter different types of information regarding the investment account you're creating.

3. The first screen contains the message, "First, assign a name to this account" (Figure 2–41). In the Account Name field, enter a name specific to this account—for example, Blue Chip Company Stock or ABC Mutual Fund. You are limited to 50 characters.

Figure 2–41

You specify an account name and description for an investment account in the first Investment Account Setup screen.

Figure 2–42

Specifying whether a new investment account should be linked to a checking account

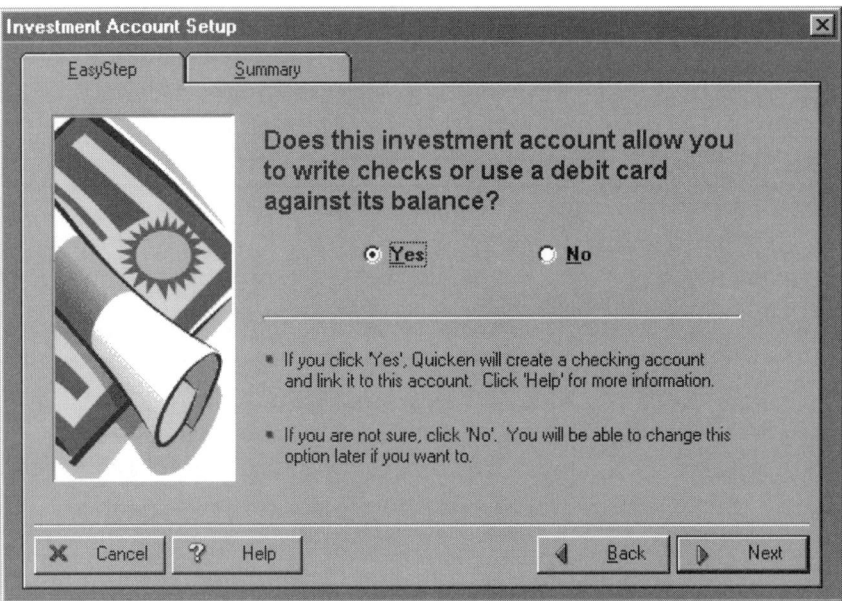

4. The Description field is optional. But it's a good idea to enter your account number here for future reference.

5. Click the Next button to continue the account setup process. The screen containing the message, "Does this investment account allow you to write checks or use a debit card against its balance?" appears (Figure 2–42).

6. Select Yes if your investment account allows you to write checks and automatically transfer funds from, or link a credit/debit card to, the account. If the investment account doesn't allow these transactions, select No. Then click the Next button to continue your account setup.

7. The next screen you see depends on whether you selected Yes or No in answer to the previous question. If you selected No, go directly to step 8. If you answered Yes, you can choose to link the investment account to a new Quicken checking account or to an existing Quicken checking account. (Figure 2–43 shows the "Set up your linked checking account" screen.) If you want to link it to a new Quicken account, enter a balance and a start date for the account. If you prefer to use an existing account, select the appropriate account from the drop-down list. Then click the Next button.

8. When you select No, a screen containing the message, "What kind of securities will this account contain?" appears (Figure 2–44). Indicate whether this investment account will track several funds or a single fund, then click the Next button.

Figure 2–43

Linking a new investment account to an existing checking account for use with checks and debit cards

Figure 2–44

Specifying the type of securities for a new investment account

9. In the screen marked "Is this a tax-deferred account?" that appears (Figure 2–45), indicate whether this investment account will track a tax-deferred investment, such as an IRA, or a non-tax-deferred investment. Then click the Next button to go to the Summary screen.

10. Use the Summary screen (Figure 2–46) to double-check the information you've entered and confirm its accuracy. When you're ready, click the Done button. You've created a new investment account.

Figure 2–45

Specifying the tax-deferral status of a new investment account

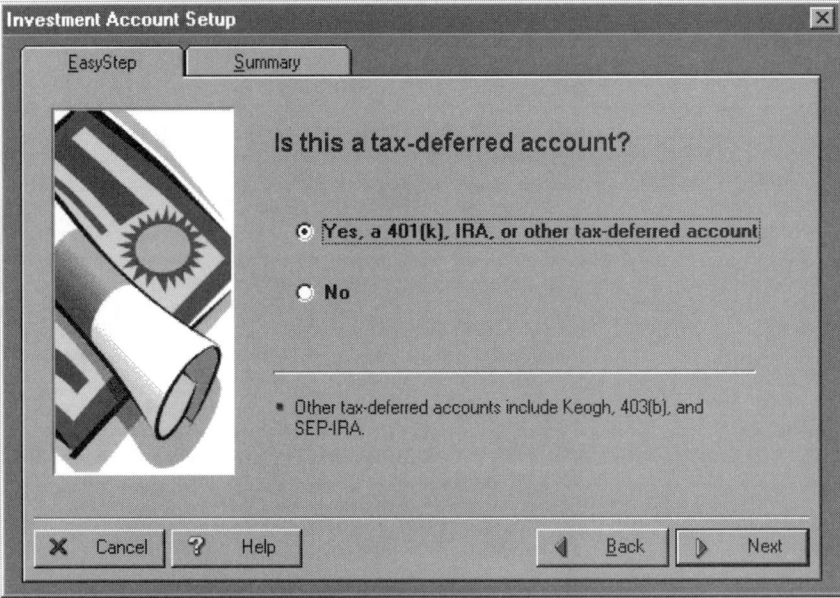

Figure 2–46

Use the Investment Account Setup Summary screen to double-check or change any information you've entered.

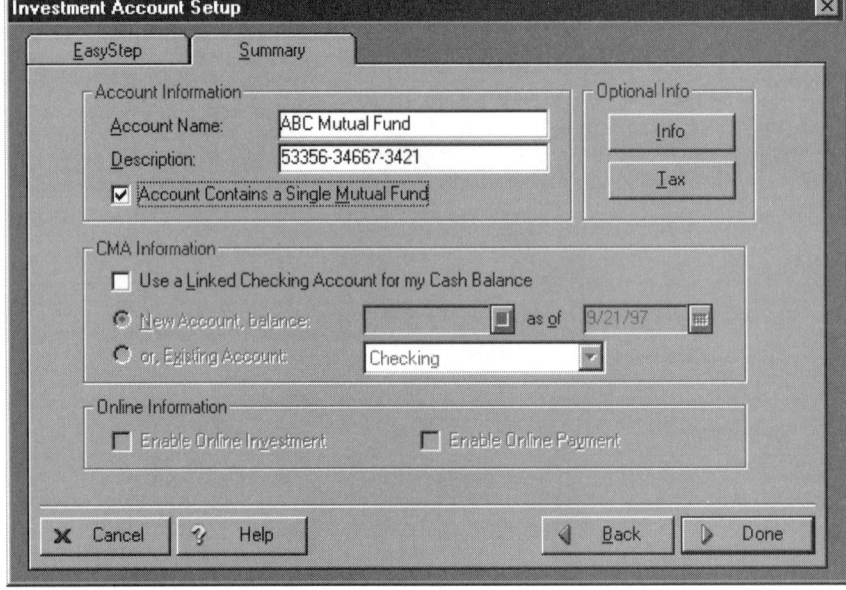

If you need to edit the account later, you can access the Summary tab by selecting Lists|Account from the menu, highlighting the account you want to edit, then clicking the Edit button in the Account List window. Quicken will open the Summary screen for that account.

401(k) Accounts

When setting up accounts, you can also choose to set up a special account to track contributions to a 401(k) plan for you or your employees. A 401(k) is a specialized type of investment account; it's a retirement account set up by an employer. Money is deducted from the employee's paycheck prior to calculating federal income tax. The money invested does not generate any taxable income as long as it remains in the 401(k) (or in its variant, the 403[b]).

You're likely to have 401(k) funds if you're an employer, if you're working for a company full-time, or if you or your spouse works part-time for a company. If you're fully self-employed (and your spouse is, too), you probably won't have a 401(k) account; you might have an IRA or a SEP instead.

Here's how you go about setting up an account in Quicken to track 401(k) funds.

1. Select the Features | Banking | Create New Account command to display the Create New Account window (see Figure 2-25). Click the 401(k) option button and then click the Next button to view a window that describes the process of setting up a 401(k) account (Figure 2–47). Click the Next button again to continue.

2. In the window that appears (Figure 2–48), enter a name and description for the account. Typically, the name of the financial institution or mutual fund suffices as an identifier in the Account Name field. For the Description field, it's a good idea to include

Figure 2–47

This EasyStep window gives an overview of the process of setting up a 401(k) account.

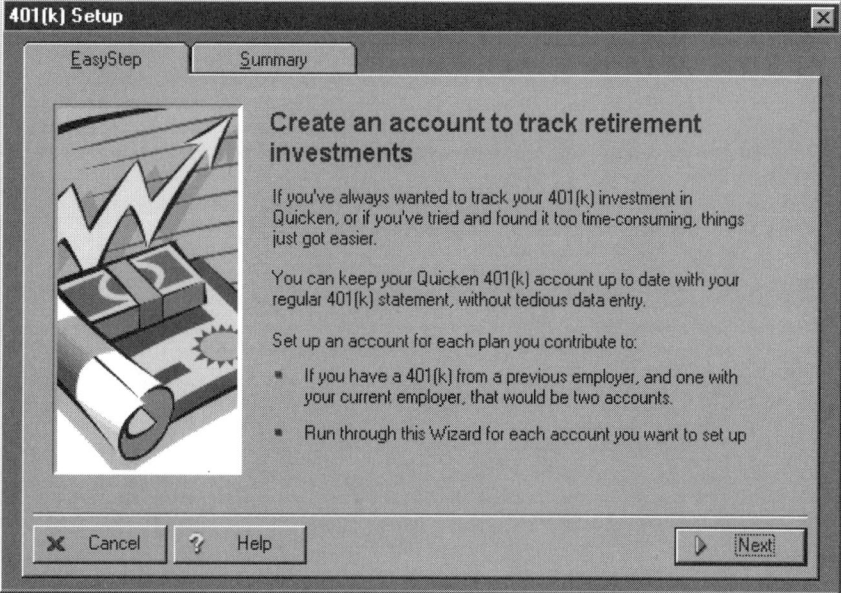

Figure 2–48

Enter the bank or mutual fund name, plus a description of the 401(k) account, in this window.

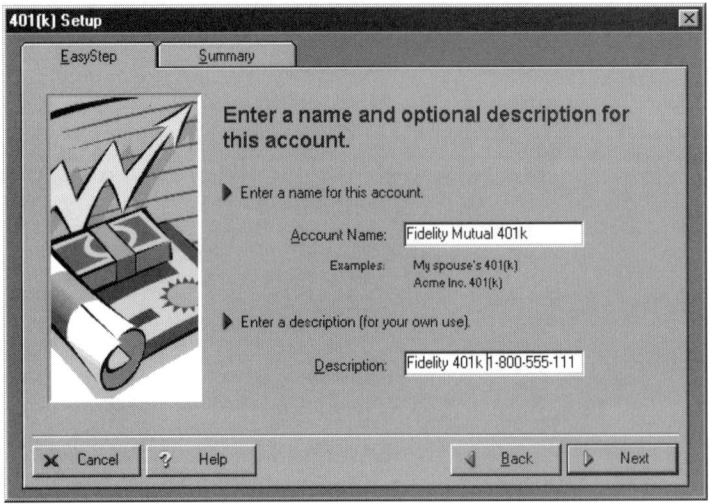

the toll-free telephone number of the 401(k) management company. Having this information handy lets you quickly make telephone queries for your current 401(k) balance or change the allocation of your 401(k)—into stocks or CDs, for example. When you're finished, click the Next button to continue.

3. At this point, you should find your most recent 401(k) statement and use the figures there to fill in the information requested in the next few windows. From then on, compare the numbers in your Quicken data file with each future statement you receive from your 401(k) plan provider. Use the EasyStep window shown in Figure 2–49 to enter the date of the last account statement and the number of funds in your plan. Then click the Next button to continue.

4. In the next two windows (Figures 2–50 and 2–51), answer questions about the name and number of shares in each fund that makes up your 401(k) plan and the ending balance for each fund. Quicken presents as many detail windows as there are funds in your plan. Continue clicking the Next button until you have entered this information for all of the component funds.

5. In the Contributions window of EasyStep (Figure 2–52), click the option buttons that specify whether your employer is also contributing to the account and whether the monthly statements you receive from your employer describe how each contribution was allocated. If you click the Yes option button for each of these options, you'll see a window like the one in Figure 2–53, asking you to provide detailed information for each fund.

Figure 2–49

Enter the last statement date and the number of funds in your 401(k) plan in this window.

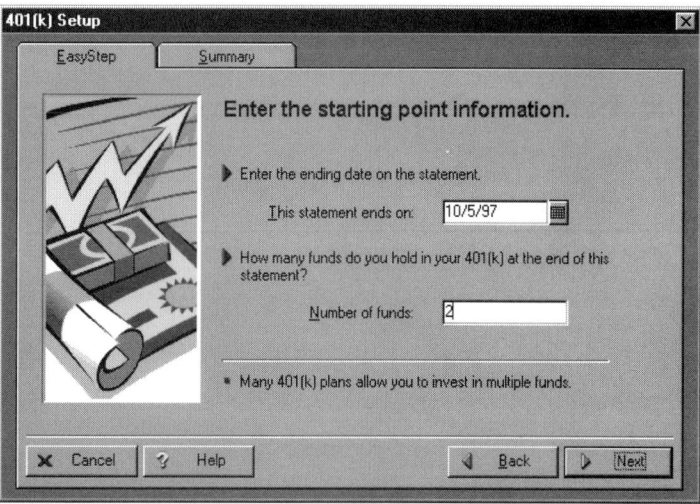

Figure 2–50

Indicate whether your 401(k) plan statement offers information about the number of shares in each fund.

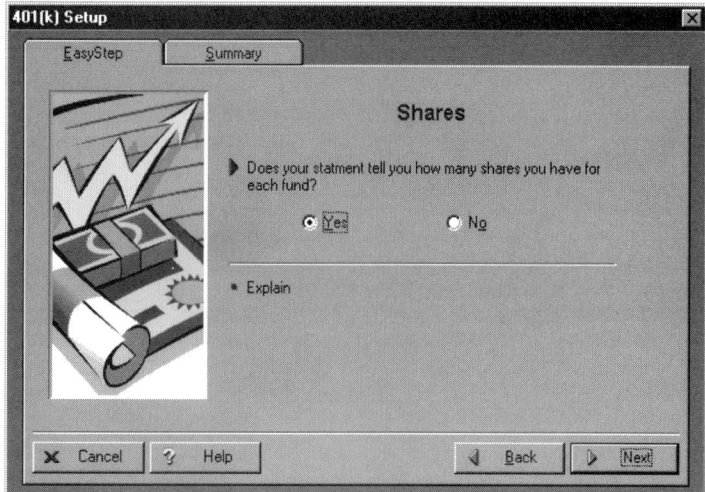

Figure 2–51

For each fund in your 401(k) plan, enter the fund name, number of shares, and ending balance.

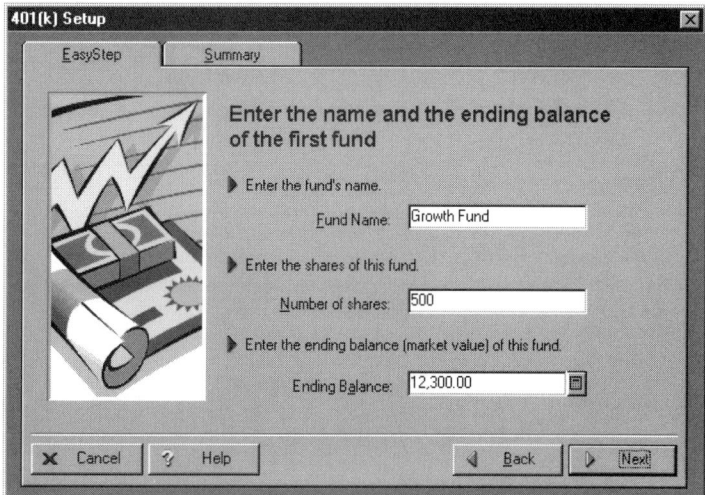

Figure 2–52

Use the Contributions window to indicate whether your employer contributes to your 401(k) plan and whether fund allocation information appears on your statement.

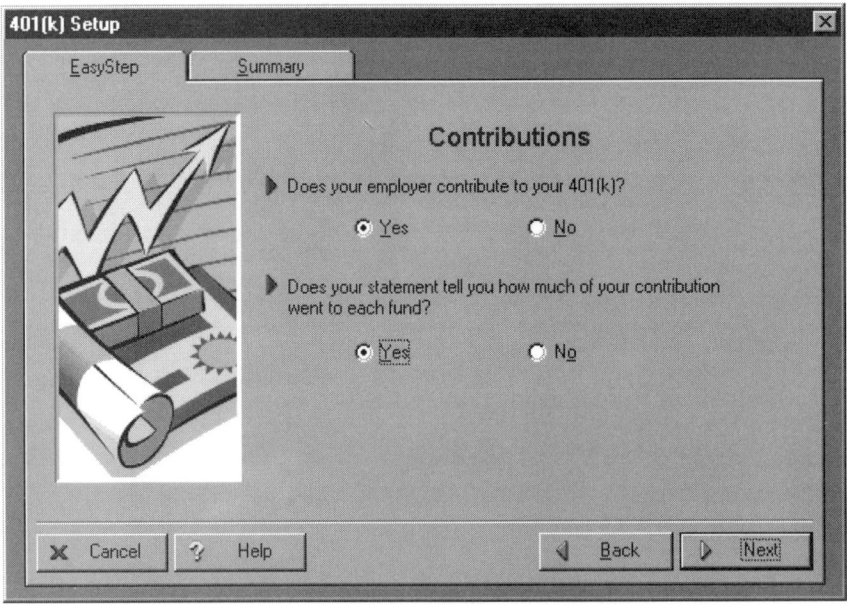

Figure 2–53

If your 401(k) plan statement gives detailed information about employer contributions and fund allocations, enter it in this window.

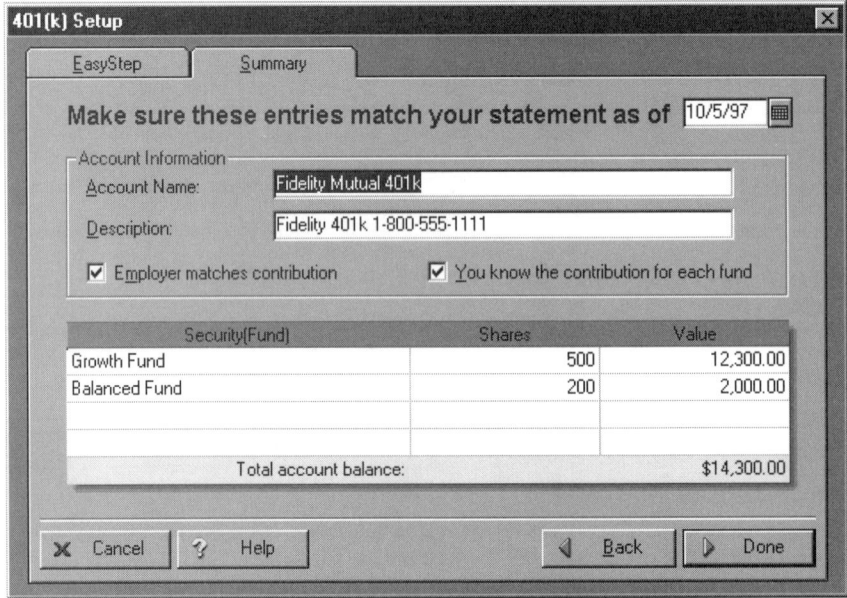

6. Finally, check your statement against what you've entered in Quicken and then click the Done button. You will be rewarded with an attractive graph that gives you a visual overview of your 401(k) holdings, like the example in Figure 2–54. Every month you update your account information, you'll see the graph grow.

Figure 2–54

Once you've entered the details about your 401(k) account, Quicken translates that information into a visual graph.

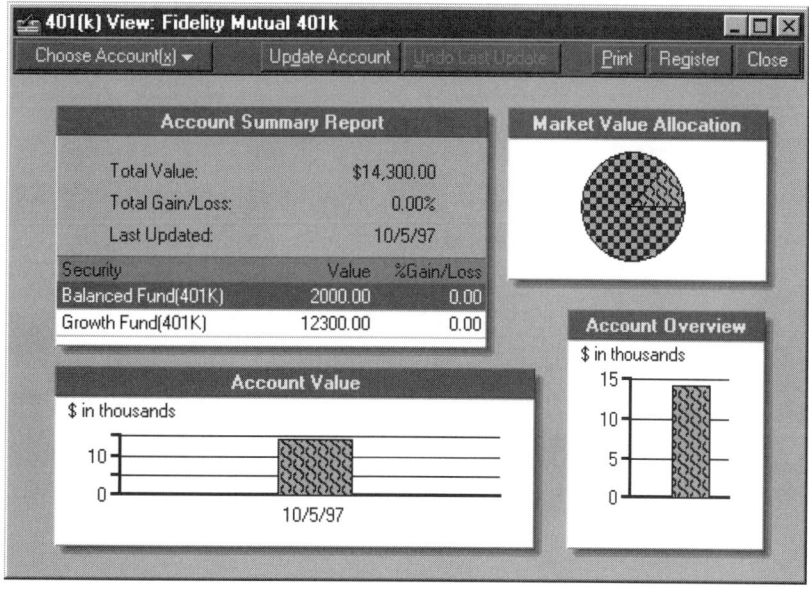

Modifying Existing Accounts

At any time, you can change the information pertaining to one of your Quicken accounts by first highlighting the account in the Account List window and then clicking the Edit button. One item that users frequently want to change is the opening balance, especially when they don't know how much the account contains at the time of setting it up. Other items you might want to edit include account name, description, tax information, account number, contact, phone number, and custom comments.

Entering Opening Balances

If you decide to use some or all of the accounts we've configured for you in the Company file, enter opening balances for these accounts using the guidelines that follow. If you're uncertain of the tax implications associated with these accounts, check with your accountant.

Automobiles & Trucks Record automobiles and trucks used exclusively in your business as assets, so you can get the tax benefits of depreciation. The Qksample and Company files we've provided have an asset account named Automobiles & Trucks. If you're unsure of the value of your vehicle(s), ask your accountant to help you determine what value to enter. Remember, you can always come back and edit the account.

To enter a value for a new truck:

1. From the menu, select Lists | Account to display the Account List window.

2. Click the Other tab in the Account List window. Locate the account with the name Asset-Auto and the description of Automobiles & Trucks. Highlight the Automobiles & Trucks account by clicking on it once.

3. Press the Open button in the Account List window to display the Automobiles & Trucks Register window shown in Figure 2–55. (The figure shows information being entered for a sample asset; the register in the Company file is blank.)

The Quicken Register window is made to look and act just like the register in your paper checkbook (see Chapter 4). It contains fields that you fill in for Date, Reference, Payee/Category/Memo, Decrease, Clr (clear), Increase, and Balance. In addition, the Register window contains function buttons that let you quickly delete information, find data, transfer amounts, update balances, edit the account, and create a report.

The Date field is where you enter the date on which a check is or was written. The Reference field is where you enter the check number or a reference to another action, such as ATM (automated teller machine) withdrawal, deposits, or transfers between accounts; or EFT (electronic funds transfers) payments (electronic checks). The Payee/Category/Memo field is really three fields. The Payee field is where you enter the name of the party you are paying. The Category field is where you specify the job and cost divisions of a project. The

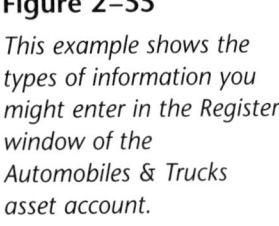

Figure 2–55

This example shows the types of information you might enter in the Register window of the Automobiles & Trucks asset account.

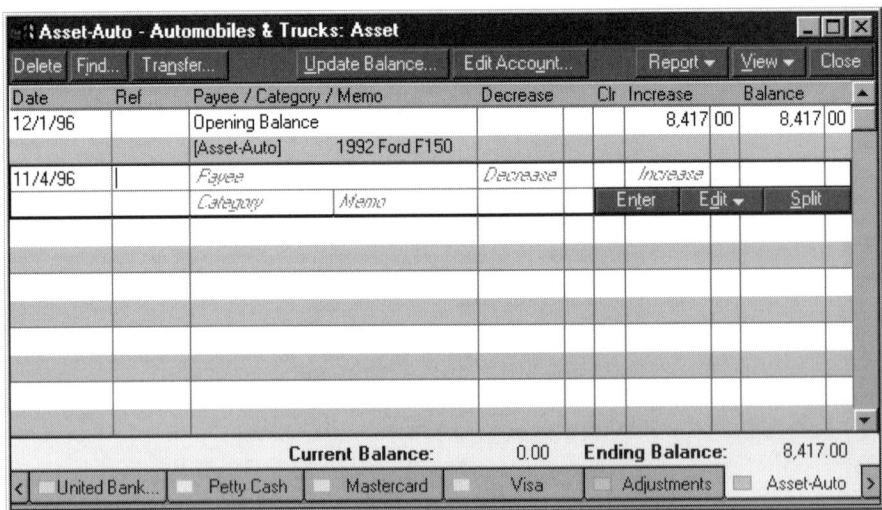

Memo field is where you can write a brief description of the expense. The Decrease field is where you fill in the amount of the check. The Clr box gets checked when you reconcile your account and indicate that the check has cleared. The Increase field is where you enter amounts that are transferred *into* your account. The Balance field, calculated by Quicken, contains your running balance.

1. Click once on the first available blank transaction record and enter the following information:

   ◆ In the Date field, enter the date on which you purchased the asset (vehicle).

   ◆ In the Ref (reference) field, enter **begbal** (short for beginning balance).

   ◆ In the Payee field, enter the name of the party from whom you purchased the asset. If you don't know the name of this company or person, simply enter **Beginning Balance.**

   ◆ In the Category field, select the asset account at the bottom of the list that begins with Transfer to/from [account name]. For example, if you are entering a balance for an automobile, you would use the [Asset-Auto] account.

   ◆ In the Memo field, enter the year, make, and model of the vehicle.

   ◆ Tab over to the Increase field and enter the value of the vehicle. If the vehicle is new, use the original purchase price of the asset. If you're entering the value of a vehicle you've owned for more than a year, ask your accountant to determine the value of the vehicle.

2. When you're finished entering the information, click Enter to record the transaction.

Liabilities If you've decided to show assets like buildings and trucks, you may benefit taxwise if you show the liabilities associated with those assets. The Qksample and Company files have a mortgage account and a loan account configured for your use. As an additional enhancement, we've created memorized transactions to run these accounts. If you're uncertain of the tax implications associated with these accounts, ask your accountant.

Mortgage — Contractors often own real estate or are buying their buildings and have to pay monthly mortgage payments.

To enter a value for a mortgage:

1. From the menu, select Lists | Account.

Figure 2-56

This example shows how you might set up an opening balance for a liability in the Mortgage Register.

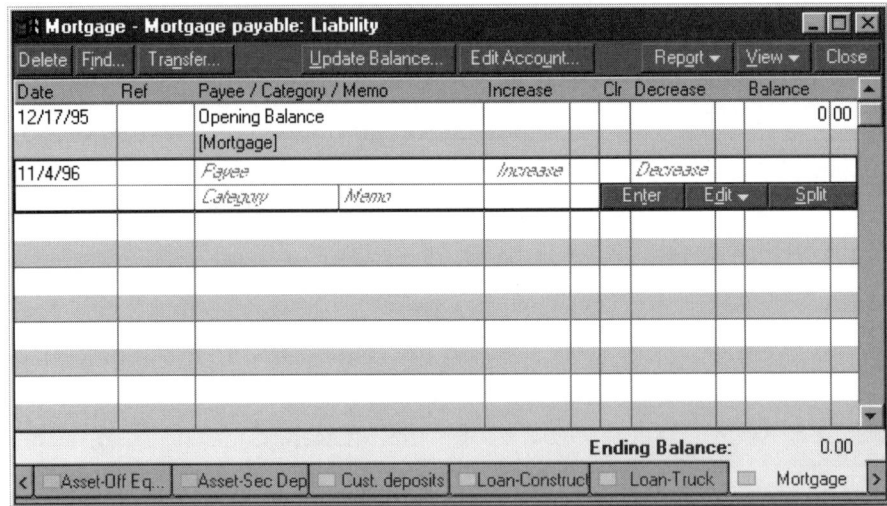

2. Click on the Other tab in the Account List window. Locate the account with the name Mortgage and the description of Mortgage Payable. Highlight the Mortgage Payable account by clicking on it once.

3. Click the Open button in the Account List window to open the Mortgage Register. Figure 2-56 shows sample information being entered in this register.

4. When the register appears, it should be blank. Click once on the first transaction and enter the following information:

   ◆ In the Date field, enter the date on which the liability was first incurred.

   ◆ In the Ref (reference) field, enter **begbal** (short for beginning balance).

   ◆ In the Payee field, enter the name of the bank or financial institution to whom you owe the liability.

   ◆ In the Category field, select the liability account at the bottom of the list that begins with Transfer to/from [account name]. For example, if you are entering a balance for a mortgage you would use the [Mortgage] account.

   ◆ In the Memo field, enter the building address; for example, Powell Street Project.

   ◆ Tab over to the Increase field. Enter the current principal balance on the loan.

5. Click Enter to record the transaction.

Figure 2–57

This example shows how to set up loan information in the Liability-Truck Loan Register window.

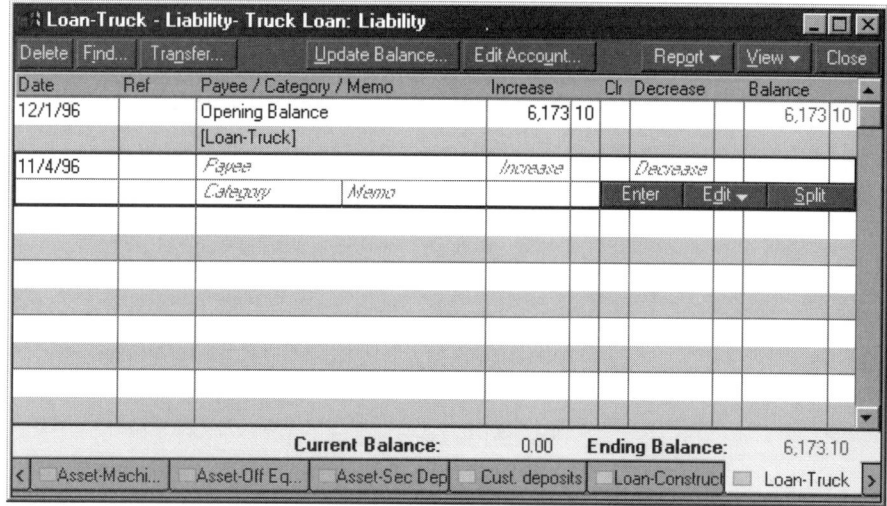

Loans—If you didn't pay cash for your truck, or for other equipment, you probably have a loan to pay. You can set up a loan account in Quicken.

To enter a value for a loan:

1. From the menu, select Lists | Account.

2. Click on the Other tab in the Account List window. Locate the account with the name Loan-Truck and the description of Liability-Truck Loan. Highlight the Liability-Truck Loan account by clicking on it once.

3. Press the Open button in the Account List window to open the Liability-Truck Loan Register, as shown in Figure 2–57.

4. When the register appears it should be blank. Click once on the first transaction record and enter the following information:

    ◆ In the Date field, enter the date on which you purchased the asset and the loan went into effect.

    ◆ In the Ref (reference) field, enter **begbal** (short for beginning balance).

    ◆ In the Payee field, enter the name of the bank or financial institution to whom you owe the liability.

    ◆ In the Category field, select the liability account at the bottom of the list that begins with Transfer to/from [account name]. For example, if you are entering a balance for an auto loan you would use the [Loan-Truck] transfer account.

    ◆ In the Memo field, enter a short description of the loan; for example, Ford F150 Loan.

◆ Tab over to the Increase field. Enter the current principal balance on the loan.

5. Click Enter to record the transaction.

Deleting Existing Accounts

You may find that the sample file we've provided has more accounts than you need. For instance, you may not be in a position to need an investment account, or perhaps you only purchase new equipment with cash so you don't need a loan account.

To delete an account:

1. From the menu, select Lists | Account.

2. Locate the account you want to delete and click on it once to highlight it.

3. Click the Delete button. You'll be prompted with a message telling you this action is permanent. If you're sure you want to delete the account, type in **yes** to confirm.

4. Click OK and the account is deleted.

Classes (Jobs)

Classes can be thought of as containers or buckets that you put job costs into. By setting up and using classes, you can later sort information for billing and reports. For instance, if you enter a budget for a class/job, you can generate a report showing actual costs versus estimated or budgeted costs for that job. For a project that is billable on a time and materials basis, tracking the project with a class will allow you to print a report, by class, that will give you a list of all the transactions for that project.

For the contractor, classes in Quicken should be thought of as jobs. For example, suppose you contract with Nancy Johnson to remodel her kitchen at 121 Grove Street. As soon as you're awarded the job you would set up a class for the Johnson remodel.

Using our system as an example, the class/job is simply J.0000; the J stands for the job, and 1002 represents the job number. An alternative way to name a job would be to include the year. For example, 97-10 would be the tenth job started in 1997. We suggest you keep the class/job name short because Quicken allows only 15 characters for this information. The *description* of the class name, on the other

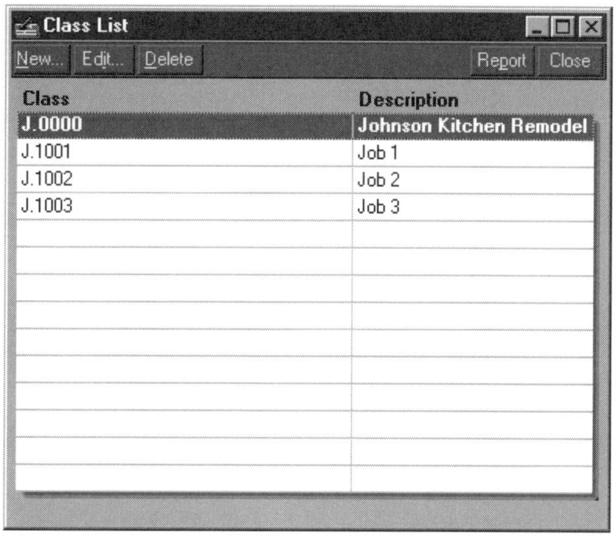

Figure 2–58

You can use the Class (job) List provided with the Company file as a model for your own projects.

hand, can be longer and more specific. In our example, the description might be the last name of the customer and the type of job, Johnson Kitchen Remodel. Figure 2–58 shows the class list from the Qksample data file.

Creating New Classes

To create a new class that you can use to track a job:

1. From the menu, select Lists | Class. You'll see displayed a list of all the classes you've previously entered.

2. Click the New button to display the Set Up Class dialog box shown in Figure 2–59.

3. In the Name field, enter a brief name for the class, such as J.1004.

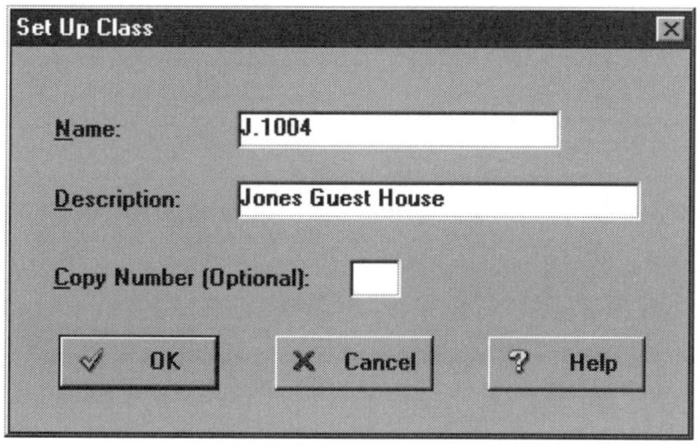

Figure 2–59

You specify a name and description for a new class in the Set Up Class window.

Figure 2–60

After you create a new class, the Class List window shows that the new class (job) has been added.

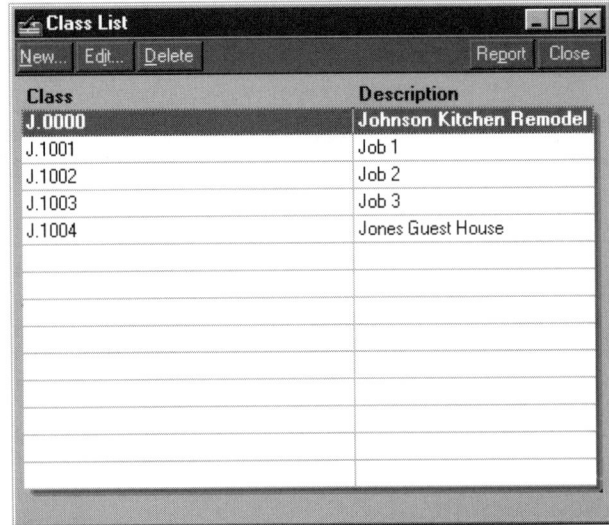

4. In the Description field, enter a description for the class, such as Jones Guest House.

5. Click the OK button to create the new class. The new class (job) now appears in the Class List window, as shown in Figure 2–60.

Modifying Existing Classes

Depending on your existing setup, you may or may not need to modify existing classes. If you have existing classes that are set up as something other than jobs (not recommended), you can keep them; however, we recommend that you change the name to push these classes to the bottom of the class list. You can do this by putting a "Z" in front of the original name. This is also a good way to identify old versus new methods of using classes.

To modify an existing class:

1. From the menu, select Lists | Class. You'll see displayed a list of all the classes you've previously entered.

2. Let's edit the J.1000 class in the Qksample file as an example. Highlight the class by clicking on it once. Then click the Edit button.

3. In the Edit Class dialog box that appears (Figure 2–61), enter a description for the class, such as Johnson Kitchen Remodel.

4. Click the OK button to save your changes. The new information about the class now appears in the Class List window, as shown in Figure 2–62.

Figure 2–61

You can edit the description for an existing class in the Edit Class dialog box.

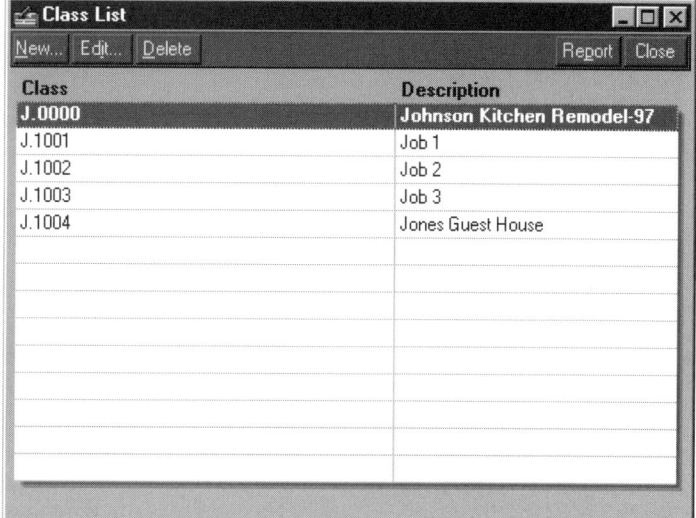

Figure 2–62

Changes you make to class information are updated in the Class List window.

Deleting Existing Classes

We suggest you avoid deleting classes. If you delete a class, all the data associated with that class will be "orphaned." It will still be in your Quicken file, but it won't show up in any class report.

A common problem with classes is that your class list becomes very long. To get around this problem, you can use a method similar to what we discussed in the "Modifying Existing Classes" section. Change the name of the class to start with a "2," followed by a two-digit year identifier. For example, when you're finished with the Johnson Kitchen Remodel job you can identify the job as completed and inactive by changing the class name from J.1000 to 297J.1000. Using this naming system will help you keep your classes organized.

3

Customizing Quicken

J ust as you'd fine-tune a new table saw, your Quicken application needs to be tuned before it will perform the job-costing functions that are so important in running a construction-industry business. In this chapter, we'll show you how to customize Quicken by editing various options that affect how Quicken looks and functions.

Customizing Quicken involves reviewing groups of related options found under the Edit|Options command and choosing to turn each option on or off. Quicken uses a check mark to designate whether an option is currently active ("turned on"). When the check box in front of an option is blank, the option is currently inactive ("turned off"). Conversely, when the check box contains a check mark, the option is active. To change the status of any option from active to inactive or vice versa, simply click into the check box.

NOTE: *Throughout this chapter, some of the options that we'll be illustrating are different from the standard (default) options in your software. That's because the options we're suggesting are the ones that make it easier for you, as a construction professional, to work in Quicken.*

To begin customizing Quicken, start the program now if it isn't currently running. To view the available options, select Edit|Options

Figure 3–1

The Options submenu shows all the different categories available for customizing Quicken.

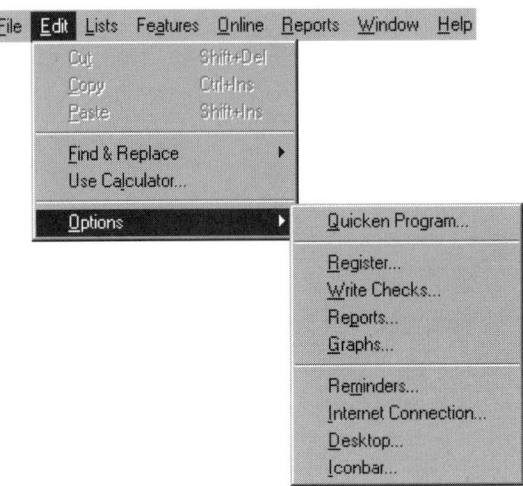

from the menu. Figure 3–1 shows the categories on the submenu that appears. The Options categories and an overview of what they do are listed below.

◆ *Quicken Program*—This group includes general options that affect basic Quicken functions and the interface (colors, keyboard shortcuts, placement of screen elements, and so on).

◆ *Register*—This group of options controls the way Quicken looks and performs when you are working in the Register window of any of your accounts.

◆ *Write Checks*—These options determine how Quicken automates the process of writing electronic checks.

◆ *Reports*—This group controls how Quicken displays and generates reports, which are important for job costing, tax preparation, and cost comparison (see Chapter 7, "Using Memorized Reports").

◆ *Graphs*—These options affect the way Quicken displays graphs on your screen.

◆ *Reminders*—Quicken can act as your personal secretary, reminding you when to pay bills and handle other financial tasks. The Reminders options let you specify exactly how to use this feature.

◆ *Desktop*—The Desktop options control how your display appears each time you run Quicken. You can choose to have Quicken always open with the same set of windows and items on the screen, or you can have Quicken open using the exact settings you had the last time you *exited* the application.

◆ *Iconbar*—These options let you customize the *iconbar*, the row of icons at the top of the Quicken screen. The iconbar gives you handy, one-click access to functions you use frequently.

The remaining sections of this chapter examine each group of options in detail to help you configure Quicken to your best advantage.

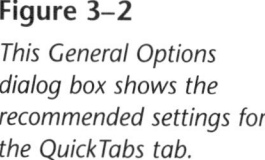 Quicken Program Options

The options found under the Edit I Options I Quicken Program command let you set up a fiscal year calendar and select other general settings that affect the look and feel of Quicken. From the Edit I Options submenu, select the Quicken Program command to display the General Options dialog box. Figure 3–2 shows the QuickTabs tab of this dialog box with our recommended settings activated.

The General Options dialog box actually contains three different groups of options—QuickTabs, General, and Settings. You can access each group by clicking on its *tab,* which looks much like the tab on a file folder (Figure 3–2).

QuickTabs Tab

The options in the QuickTabs tab of the General Options dialog box directly affect which elements appear on your screen each time you work in Quicken. Figure 3–2 shows the options in this section of the dialog box.

Figure 3–2

This General Options dialog box shows the recommended settings for the QuickTabs tab.

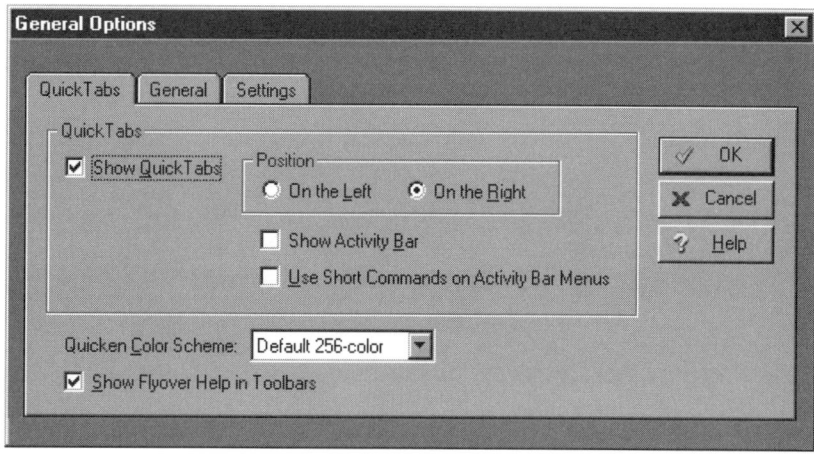

Show QuickTabs

When the Show QuickTabs option is active (the default setting), a tiled list appears at the right or left side of the Quicken application window (see the "Position" section that follows). Each time you open a new window, a labeled QuickTab corresponding to the name of that window is added to the list. QuickTabs are convenient; instead of having to open and close the same windows repeatedly, you can just click on a QuickTab tile to quickly move from one open window to another. For example, it is very handy to be able to move from your check register to the Category & Transfer List window when you have to choose a new category for a check. The example in Figure 3–3 shows that the Category & Transfer List window, Register window, and Account List window are all open and can be accessed by clicking on the Register, Accounts, or Categories QuickTab, respectively.

When Show QuickTabs is turned off, your Quicken window displays all currently open windows in a cascaded format, with the window in which you're working on top (Figure 3–4).

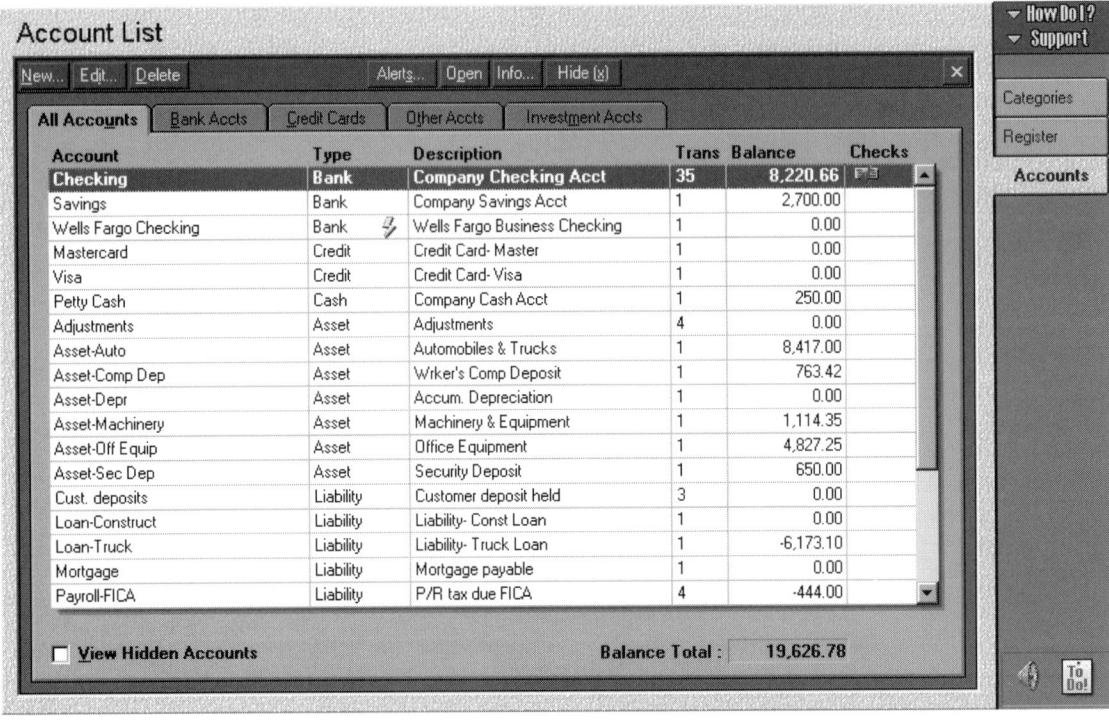

Figure 3–3

With QuickTabs turned on, you can view a handy list of all Quicken windows that are currently open and move quickly between them with a single click.

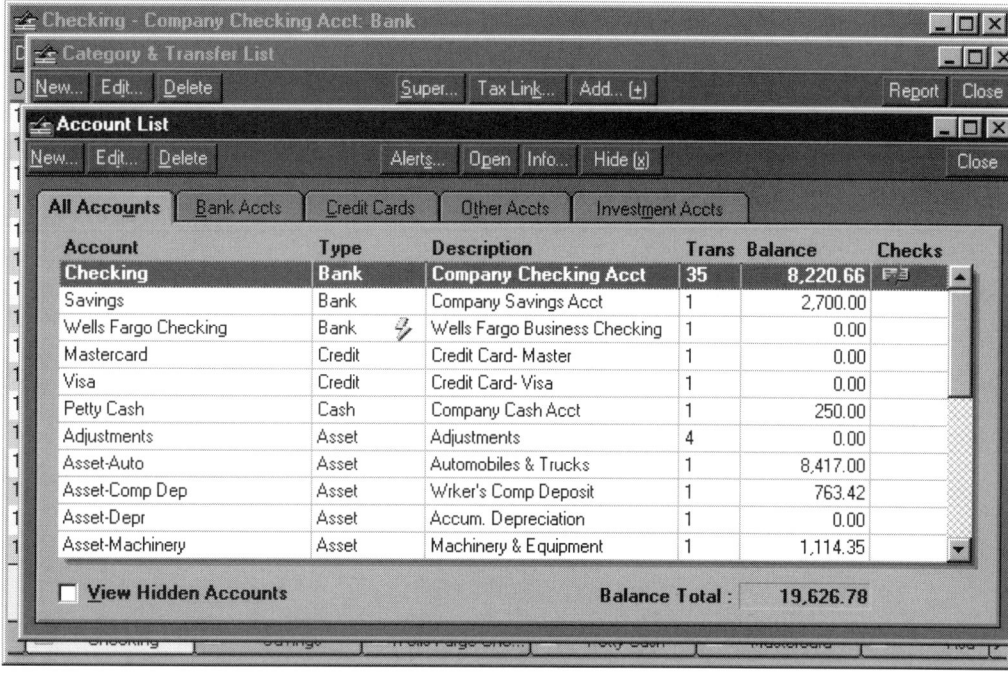

Figure 3-4

With Show QuickTabs turned off, all currently open windows in Quicken appear in cascaded format, with the active window on top.

Position

The Position option is available only when Show QuickTabs is turned on. It lets you select where you would like to display Quick-Tabs. You can choose to have QuickTabs appear on either the right or left side of the screen. On the Right is the default option.

Show Activity Bar

The Show Activity Bar option is available only when Show Quick-Tabs is turned on. When this option shows a check mark, Quicken displays a row of icons along the bottom of the screen. These icons—My Accounts, Bills, Planning, Investments, Home & Car, Online, and Reports—relate to common user activities. Moving your mouse over one of these icons causes a pop-up menu to appear, as shown in Figure 3-5. All the menu choices from these icons are also available from the menus at the top of the Quicken screen. If you have a small monitor (say, 15 inches or less) and would prefer to have more space to see your register or other account windows, keep the Show Activity Bar option turned off.

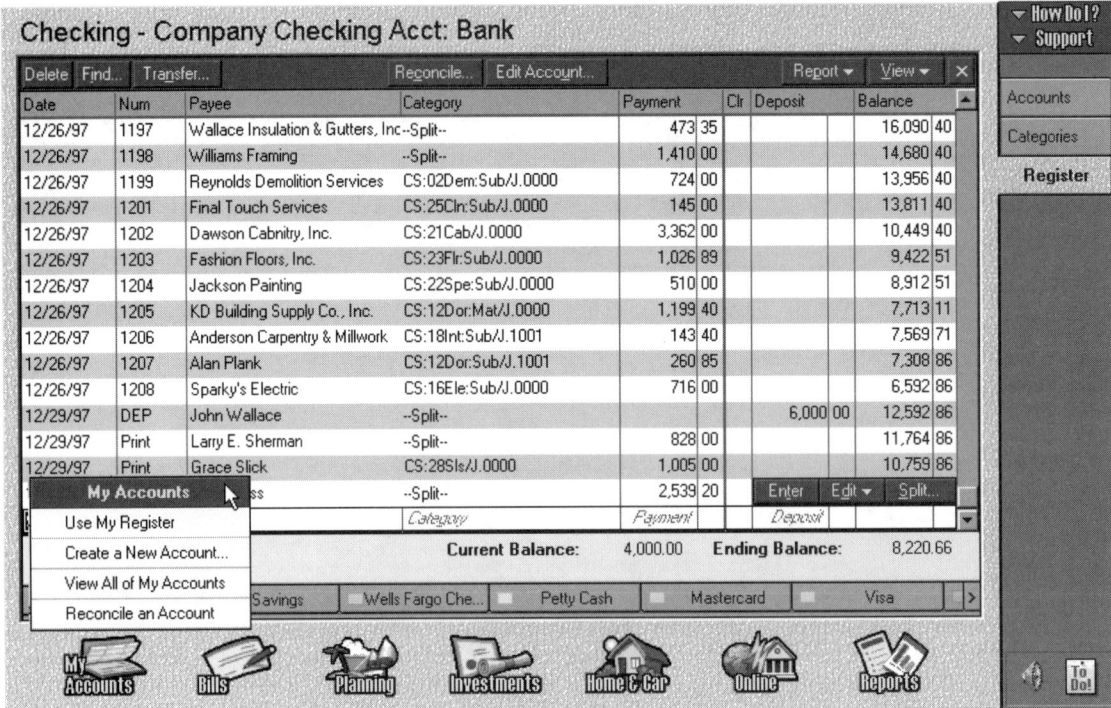

Figure 3–5

When the Activity Bar icons are active, you can quickly access common functions by moving the mouse over an icon and then clicking on the desired function.

Use Short Commands on Activity Bar Menus

With this option active, the Activity Bar pop-up menu will display a very brief description of the available commands. For instance, when you move your mouse over the icon labeled My Accounts with this option on, the first command on the pop-up menu is Register. If you turn off the Use Short Commands on Activity Bar Menus option, the same pop-up menu command would be Use My Register.

Quicken Color Scheme

This is a "just for fun" option that you can change whenever you want a different look for your Quicken display. Quicken supplies a number of different preconfigured color schemes. To select one other than the Default 256-color option, scroll through the drop-down menu and click on the one you want to try.

Show Flyover Help in Toolbars

When this option is turned on, you never have to memorize the meaning of the on-screen icons in the iconbar or elsewhere. Moving the cursor over an icon causes a description of the icon to pop up, as shown in Figure 3–6. Show Flyover Help in Toolbars is active by default; to turn this option off, just click into the check box.

General Tab

The options in the General tab of the General Options dialog box (Figure 3–7) determine how Quicken manages backups, tax information, and memorized transactions. To access the General tab if you're in the QuickTabs tab, click on the word "General."

Prompt to Backup Files on Shutdown

With this option active, each time you exit Quicken you'll see a prompt suggesting that you back up your files. You can click on the Backup button in the dialog box that appears and Quicken will step

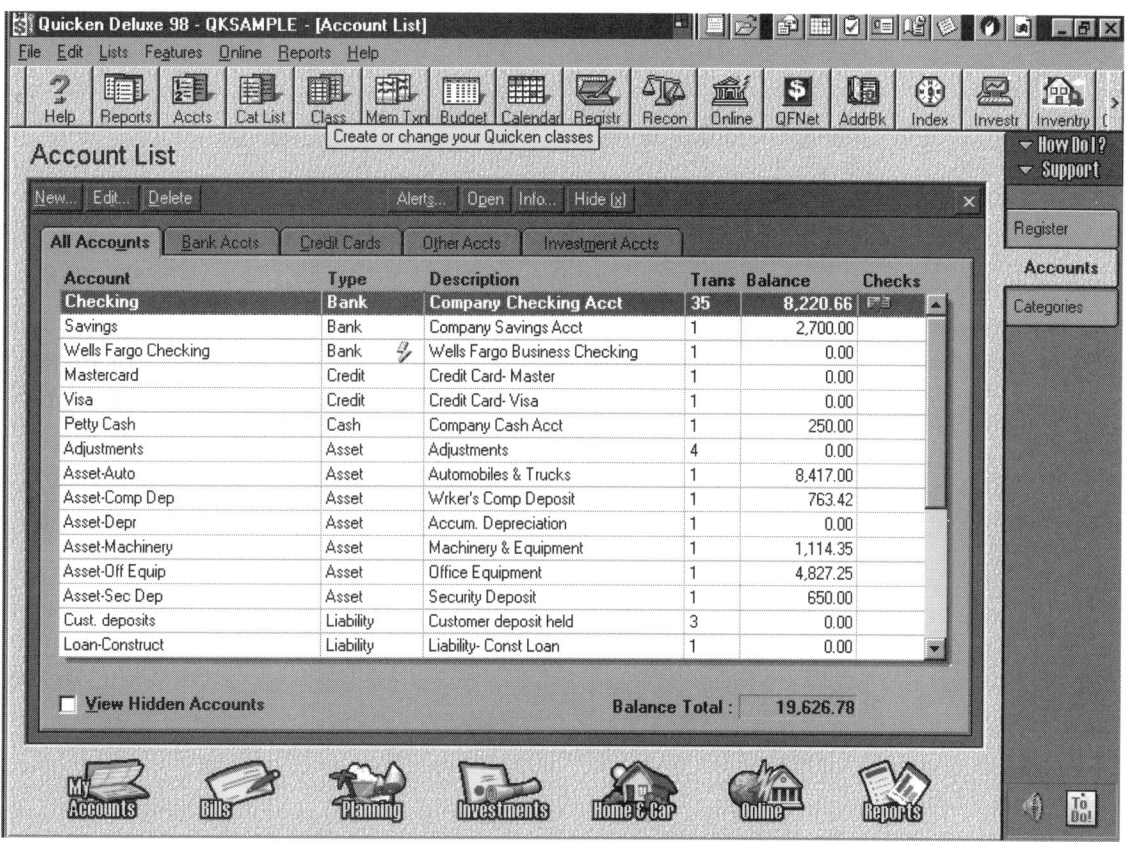

Figure 3–6

The Show Flyover Help in Toolbars option lets you view pop-up descriptions of the function of any icon over which you move the mouse.

Figure 3–7

This General Options dialog box shows the recommended settings for the General tab.

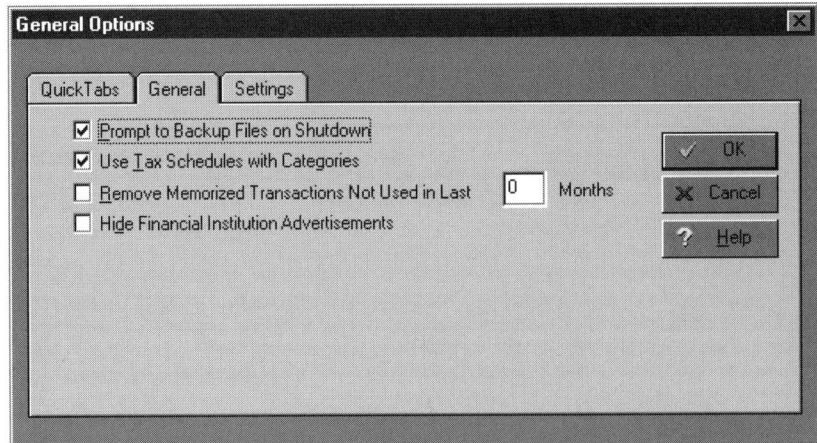

you through backing up your files. This option is active by default, and we suggest that you leave it turned on.

 NOTE: *Here's an efficient method for backing up your files. Back up every day at the end of your session, using a different diskette for each day of the week. Using this method, you will not have to rely on a single backup diskette in the case of data loss.*

Use Tax Schedules with Categories

With this option active, you can choose to link specific tax schedules to the appropriate categories within your Quicken file. This option is active by default.

Remove Memorized Transactions Not Used in Last *XX* Months

When active, this option turns off memorized transactions that you haven't used within the number of months you specify. By default, the option is inactive, meaning Quicken won't delete any memorized transactions. Refer to Chapter 6, "Using Memorized Transactions," for more information.

Settings Tab

The options in the Settings tab of the General Options dialog box control keyboard commands and your fiscal calendar (Figure 3–8). To access the Settings tab when some other tab of the dialog box is visible, click on the word "Settings."

Figure 3–8

This area of the General Options dialog box shows the recommended settings for the Settings tab.

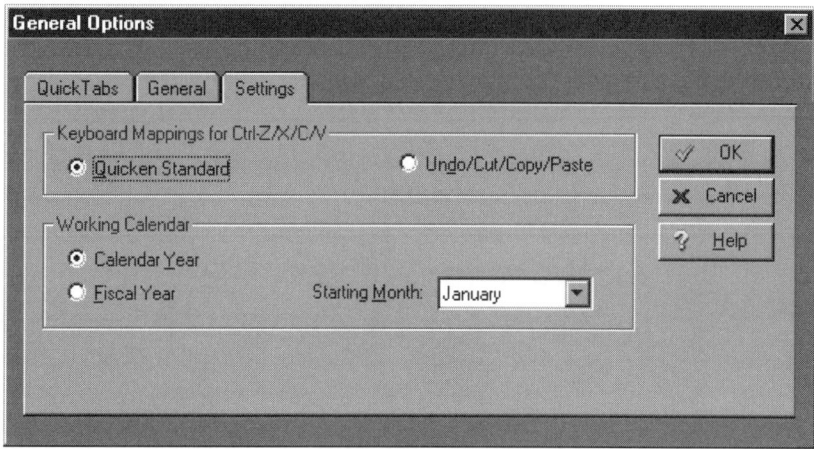

Keyboard Mappings for Ctrl-Z/X/C/V

This option lets you select either Windows standard Ctrl-key sequences or Quicken's key sequences, which are different. If you work with many other Windows programs besides Quicken, you may find it more convenient to turn on the Undo/Cut/Copy/Paste option. With this option active, pressing the Ctrl key in combination with X, C, V, or Z performs the following Windows actions:

Ctrl-X	Cut
Ctrl-C	Copy
Ctrl-V	Paste
Ctrl-Z	Undo

If, on the other hand, Quicken is your main application and you don't work with many other Windows programs, you may wish to leave the Quicken Standard option (the default setting) active. Pressing the Ctrl key in combination with X, C, V, or Z when this option is turned on performs the Quicken-specific actions shown in the list that follows:

Ctrl-X	Immediately takes you to the Register window of the transfer account when you're transferring amounts from one account to another; equivalent to selecting the Edit I Transaction I Go to Transfer command.
Ctrl-C	Displays the Category & Transfer List window; equivalent to selecting the Lists I Category/Transfer command.
Ctrl-V	Voids the current transaction; equivalent to selecting the Edit I Transaction I Void Transaction command.

Ctrl-Z   When viewing a report, zooms in to show a detailed report related to the amount over which your mouse is located; equivalent to double-clicking on the amount.

Most of the functions described above can also be performed by using commands in the Edit and Lists menus.

Working Calendar

This section of the dialog box lets you choose whether your business is run on a Fiscal Year or a Calendar Year (the default option). A calendar year is 12 months from January through December. A fiscal year is 12 continuous months starting at any month except January. If you chose a special fiscal year at the time of starting up your business, activate the Fiscal Year option and select a start month from the Starting Month drop-down menu.

⌂ Register Options

Register options let you personalize the way Quicken displays and operates your account registers. From the Edit I Options submenu, click on Register to display the Register Options dialog box. Figure 3–9 shows the recommended settings for the Display tab of this dialog box.

Display Tab

The options in the Display tab of the Register Options dialog box affect the visuals that appear in your account registers.

Show Date in First Column

This option, which is turned on by default, controls the display of the check number (Num) and Date fields in your account registers. With this option active, the date appears in the first column on the left. When it's turned off, the check number appears in the first column of each transaction.

Show Memo before Category

This option controls the display of the Category and Memo fields. When active, the Memo field always appears before the Category field in the Register window. When this option is turned off (the default), the Category field always appears before the Memo field of each transaction.

Figure 3–9

This Register Options dialog box shows the recommended settings for the Display tab.

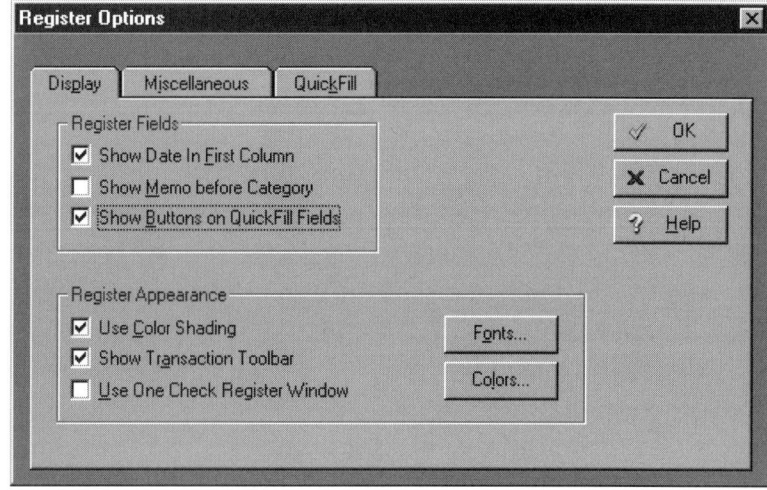

The effect of turning on this option is apparent only when your Register window is set up for a two-line display (the default is one line). If your Register window shows only a one-line display and you want to switch to a two-line display, click the View button in the upper-right area of the Register window and then click One-Line Display to deactivate that setting.

Show Buttons on QuickFill Fields

Some of the fields in the Register window are considered QuickFill fields, which means that when you click into those fields you'll see a down-facing arrow. Clicking the arrow presents a drop-down list of choices. For example, if you're in the Check Register window and click the arrow in the Payee field, you'll see a list of everyone you've previously written a check to. When the Show Buttons on QuickFill Fields is not active, no drop-down arrow appears in these fields, and no list appears when you click into the field.

Use Color Shading

Using color shading in Register windows lets you visually distinguish between transactions—alternate transactions appear in darker and lighter shades of the same color. This option is turned on by default. If you turn Use Color Shading off, the background color for all the account registers is white.

 NOTE: *Use a different color for each type of account register (bank accounts, credit card accounts, and so on) and you'll recognize which register you are in at a glance. See the section on "Colors" options for more details.*

Show Transaction Toolbar

With this option active (the default), Quicken shows a row of buttons (Enter | Edit | Split) at the right edge of the current transaction. These buttons give you point-and-click access to transaction editing functions—recording the transaction, editing the transaction, or splitting the transaction among multiple items. These buttons are absent when you turn Show Transaction Toolbar off.

Use One Check Register Window

When this option is turned on, Quicken displays a single Register window, no matter how many accounts are currently open. The appearance of this single Register window changes depending on which account you're currently viewing. When Use One Check Register Window is turned off, a separate Register window will be opened for each account that you currently have open.

Fonts

Quicken uses a standard set of fonts to display its interface. If you have additional fonts in your system, click the Fonts button in the Display tab to select the fonts and type sizes you want Quicken to use in your register. Figure 3–10 shows the Choose Register Font dialog box that appears when you click this button.

Colors

By default, Quicken uses one color for bank account registers, another for cash account registers, and so on. If you wish to customize the colors displayed in each type of account register, click the Colors button in the Display tab and select the colors you want. Figure 3–11 shows the Choose Register Colors dialog box.

Miscellaneous Tab

The options in the Miscellaneous tab of the Register Options dialog box let you indicate when Quicken should notify you of something (Figure 3–12). Notifications are useful because they can help prevent you from accidentally making errors when working in an account register. By default, all the options are active except for Beep When Recording and Memorizing.

Beep When Recording and Memorizing

Activating this option makes Quicken beep when you record, memorize, or delete transactions or reports.

Figure 3–10

The Choose Register Font dialog box lets you customize the fonts that Quicken uses to display transactions in the Register window.

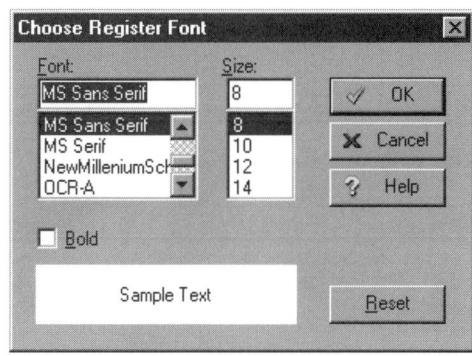

Figure 3–11

You can pick custom colors for each type of account register using the Choose Register Colors dialog box.

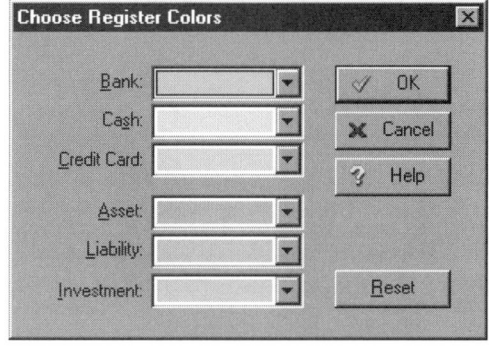

Figure 3–12

This Register Options dialog box shows the recommended settings for the Miscellaneous tab.

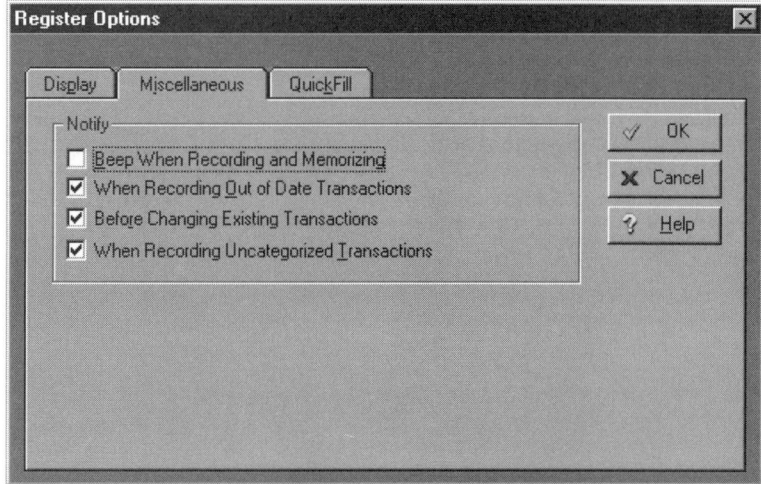

When Recording Out of Date Transactions

With this option active, Quicken displays a warning message if you try to record a transaction for a year other than the current year. This is especially helpful at the beginning of a new year.

Before Changing Existing Transactions

With this option active, Quicken asks you to confirm a change to a transaction if you try to move to another transaction before you've recorded the change.

When Recording Uncategorized Transactions

Keeping this option turned on ensures that you assign categories to all your transactions. This is important to ensure the accuracy of the reports you generate in Quicken—if some transactions remain uncategorized, they will not show up in any report.

QuickFill Tab

Figure 3–13 shows the QuickFill tab of the Register Options dialog box. These options let you control features that affect the degree to which Quicken automatically fills in data for each transaction. The more you automate data entry, the more time you can save.

Use Enter Key to Move Between Fields

By default, you use the Tab key in Quicken to move from one field to the next in account registers. If you'd prefer to use the Enter key instead, activate the Use Enter Key to Move Between Fields option.

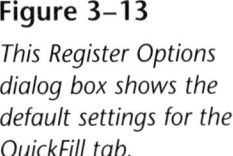

Figure 3–13

This Register Options dialog box shows the default settings for the QuickFill tab.

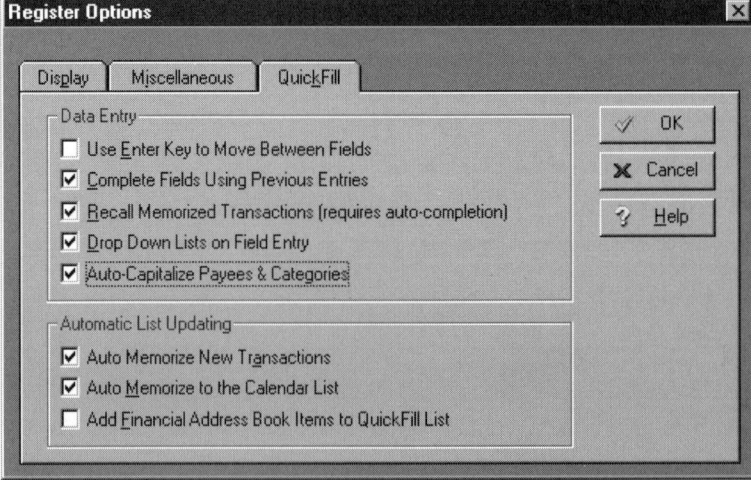

Complete Fields Using Previous Entries

If you repeatedly pay bills to the same creditor every month for the same purpose and in the same amount, keep both this option and the Auto Memorize New Transactions option activated. Then, when you type the first few characters of a transaction, Quicken completes the remainder of the transaction automatically, using the data from the *last* time you entered this same transaction. If you turn off this option, you won't be able to use the Recall Memorized Transactions option. On the other hand, if the amounts of a repeated transaction vary each time, or if the job varies, you may find Complete Fields Using Previous Entries annoying. To avoid problems, be sure to make any necessary changes to the class (job) and amount of the transaction before recording the transaction.

Recall Memorized Transactions

With this option turned on (the default), Quicken will finish a transaction when you leave the Payee field using the Tab key (or the Enter key if that option is enabled). When turned off, this option disables Complete Fields Using Previous Entries.

Drop Down Lists on Field Entry

Activate this option to have Quicken automatically display a drop-down list when the cursor enters a drop-down field. This eliminates having to click into the field to see the possible choices.

Auto-Capitalize Payees & Categories

When this option is turned on, Quicken automatically capitalizes the first, last, and company name of a vendor, even if you enter it in lower case. Initial caps are also applied to new category names. This option is active by default.

Auto Memorize New Transactions

Leave this option activated (the default) to add each transaction for a new payee to the Memorized Transaction list. See Chapter 6 for more information about using memorized transactions.

Auto Memorize to the Calendar List

This option, which is active by default, prevents you from paying bills late or forgetting payments. It tells Quicken to memorize transactions and schedule them on the Financial Calendar. Quicken then automatically issues a payment on schedule and tells you that a check needs to be written.

Add Financial Address Book Items to QuickFill List

When activated, this option makes names from Quicken's Financial Address Book available to the internal database. When you begin to type one of these names, Quicken automatically fills it in for you.

Check Options

The Check Options dialog box lets you personalize the display and operation of your check register and the way Quicken prints your checks. To access these options, select Edit | Options | Write Checks. Figure 3–14 shows the Checks tab of this dialog box.

Checks Tab

The options in the Checks tab of the Check Options dialog box control the look of electronic checks, both on screen and when printed.

Printed Date Style

This option determines whether Quicken prints check dates using four-digit years (the default 4-digit Year option) or two-digit years (the 2-digit Year option).

Allow Entry of Extra Message on Check

Activating this option adds an extra message field, which is printed on your checks. A typical message that a business might include in

Figure 3–14

The Checks tab of the Check Options dialog box is where you customize your electronic checks.

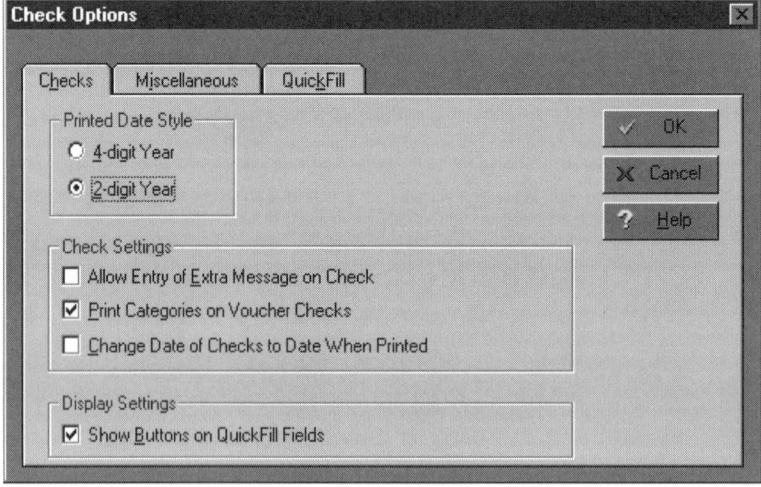

this message field is "For inquiries, contact Accounts Payable at extension 100."

If you use window envelopes to send checks, the extra line will not be visible in the address window.

Print Categories on Voucher Checks

Keeping this option active prints up to 16 lines of information on the attachment to voucher checks (the attachment is the part of the check below the perforation). This lets you easily identify how the amount of the check is split between two or more categories.

Change Date of Checks to Date When Printed

Activate this option if you wish to print the check using the date on which it was printed rather than the date on which it was issued. This can be useful if you enter payments in advance of actually printing and issuing checks. For instance, suppose you want to create a check to show a committed cost on your job-cost reports. You would write a check using a future date for materials that you have ordered but haven't been billed for yet. When you receive the bill and print the check, Quicken will change the date on the check from the date on which you created the record to the date on which the check is printed.

Show Buttons on QuickFill Fields

With this option turned on, QuickFill fields in check register windows display drop-down arrow buttons that make available a list of choices based on entries you've made previously. When this option is turned off, no drop-down buttons or lists appear in the QuickFill fields.

Miscellaneous Tab

The options in the Miscellaneous tab of the Check Options dialog box let you control when and how Quicken alerts you when you're writing checks. Figure 3–15 shows the recommended settings for this tab.

Beep When Recording and Memorizing

Leave this option activated to make Quicken beep when you record, memorize, or delete transactions or reports.

When Recording Out of Date Transactions

When this option is turned on (the default), Quicken displays a warning message if you try to record a transaction for a year other than the current one.

Figure 3–15

This Check Options dialog box shows the recommended settings for the Miscellaneous tab.

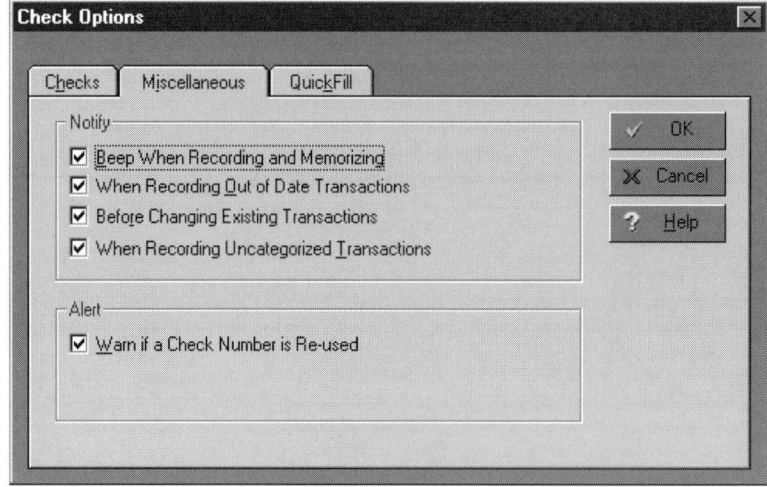

Before Changing Existing Transactions

With this option active (the default), Quicken asks you to confirm a change to a transaction if you try to move to another transaction before you've recorded the change.

When Recording Uncategorized Transactions

Leave this option turned on to ensure that you categorize all your transactions. Transactions not assigned to any category don't show up in any Quicken reports, which could compromise the accuracy of those reports.

Warn if a Check Number is Re-used

When activated (the default), this option displays a warning message if you enter a previously-used check number. It's important to leave this option turned on to prevent accidental use of duplicate checks.

QuickFill Tab

The QuickFill tab of the Check Options dialog box contains options that affect how Quicken automates the check writing process. Figure 3–16 shows this tab with the recommended settings activated.

Use Enter Key to Move Between Fields

By default, you use the Tab key in Quicken to move from one field to the next in the Write Checks window. If you'd prefer to use the Enter key instead, activate the Use Enter Key to Move Between Fields option.

Figure 3-16

This Check Options dialog box shows the recommended settings for the QuickFill tab.

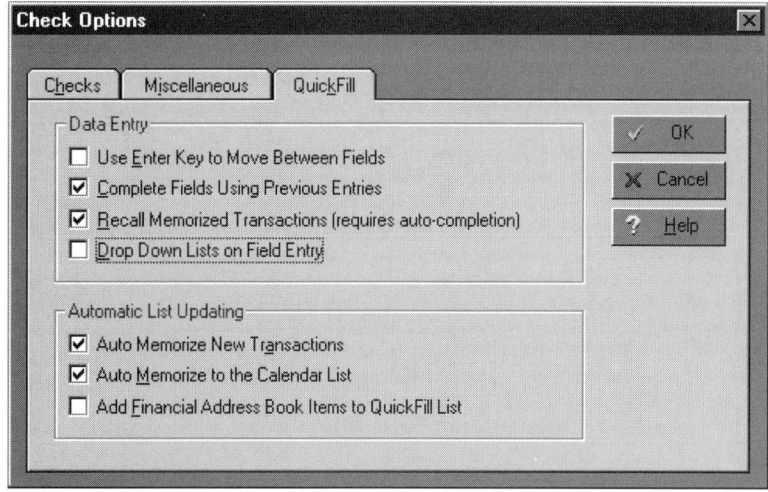

Complete Fields Using Previous Entries

If you repeatedly pay bills to the same creditor every month for the same purpose and in the same amount, keep both this option and the Auto Memorize New Transactions option activated. Then, when you type the first few characters of a transaction, Quicken completes the remainder of the transaction automatically, using the data from the *last* time you entered this same transaction. If you turn off this option you won't be able to use the Recall Memorized Transactions option. On the other hand, if the amounts of a repeated transaction vary each time, or if the job varies, you may find Complete Fields Using Previous Entries annoying. To avoid problems, be sure to make any necessary changes to the class (job) and amount of the transaction before recording the transaction.

Recall Memorized Transactions

With this option turned on (the default), Quicken will finish a transaction when you leave the Payee field using the Tab key (or the Enter key if that option is enabled). When turned off, this option disables Complete Fields Using Previous Entries.

Drop Down Lists on Field Entry

Activate this option to have Quicken automatically display a drop-down list when the cursor enters a drop-down field. This eliminates having to click into the field to see the possible choices.

Auto Memorize New Transactions

Leave this option activated (the default) to add each transaction for a new payee to the Memorized Transaction list. See Chapter 6 for more information about using memorized transactions.

Auto Memorize to the Calendar List

This option, which is active by default, prevents you from paying bills late or forgetting payments. It tells Quicken to memorize transactions and schedule them on the Financial Calendar. Quicken then automatically issues a payment on schedule and tells you that a check needs to be written.

Add Financial Address Book Items to QuickFill List

When activated, this option makes names from Quicken's Financial Address Book available to the internal database. When you begin to type one of these names into a check, Quicken automatically fills it in for you.

Report Options

The Report Options dialog box lets you customize the way your reports appear and function in Quicken. (If you'd like more information about preparing and automating reports, see Chapter 7.) To access the Report Options dialog box shown in Figure 3–17, select the Reports command from the Edit | Options submenu.

Account Display

The three options in this section of the dialog box control how much information about an account Quicken displays in your reports. You can choose to display the Name, the Description, or Both. Using the name alone leaves more room on the report for other fields.

Category Display

The three options in the Category Display section of the dialog box control how much information about each category Quicken displays in your reports. Choose Description, Name, or Both. Using the category name alone leaves more room on the report for other fields; if

Figure 3-17

The Report Options dialog box lets you customize the way Quicken displays and prepares automated reports.

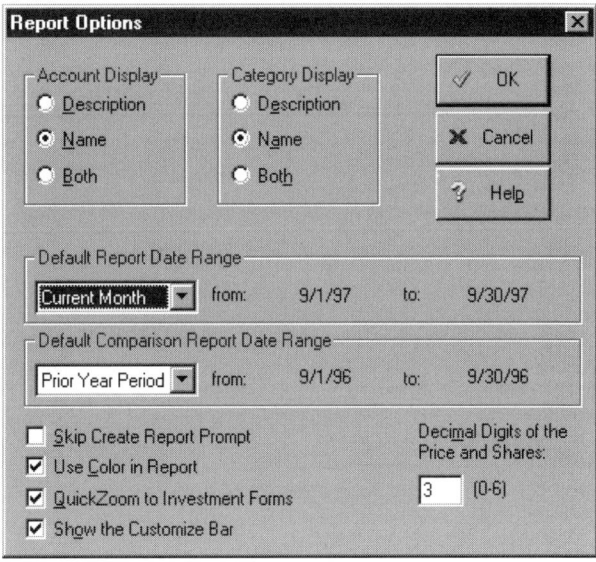

your category names are very short, you may prefer to view category descriptions, too.

Default Report Date Range

The date range you select from the drop-down list in this section of the dialog box becomes the default date range for all your Quicken reports. (You can always change the date for individual reports in the Create Report window.) The options are: Include all dates, Current Month, Current Quarter, Current Year, Month to date, Quarter to date, Year to date, Earliest to date, Last Month, Last Qtr, Last Year, Last 12 Months, and Custom Date. Year to date is the default setting. When creating reports for specific jobs, however, you may need to change the default setting, especially when the job crosses over the calendar year.

Default Comparison Report Date Range

When you want to compare finances for two different time periods (for example, between last year to date and this year to date), you generate a comparison report. The date range you select from the drop-down list in this section of the Report Options dialog box becomes the default date range for all comparison reports. (You can change the date for individual reports in the Create Report window.) The options are the same as for Default Report Date Range, with the addition of Prior Year Period (the default setting).

Skip Create Report Prompt

Activate this option if you want Quicken to create reports without first displaying the Create Report window. With this option turned off (the default), the Create Report window appears every time you run a report. Until you are very familiar with Quicken reports, it is a good idea to leave this option turned off.

Use Color in Report

With this option active (the default), Quicken displays report titles and negative amounts in color.

QuickZoom to Investment Forms

This option, which is activated by default, lets you jump from a specific transaction on an investment report to the investment form used to enter the transaction. If this option is not selected, Quicken moves you from a specific transaction on an investment report to the entry in the investment register.

Decimal Digits of the Price and Shares

This option lets you specify how you would like to see your investment price and shares displayed on reports. Suppose you have created an investment account that contains 1,000 shares of stock each worth $18, and you're using the default setting of 3 digits. When you run an investment report, this account would display 1000.000 shares of current stock with a current value of $18.000.

🏠 Graph Options

Quicken can display financial data in graph form. The Graph Options dialog box lets you customize the way Quicken displays these graphs. From the Edit I Options submenu, click on Graphs to display the Graph Options dialog box (Figure 3–18).

Figure 3–18

This Graph Options dialog box shows the settings recommended for speed and ease of use.

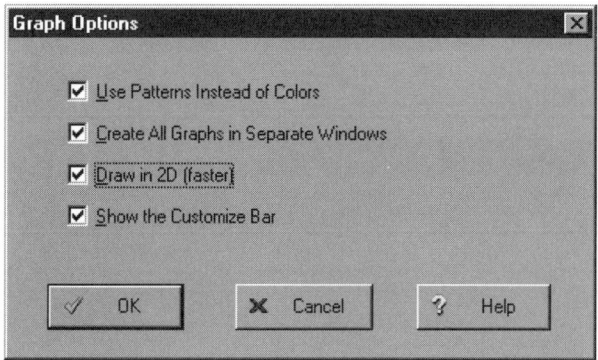

Use Patterns Instead of Colors

By default, Quicken displays graphs using multiple colors. Activate this option if you'd prefer to display graphs using black-and-white patterns instead. Using patterns is recommended if you typically output your graphs on a black-and-white printer.

Create All Graphs in Separate Windows

By default, Quicken is set up so that when you create multiple graphs, they all display in a single window. The window changes each time you revise a graph or activate a different one. If you activate the Create All Graphs in Separate Windows option, you can then create one graph after another—each in a separate window. Quicken cascades the windows in which you create multiple graphs; if you close the current graph, the previous graph remains open in the window behind it.

Draw in 2D

The default mode of graph display in Quicken is 3D (three dimensions). If you activate Draw in 2D, you tell Quicken to display graphs in two dimensions instead. If you find that it takes a long time for a graph to display, choosing the 2D option may speed things up.

Show the Customize Bar

When you activate this option, a bar appears above your graph, allowing you to change the graph dates interactively. When this option is not activated, you can still edit your graph by clicking the Customize button in the graph window.

Figure 3-19

The Reminder tab of the Reminder Options dialog box instructs Quicken on how and when to send you reminder messages other than Billminder messages.

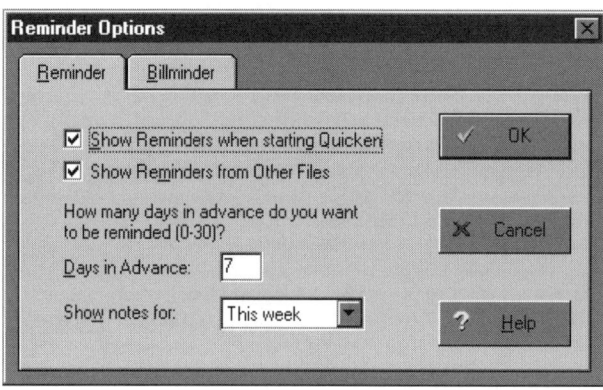

Figure 3-20

The Billminder tab of the Reminder Options dialog box instructs Quicken on how and when to send you Billminder reminder messages for the tasks you select.

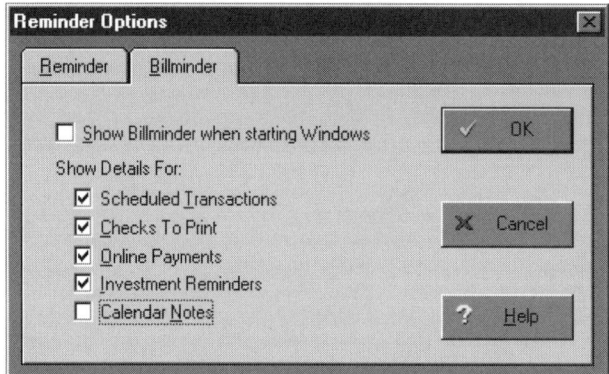

🏠 Reminder Options

The Reminder Options dialog box helps you make the most of Quicken as a personal financial secretary. To access this dialog box (Figures 3-19 and 3-20), choose the Edit I Options I Reminders command. The Reminder Options dialog box contains two tabs: one for general reminders and one for Billminder.

Reminder Options

The options in the Reminder tab (Figure 3-19) pertain to reminder messages from Quicken *other* than Billminder messages.

Show Reminders when starting Quicken

When activated, this option causes financial reminder messages to appear on your screen each time you start Quicken. You are reminded of upcoming due dates, including scheduled bill payments, checks to print, and future transactions. For example, if you schedule a rent transaction for the first day of every month, an automatic alert appears monthly, reminding you to write a check for the rent.

Show Reminders from Other Files

Many Quicken users maintain financial data in more than one file. If you have more than one business, or if you keep your business data separate from your personal financial data, you might have multiple Quicken files. If so, then activate this option (along with Show Reminders when starting Quicken) to make sure that Quicken shows up-to-date reminders from all of your data files, regardless of which file you currently have open.

Days in Advance

This option lets you determine how many days before the due date you want Quicken to remind you about scheduled financial events. The default value is 7 days. This option has no effect if Show Reminders when starting Quicken is not turned on.

Show notes for

This option works in conjunction with the setting for the Show Calendar Notes check box in the Billminder tab; it's available only if Show Calendar Notes is turned on. Use the Show notes for field to select a time range for the calendar notes that Quicken displays. With the default value of This week, the calendar displays notes for the current week only.

Billminder Options

The Billminder options tab (Figure 3–20) contains options that pertain to Quicken's Billminder feature. Even when you're not running Quicken during a computer session, Billminder can automatically notify you of upcoming due dates, including scheduled bill payments, checks to print, online payments, investment reminders, and calendar notes.

Show Billminder when starting Windows

When activated, this option causes current Billminder reminders to appear on screen every time you start Windows—even if you don't run Quicken right away. The other options in the Billminder options tab are available *only* if this option is active.

Scheduled Transactions

Activate the Scheduled Transactions check box if you want Billminder to notify you automatically of scheduled transactions. Refer to Chapter 6 for more information about memorizing and scheduling transactions.

Checks To Print

Activate this check box if you write checks with Quicken and want to receive reminders when scheduled checks are due to be written. For example, if you schedule a rent transaction for the first day of every month and Checks To Print is turned on, an automatic alert will appear on every due date reminding you to write a check for the rent.

Online Payments

If you're signed up for online banking and electronic payments (see Chapter 2), activate this option to make sure that Quicken reminds you of when scheduled electronic payments are due.

Investment Reminders

If you track investment accounts with Quicken, activate the Investment Reminders check box to have Quicken prompt you for investment due dates and other pertinent investment milestones.

Use the options in this section of the dialog box to select the type or types of transactions—Scheduled Transactions, Checks To Print, Online Payments, and Investment Reminders—that you want Billminder to remind you about. This option is unavailable if Billminder is not turned on.

Calendar Notes

Quicken's Financial Calendar (Figure 3–21) is a tool that you can use for tasks such as automatically creating new check transactions based on scheduled financial events. Since it's not specifically a tool for construction professionals, we don't discuss it in detail in this book, but you might want to explore its uses on your own. You can open the Financial Calendar window by choosing the Features | Paying Bills | Financial Calendar command.

Activate the Show Calendar Notes option if you want to display Financial Calendar notes in the Billminders window each time you start Windows. This option is turned off by default.

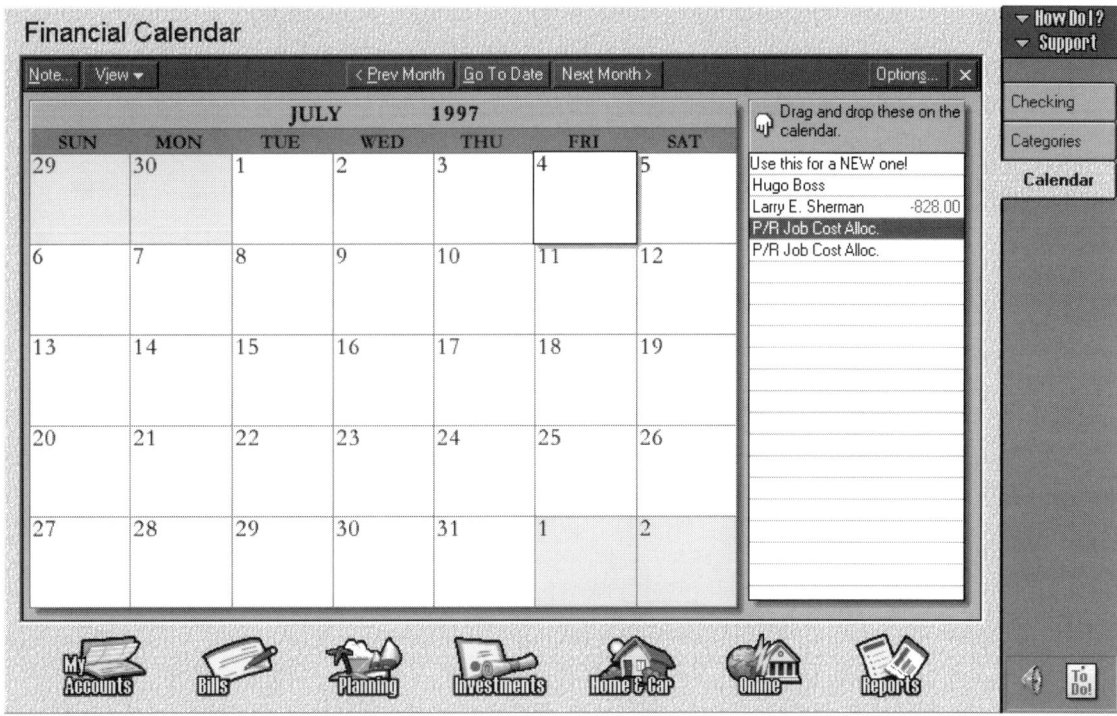

Figure 3–21

Quicken's Financial Calendar window helps you schedule various financial events.

💲 Internet Connection Options

Beginning with Quicken 98, Intuit makes its software updates available through the Internet for registered users of Quicken. The Internet Connection Options let you decide whether and how to update Quicken while online. These options apply only if you use Quicken's online banking features (see Chapter 2). To access the Internet Connection Options dialog box shown in Figure 3–22, select the Edit I Options I Internet Connection command.

Prompt me to update Quicken '98 on startup

Some users prefer to update their software by mail order or at specified times only; others want it to happen automatically and online. If you'd like to have your Quicken software updated automatically, activate this check box. Quicken then issues a message each time you

Figure 3–22

Use the Internet Connection Options dialog box to specify how and when to update your Quicken software while online.

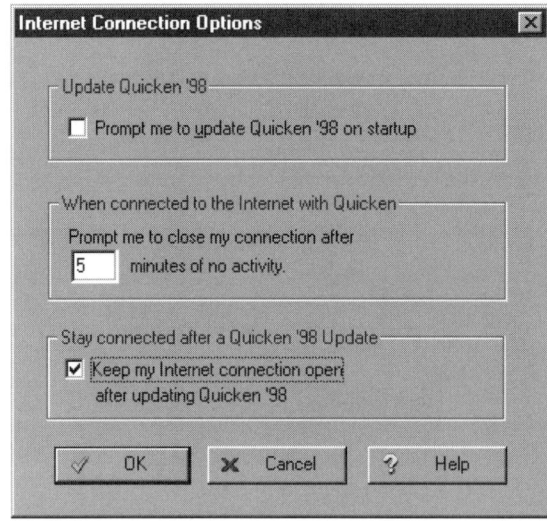

start the software, asking whether you want to go online to check for available updates.

Prompt me to close my connection after XX minutes of no activity

If you're online running Quicken and no activity has taken place for some time, Quicken displays a message asking whether you want to terminate your Internet connection. You specify how many minutes of idle time must pass before this message appears.

Keep my Internet connection open after updating Quicken '98

When this check box is activated, you remain online automatically after completing an online update of your Quicken software.

🏠 Save Desktop

The Save Desktop dialog box lets you customize the way Quicken displays your desktop on startup. From the Edit I Options submenu, click on the Desktop command to display the Save Desktop dialog box (Figure 3–23).

Figure 3–23

The Save Desktop dialog box is set to Save Desktop on Exit by default.

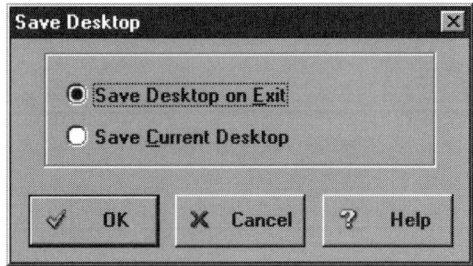

Save Desktop on Exit

With this option active (the default setting), Quicken remembers the state of your desktop each time you close the application. When you start Quicken again, the same windows will be open and arranged just as you left them. This setting is especially useful if you often have to close Quicken in the midst of a financial session.

Save Current Desktop

If you prefer to always start Quicken with the same windows open on the desktop, open and arrange the windows the way you want them to be. Then activate this option after the arrangement is just the way you want it. Thereafter, your desktop will look the same every time you open the Quicken application. Save Current Desktop is turned off by default.

Customize Iconbar

The iconbar is the horizontal row of symbols at the top of the Quicken application window. It gives you convenient, one-click access to commonly-used functions. The options in the Customize Iconbar dialog box, shown in Figure 3–24, let you add, delete, and edit what appears in the iconbar.

In this book, we stress using menu commands rather than icons when working with Quicken features. But if you wish to customize the iconbar for your own use, you can access this dialog box from the Edit | Options submenu by clicking on the Iconbar command.

The Customize Iconbar dialog box displays all the default icons and their names in a horizontal scroll bar. To edit or delete an existing icon, click it once to select it, and then click on the appropriate button.

Figure 3–24

*The Customize Iconbar
dialog box lets you add,
delete, and edit the icons
that appear at the top of
your Quicken window.*

New

The New button lets you add new icons to the existing iconbar. You can add as many icons as you'd like. When you've added so many that they can't all be displayed at once, you'll see scroll arrows to the left and right of the iconbar. Use these arrows to view additional icons.

To add icons to the iconbar:

1. Click the New button. The Add Action to Iconbar dialog box (Figure 3–25) appears, containing a scroll list of preset icon actions above and beyond those in the standard iconbar.

2. To specify a new icon action, scroll down the Icon Action list and click once on the name of the desired action to highlight it.

3. Next click the Change button. Quicken displays the Change Iconbar Item dialog box (Figure 3–26) with the chosen action and the corresponding icon selected.

4. If you want to add a keyboard shortcut for this icon (an Alt-Shift key combination), enter the desired key letter in the Speed Key field.

Figure 3–25

*The Add Action to Iconbar
dialog box contains a list
of icon actions that can
be added to the
standard iconbar.*

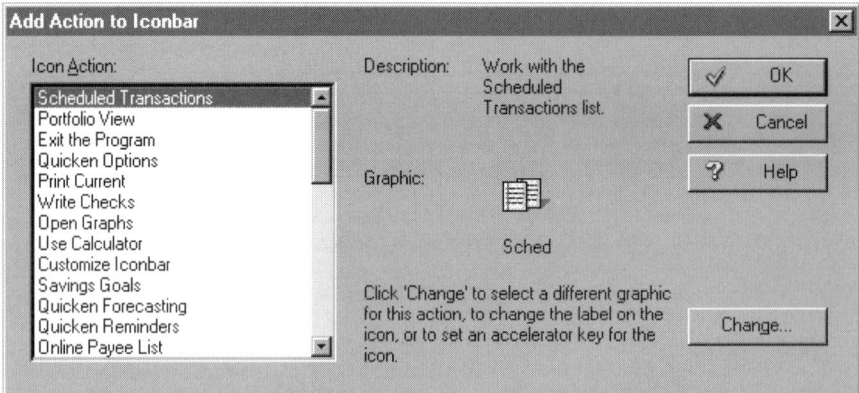

Figure 3–26

The Change Iconbar Item dialog box lets you customize new icons before you add them to the iconbar.

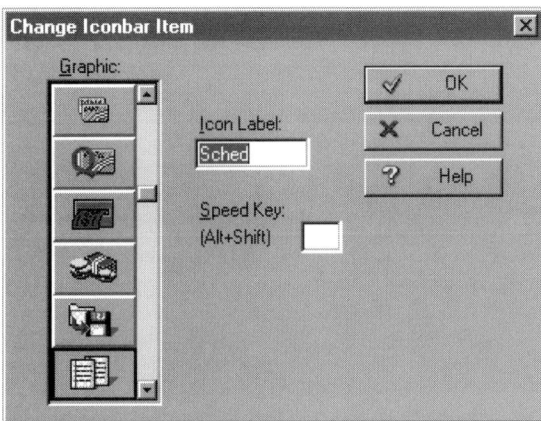

5. Click the OK button to assign the new icon to the iconbar and to return back to the Customize Iconbar dialog box.

6. Repeat the process to assign other new icons if desired, or click the Done button if you're finished.

Edit

Use the Edit button to change the label and graphic display of an existing icon. Clicking this button makes available the same dialog boxes as clicking the New button does, with the exception that the first dialog box is called Edit Action on Iconbar.

Delete

Use the Delete button to remove the currently selected icon from the iconbar.

Reset

This option clears any changes you make to the iconbar and resets the iconbar to the way it was before you made the current changes.

Show Icons

When this check box is active (the default), Quicken displays the iconbar at the top of the Quicken application window. If you have a small monitor, need to save screen space, or prefer to use menus

instead of icons to access common functions, turn this option off to
hide the iconbar.

Show Text

By default, Quicken's iconbar displays only the icons, not their
names or functions. If you find memorizing icon functions using pictures alone difficult, you may appreciate having short descriptive
names appear beneath the icons. Turn on the Show Text option to
display text names beneath each icon in the iconbar.

Now that you've fine-tuned your Quicken application, you're
ready to start entering transactions in Quicken. That's the subject of
the next chapter.

Entering Transactions in Quicken

O nce you've defined your preferences for Quicken (see Chapter 3, "Customizing Quicken"), you're ready to enter actual transactions for your business into the Company file provided on the diskette that accompanies this book. In this chapter, we'll provide an overview of the most common types of transactions that contractors need to know about: writing checks, recording deposits, generating invoices, and handling payroll. We'll also include information about how to schedule transactions so that Quicken automatically reminds you when they are due.

We'll base our examples in this chapter on entries in the Qksample and Company files provided on the diskette that accompanies this book. For more in-depth information about how to use the memorized transactions, classes, and memorized reports mentioned throughout this chapter, refer to Chapter 6, "Using Memorized Transactions"; Chapter 5, "Budgeting with Quicken: Job Costing and Estimating"; and Chapter 7, "Using Memorized Reports," respectively.

🏠 Writing Checks

For many small- to medium-sized contractors, the checkbook is the accounting and job-cost system all rolled into one perforated package. The Pay to the Order of field defines the vendor, the Amount field shows the cost, and the Memo field earmarks the job—a simple job-costing system.

A notch up in sophistication is the extended check register, such as the Safe Guard check register, that has a columnar table extending out from the side of the check. You first define the columns using job names. Then, when you fill out the check, you assign the check amount to one of these columns. Later, you go back and add up all the checks for a certain job, selectively total the job divisions, and —after an agonizing effort—you know your job costs.

The good news is Quicken does the same thing with much less effort. In fact, if you use the QuickFill feature (discussed in Chapter 3), the effort can amount to just a few keystrokes for each transaction.

If you've ever written a check (and even if you haven't), you'll be comfortable filling out one in Quicken. When you choose the Features | Paying Bills | Write Checks command, the screen displays a facsimile of a paper check (see Figure 4–1). The check has spaces for entering Date, Pay to the Order of, Address, Memo, Category, and the amount. If you've set up your preferences according to our recommendations in Chapter 3, you'll find Quicken's QuickFill memory feature especially efficient. When you begin to fill in the Pay to the Order of field, Quicken anticipates what you're going to type based on your first few keystrokes and your past entries. So, for example, if you have previously made out a check to Adams HVAC, as soon as you begin to type the first few letters, Quicken fills in the rest of the field. It also fills in all the remaining fields, duplicating the data you entered the last time you wrote a check to Adams HVAC. The entire transaction, including the job-cost category and class, is duplicated and entered into the check, ready to be accepted or modified as needed.

Figure 4–1

When you begin to fill in a memorized check in the Write Checks window, the rest of the data is entered automatically by Quicken.

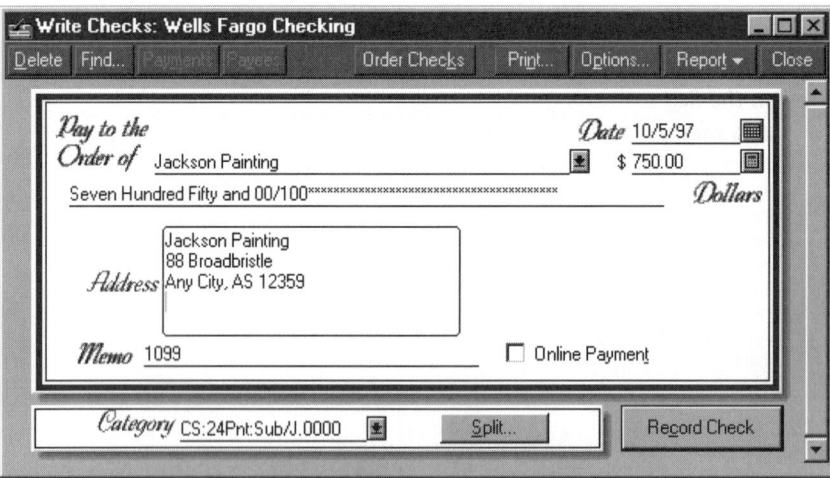

NOTE: *When the amount to be paid to a given payee varies each time you write a check to that payee, be sure to change the amount manually before you record the check entry. Otherwise, Quicken automatically assigns the same amount that you specified the last time you wrote a check to that payee.*

This ability to remember a transaction and "play it again" is the real strength of Quicken. In fact, the program lets you further increase the usefulness of the basic QuickFill function by memorizing a transaction and giving it a name. See Chapter 6 to learn more about the power of using memorized transactions.

Assigning Classes

In Quicken, you can use classes to earmark the job name for each check you write. You enter the class designation in the Category field of a transaction by following the category entry with a forward slash (/), then selecting the class from the Class List window. For example, after entering a category such as 01 Plans and Permits, you would type a forward slash and press Ctrl-L. This will display the Class List window shown in Figure 4–2. Double-click the appropriate class (job), and then complete the transaction and record the entry.

Look ahead to Chapter 5 if you'd like more information on how to use Quicken to organize your business finances on a job-by-job basis.

Figure 4–2

Use the Class List window to assign specific jobs to a transaction in the Register or Write Checks windows.

Class List		___ □ X
New... Edit... Delete		Report Close
Class		**Description**
J.0000		Johnson Kitchen Remod...
J.1001		**Job 1**
J.1002		Job 2
J.1003		Job 3
J.1004		Jones Guest House

Writing a Check to Pay a Job Expense

The Qksample and Company files on the diskette that accompanies this book contain many preconfigured categories, which are subcategories of a CS (cost of goods sold) category. Expenses which are directly related to a specific job should only be allocated to these CS categories and subcategories. The key to successfully capturing job-cost information for each transaction is to use the Category field to designate both the desired cost of goods sold subcategory *and* the job number (which is represented by the class). You can refer to Chapter 2, "Using Quicken Categories, Accounts, and Classes," for information about setting up classes. Assigning classes to transactions is also covered in Chapter 5, but we'll walk you through the basic process here.

To write a check for one job-related expense item:

1. From the menu, select the Features | Paying Bills | Write Checks command. The Write Checks window appears, showing a blank check.

2. In the appropriate fields, enter the Date (the date on which you want to print the check), the name of the Payee, and the Amount.

3. In the Memo field, indicate an appropriate description of the transaction, if desired.

4. Click the down arrow at the right of the Category field to display the category list. Scroll through the list to find the appropriate job-cost category and click on it to enter it in the Category field.

5. Press Ctrl-L to display the Class List window. Click on the job number you want to earmark the check for and click the Use button. If the job number is not listed, click the New button and enter a new job, as described in Chapters 2 and 5. The Category field will now display the job-cost category and the job separated by a forward slash (see Figure 4–3).

6. Click the Record Check button on the Write Checks window to record the check in the register. Figure 4–3 shows an example of a fully filled-out Quicken check.

To write a check for more than one job-related expense item:

1. From the menu, select the Features | Paying Bills | Write Checks command. The Write Checks window appears showing a blank check.

2. In the appropriate fields, enter the Date (the date on which you want to print the check), the name of the Payee, the Amount, and any pertinent Memo information.

Figure 4–3

This Write Checks window shows a fully filled-out check.

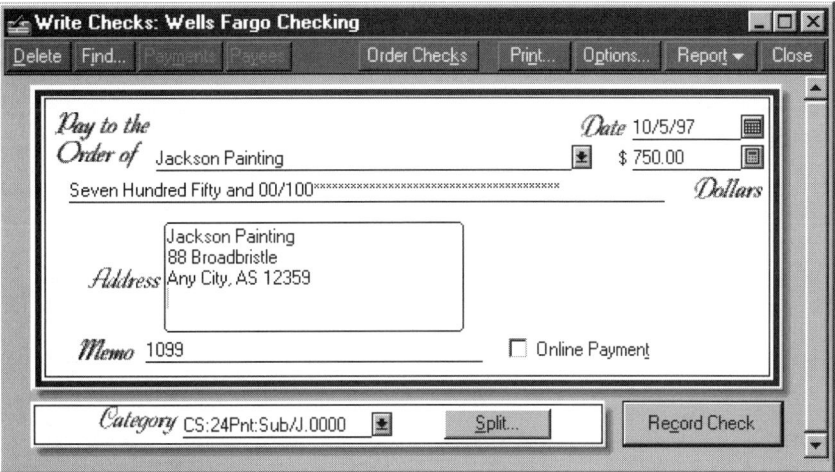

Figure 4–4

This Split Transaction Window shows how you can enter multiple line items for a check.

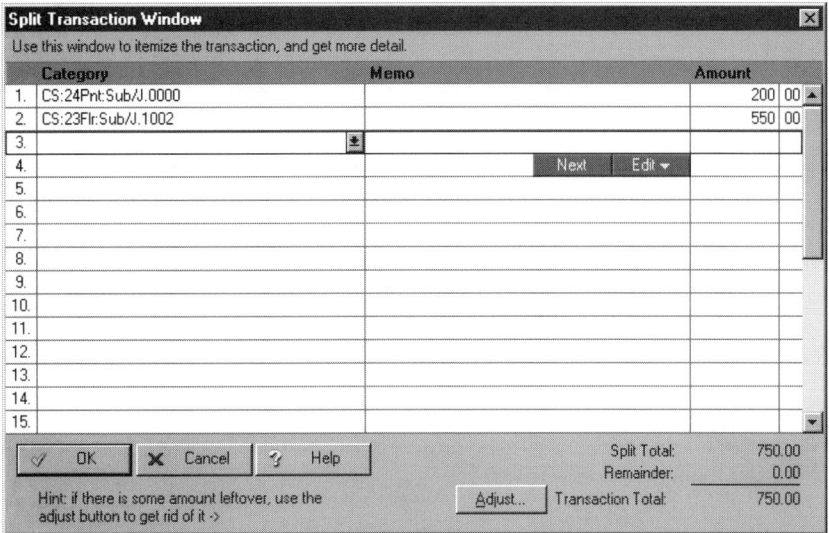

3. Click the Split button to display the Split Transaction Window (Figure 4–4).

4. Click the down arrow at the right of the Category field of the first line to display the category list. Scroll through the list to find the appropriate job-cost category and click on it to enter it in the Category field.

5. Press Ctrl-L to display the Class List window. Click on the job number you want to assign to the transaction and click the Use button. If the job number is not listed, click the New button and enter a new job. The Category field will now display the job-cost followed by a forward slash and the job number.

Figure 4–5

When you write a check that covers more than one expense, the Category field for the check displays the designation SPLIT.

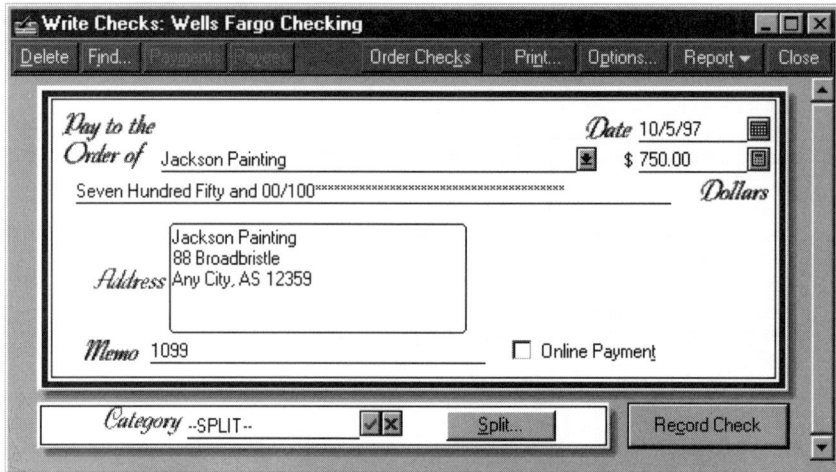

6. Tab to the Memo field and enter a description for the item, if desired.

7. Tab to the Amount field and enter the amount for that line item.

8. Repeat steps 4 through 7 to complete any other split line items that are associated with the check. Figure 4–4 shows a Split Transaction Window with multiple line items entered.

9. Click the Adjust button when you have finished entering the split transactions. The Adjust button totals the amount of the split line items and enters that total in the Amount field of the check.

10. Click the Finished button to close the Split Transaction Window and return to the Write Checks window. The Category field of the Write Checks window now displays the SPLIT indicator, as shown in Figure 4–5.

11. Click the Record Check button to record the check.

If you are using the QuickFill feature (see the "Check Options" section in Chapter 3), entering the payee's name causes Quicken to automatically fill in the category, job, amount, and any split transaction details based on the data from the last check you wrote to this payee. You'll need to change the details manually if any of them are different for the current payment.

Printing Checks

Contractors write a lot of checks during their day-to-day business transactions. Checks go out to material suppliers, to subcontractors, and for labor. The fastest way to write and send a group of checks is to let Quicken use your printer to fill out preprinted checks. Then all you have to do is stuff them into window envelopes, stamp them, and drop them in the mail. (Electronic payments are even faster—see page 116 for a short description.) You can purchase preprinted checks from Intuit, from forms companies such as NEBS, or even from some of the estimating software companies. And that old dot matrix, tractor-feed printer that's been sitting in the back room can now be brought out for a second useful life—writing checks on demand for your company.

To get Quicken to properly print your checks, you need to choose the correct Quicken options and change your printer settings to match the checks you are using. The Help file on the Print Checks window will walk you through any serious customizations you may need, but here is a nutshell account of how to perform this setup.

Setting Check-Printing Options

To print checks, select Features | Paying Bills | Write Checks from the main menu. The Write Checks window shown in Figure 4–6 appears. When you write a check using this window, Intuit sends it to the Register window. The check also shows up on the Checks to Print list, which appears below the image of the check you are currently filling out.

The upper-right corner of the Write Checks window contains three buttons to help you print checks. From left to right, they are Order Checks, Print, and Options. When you click the Order Checks button, you're taken to an Internet sign-on screen where you can connect to Intuit's Web site and order checks.

The Print button opens a dialog box called Select Checks to Print: *Checking* (Figure 4–7), where *Checking* stands for the name of your actual business checking account. If you have more than one checking account set up in Quicken, be sure to notice the title of the dialog box to make sure you are writing checks from the correct account.

At the top of the Select Checks to Print dialog box there's a message telling you how many checks are "batched" or ready to be printed. Below that is a text box that indicates the first check number in the batch. You need to confirm that the number in that box matches the number on the first check you place in your printer. If it doesn't match, you can enter the correct starting number manually.

The Print section of the Select Checks to Print dialog box contains three option buttons:

◆ *All Checks*—If you select the All Checks option, Quicken prints all the checks listed in the Checks to Print list (below the check in the Write Checks window only).

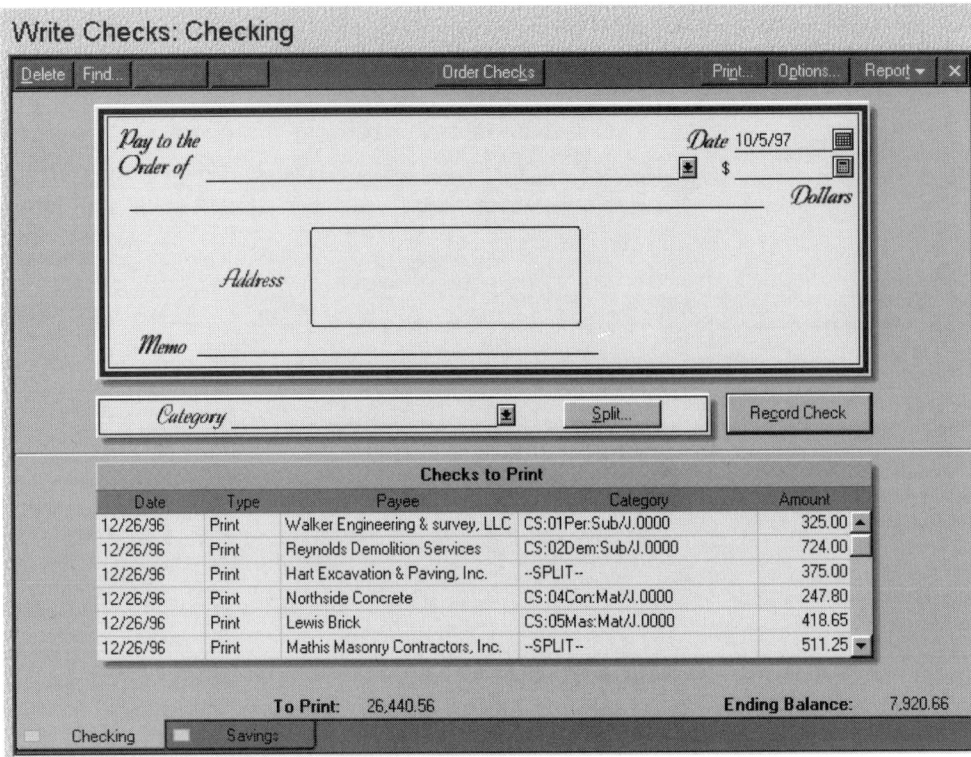

Figure 4-6

The Write Checks window showing the Checks to Print list

Figure 4-7

Use the Select Checks to Print dialog box to specify the number and style of checks to print.

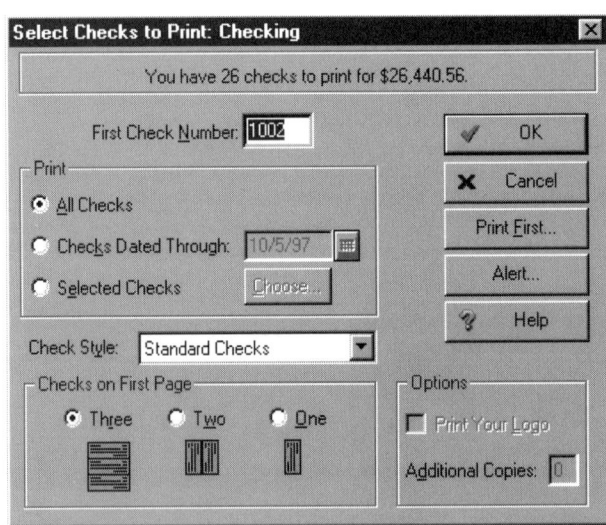

◆ *Checks Dated Through*—If you select the Checks Dated Through option, you can pick a date through which the checks will print. For example, the checks in your list might have different payment dates, but you might want to print only the checks with the latest dates. By choosing the appropriate date you can selectively decide which checks to print and send.

◆ *Selected Checks*—Choosing the Selected Checks option opens another window that lets you visually pick out the checks you want to print.

Another important setting in the Select Checks to Print dialog box is the Check Style drop-down list. Quicken handles three types of pre-printed checks: Standard Checks, Wallet Checks, and Voucher Checks. Standard Checks are the large-format checks that businesses typically use. Wallet Checks have a stub on the end, and Voucher Checks have an entire information sheet that can be attached to the check.

NOTE: *When you choose Standard Checks or Wallet Checks, you can use the Checks on First Page option to specify whether one, two, or three checks are on the first page that prints. This option lets you print on partially used pages of checks. If you select one or two checks, be sure to position that partial sheet in the print tray so that it will be the first one printed.*

Here are some of the other important options in the Select Checks to Print dialog box:

◆ The Print First button in the Select Checks to Print dialog box lets you print only the first check as a test. Click this button if you are reasonably certain the checks are aligned and in the printer correctly.

◆ The Alert button takes you to the Set Up Alerts dialog box (Figure 4–8), where you can instruct Quicken to alert you when certain account balances reach the limits you specify. For example, you may not want to print checks when your account balance reaches $100 or less. Or conversely, you might want Quicken to notify you when a checking account balance gets too high so that you can transfer some money to either a higher-interest-bearing account or a money market account.

◆ If you are printing Voucher checks, you can choose to print extra copies of them by entering a number next to Additional Copies (at the lower-right corner of the Select Checks to Print dialog box).

Figure 4–8

Use alerts to have Quicken notify you of high or low account balances.

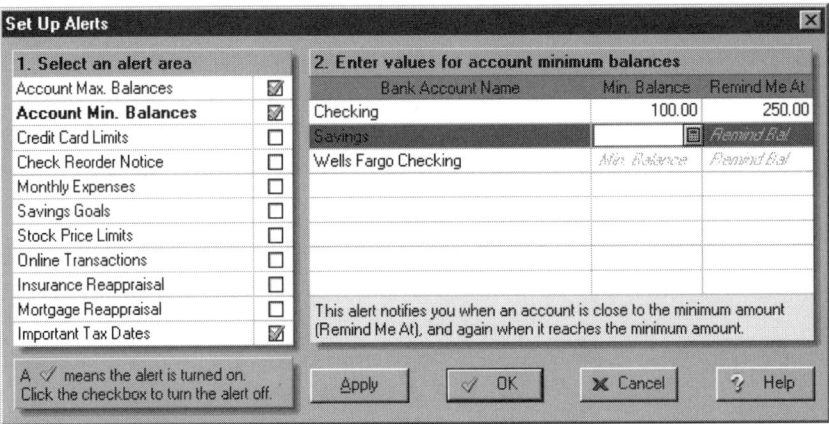

Preparing the Printer

Printers from different manufacturers handle forms such as letterhead stock and preprinted checks differently. Depending on the path the paper takes through the machine, some printers print on the top of the paper as it enters the printer, while others print on the bottom and flip side of the paper. Most people are familiar enough with their printers to know which way to insert a piece of letterhead paper, and inserting checks is no different. Test your printer with a blank sheet of paper first.

For the purposes of printing checks, you'll be using one of two basic types of printers. There's the single-page printer (Quicken calls them "page-oriented" printers), a category that includes laser, inkjet, and even dot matrix printers that pick up paper from a tray and print one page at a time. The other category is the "continuous-feed" printers, which use tractor-feed mechanisms to feed perforated paper or checks to the printer.

Before you print any checks, you should print one sample check to make sure the checks are properly aligned in the printer. If adjustments are needed, you can then use the alignment feature to tweak the alignment until your printing looks right.

To create sample checks in a continuous-feed printer, use blank paper. Place the sample check on top of the real check and then hold them both up to a light or a window to see if the text has printed in the correct location.

To set up the printer, follow these basic steps:

1. Choose the File | Printer Setup | For Printing Checks command to display the Check Printer Setup dialog box (Figure 4–9).

2. Select your printer from the drop-down list of printers. If your printer doesn't show up in the list, it probably means that the

Figure 4–9

Use the Check Printer Setup dialog box to ensure that checks will print properly on your printer.

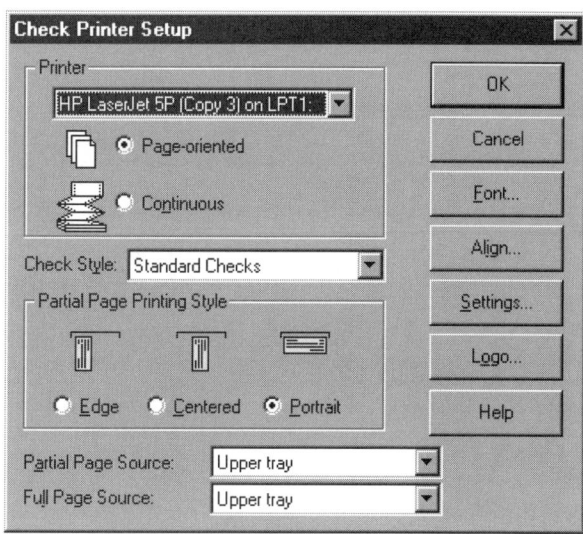

printer's driver isn't installed and you'll have to install it. (See Win95 Help or the Quicken Help file to learn how to install a printer driver.)

3. Next, choose either the Page-oriented or Continuous option.

4. Use the Check Style drop-down list to specify Standard Checks, Wallet Checks, or Voucher Checks.

5. If you are printing a page on which some of the checks have already been used, you must choose an option in the Partial Page Printing Style area of the dialog box. The Edge, Centered, and Portrait options tell the printer how to align the checks. Typically, partial pages are handled just like an envelope, so if you are not sure which choice to make, consult your printer manual and follow its directions on how to print an envelope.

6. Select one of the two settings at the bottom of the window. Partial Page Source and Full Page Source tell the printer where the checks are coming from depending on whether the page is partial or full.

7. Finally, make any changes to printer font, alignment, settings, and logo if you so desire, using the buttons along the right side of the Check Printer Setup screen.

    ◆ The Font button allows you to change the typestyles that the printer uses when printing the checks.

    ◆ The Align button lets you make changes to the way Quicken positions the print on the checks. This option also lets you create different settings for pages with one, two, and three checks per page.

◆ The Settings button covers more basic printer settings such as portrait and landscape orientation.

◆ The Logo button opens a dialog box that lets you assign a .BMP file so that Quicken will print your company's logo on each check.

The Options button near the upper-right corner of the Write Checks window opens up a three-tabbed window; the Checks tab lets you set preferences for check printing. There are three sections to the Checks Tab: Printed Date Style, Check Settings, and Display Settings. Use the Printed Date section to select either a four-digit year or a two-digit year. (You may find that the two-digit year works better because it fits better on most checks.) The Check Settings options let you add an extra message to your checks, print the categories on the checks, and change the date of the check to the date on which it was actually printed (not when it was written). Finally, in the Display Settings section of the window, you can choose to display the buttons on Quick-Fill fields when you write a check.

Electronic Checks

Printing checks will save you lots of time if you write many checks at the end of the month. If you are comfortable with electronic transfer of money (for example, paying your water bill automatically), you should consider using one of the electronic banking options that Quicken provides. We have been using Checkfree, an electronic check writing service that works within Quicken, for several years. When you are finished writing checks in Quicken, you simply transmit them to Checkfree and your checks are automatically sent to the vendors. The charge of $12 a month for up to 30 checks is well worth the savings in time and effort.

In addition, Intuit offers electronic banking services in conjunction with many national banks. Ask your local bank or go online to Intuit's Web site (*www.intuit.com*) for more information. Or select Online Financial Services Setup from the Online menu and follow the directions.

Tracking 1099 Vendors and Subcontractors

To designate a payment to a vendor who is expected to receive a Form 1099, tab to the Memo line of the transaction and enter **1099.** If

Figure 4–10

You can enter a check to a 1099 vendor in the Write Checks window by using the generic memorized transaction Job Vendor "1099."

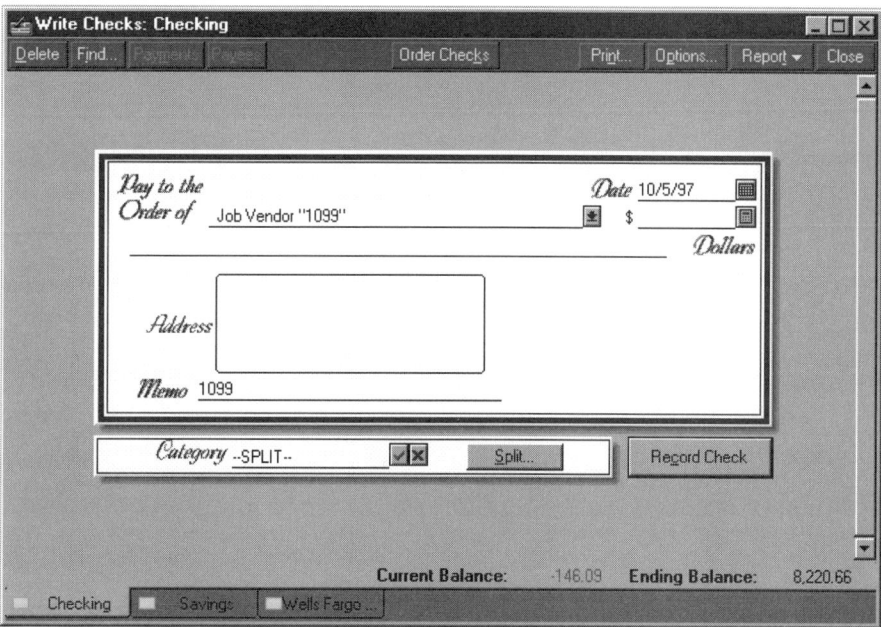

this is not a 1099 vendor, enter your account code for the vendor payee or include some relevant description for the payment.

If you're using the Company file from the diskette that accompanies this book to set up your own Quicken records, you can create a new memorized transaction for each separate vendor by starting with our generic memorized transaction Job Vendor "1099." See Figure 4–10 and refer to the "Job Vendor Payments" section of Chapter 6 for more information on how to create custom memorized transactions.

1099 Detail Report

The files we've included on the accompanying diskette include a group of memorized reports that are already set up (see Chapter 7 for more about working with memorized reports). The 1099 Detail Report will create a report showing all the payments made to your 1099 vendors during the current year. Figure 4–11 shows an example of a 1099 Detail Report that includes actual data.

Quicken does not print the 1099 form for you at tax time. You will need to print out the 1099 Detail Report and transfer the information to the IRS 1099 form.

Figure 4–11

*This report was created
with the memorized 1099
Detail Report included in
the files provided with the
companion diskette.*

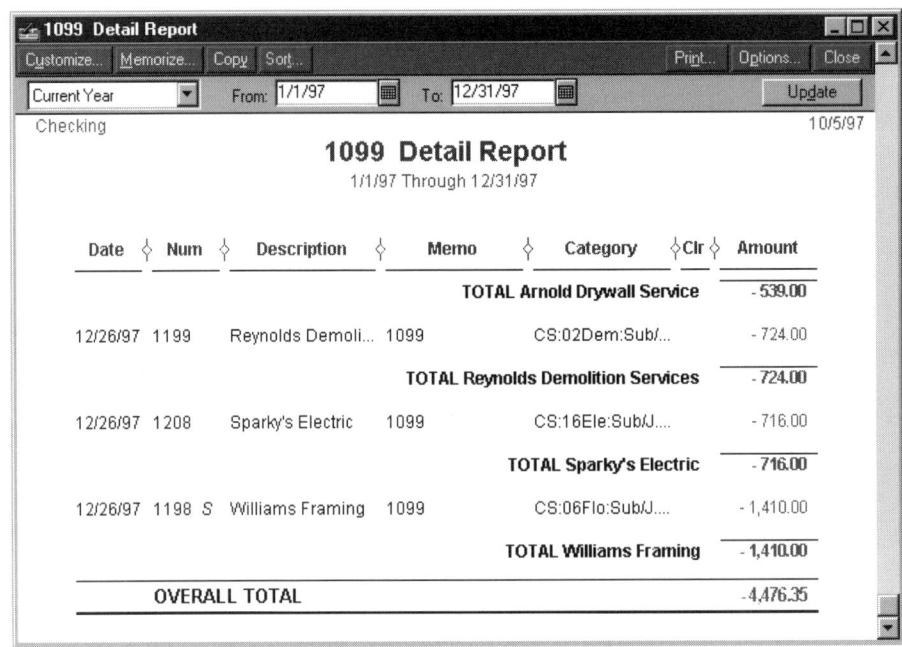

Figure 4–11

*This report was created
with the memorized 1099
Detail Report included in
the files provided with the
companion diskette.*

🏠 Entering Deposits

In the Qksample and Company files included on the diskette that
accompanies this book, we have set up three possible job-related
income scenarios that are typically encountered in a construction
business:

- ◆ customer payments based on your invoices
- ◆ deposits received from customers
- ◆ advances received from customers

We'll review each of these cases briefly in this chapter. Chapter 6
includes more detailed, step-by-step information on how to use our
preset memorized transactions when entering deposits.

Customer Payment on Invoice

The most common situation occurs when you receive payments from
customers based on invoices you sent them. We have set up a memorized transaction called Customer pmt. on Invoice (found under the
4.DEPOSITS heading of the Memorized Transaction List window) that
you can use to record such payments. The memorized transaction is
set up as a split transaction so that you can also record sales tax. Most
contractors don't charge sales tax, but some subcontractors are required

Figure 4–12

This Split Transaction Window shows the default information for the memorized transaction Customer pmt. on Invoice.

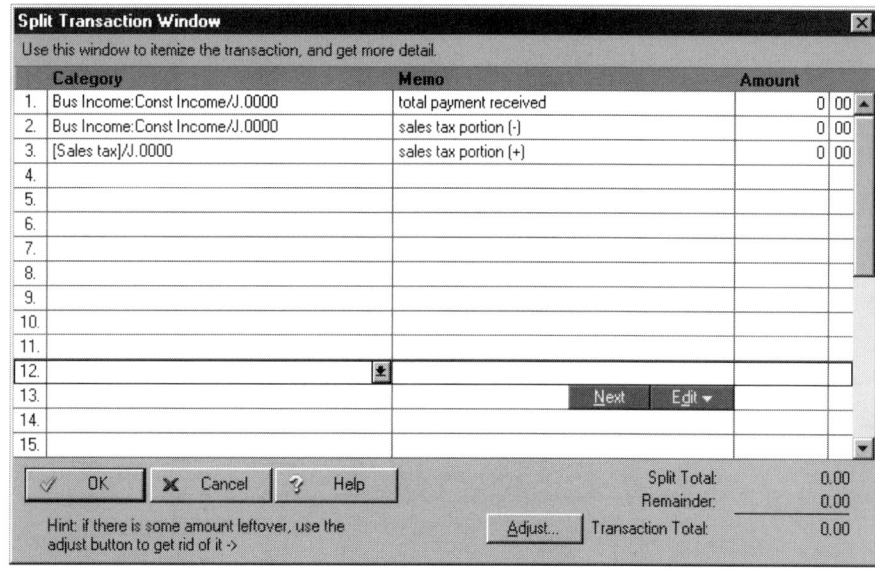

to do so by state laws or local ordinances. If you don't charge sales tax, just delete the two sales tax lines in the memorized transaction.

To record a customer payment on invoice using the Company file:

1. From the menu, select the Lists | Account command to display the Account List window.

2. Double-click the name of the account you want to use. This will open the Register window for that account.

3. From the menu, select the Lists | Memorized Transaction command to display the Memorized Transaction List window.

4. Double-click the memorized transaction entitled Customer pmt. on Invoice, which is listed under 4.DEPOSITS. This enters the default information for the memorized transaction into the account register.

5. Click the Split button to view the default information in the Split Transaction Window, shown in Figure 4–12.

6. In the Category field of each line item, modify the job number to reflect the appropriate job for the payment.

7. In the Amount field for the first line item, substitute actual values for the default 0.00.

8. If you charge sales tax, use line items 2 and 3 to add the tax information. Enter the tax amount as a negative value in line 2 and as a positive value in line 3, so that the amount transfers to the appropriate accounts in the correct amounts. Figure 4–13 shows an example of how this might look in an actual transaction.

Figure 4–13

This Split Transaction Window for the memorized transaction Customer pmt. on Invoice shows how sales tax is deducted from income and transferred to a liability account.

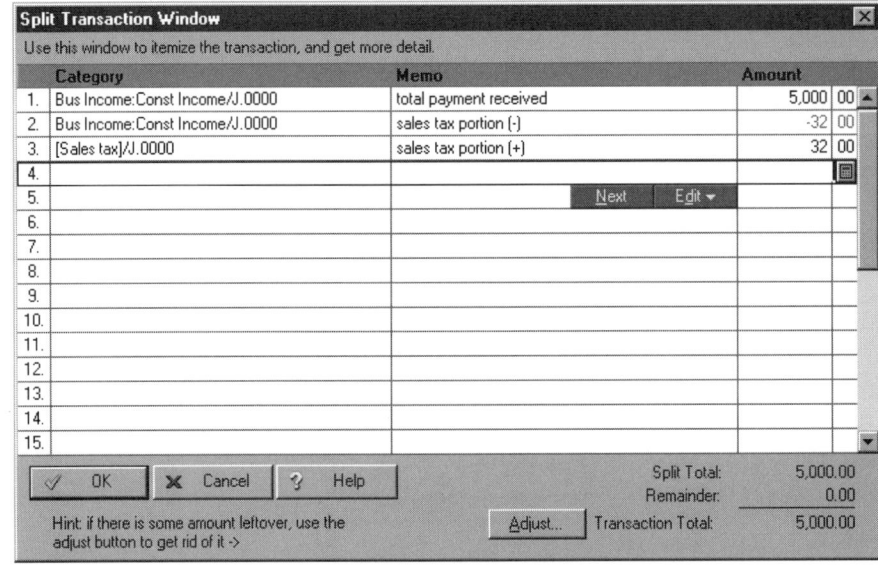

Figure 4–13

This Split Transaction Window for the memorized transaction Customer pmt. on Invoice shows how sales tax is deducted from income and transferred to a liability account.

9. Click the OK button to exit the Split Transaction Window and return to the record in the account register.

10. Press Enter or click the Enter button to record the transaction.

Customer Deposits

For those of you who take deposits from clients, we have set up a memorized transaction called Customer deposit taken to help you track these deposits and apply them to the job as you do the work. Figure 4–14 shows the default information entered into the Split Transaction Window of a record when you use this memorized transaction.

A customer deposit should be treated differently from an advance on a job (see Chapter 6). If a customer gives you a deposit, you are technically holding the customer's money. It can later be applied to the first or last invoice, but until then it should be treated as a liability rather than as income.

When you apply the customer deposit later on, you can use the memorized transaction called Customer deposit applied (found under the 5.SPECIAL TRANSACTIONS heading in the Memorized Transaction List window) to record the amount as income and remove it as a liability. Figure 4–15 shows an example of how the Split Transaction Window looks for this memorized transaction.

Figure 4–14

This Split Transaction Window shows an example of the default information for the memorized transaction, Customer deposit taken.

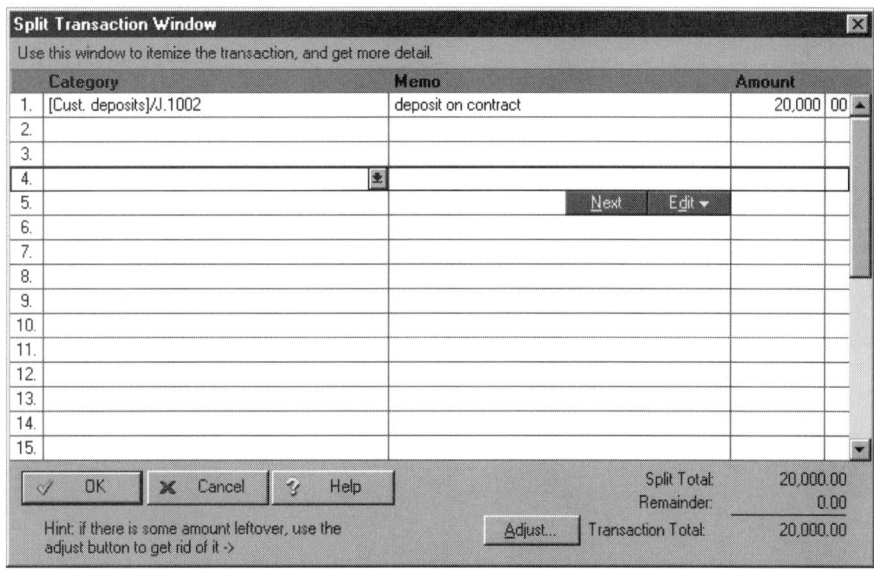

Figure 4–15

This Split Transaction Window shows how the memorized transaction, Customer deposit applied, designates deposit amounts as a liability rather than as income.

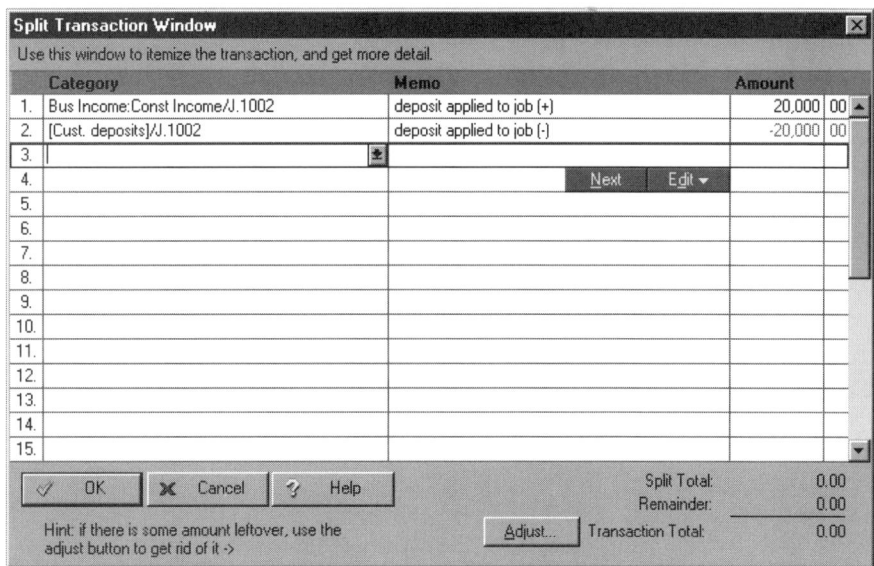

Customer Advance on Job

When customers give you an advance, they are giving you a payment in anticipation of completed work. Customer advances, unlike customer deposits, are treated as income at the time you receive them. We have set up a memorized transaction in the Company file called Customer advance on job to help you track these deposits and apply them to the job as you do the work. Figure 4–16 shows an example of how the Split Transaction Window looks when you use the Customer advance on job memorized transaction.

Figure 4-16

This Split Transaction Window shows how you can use the memorized transaction Customer advance on job.

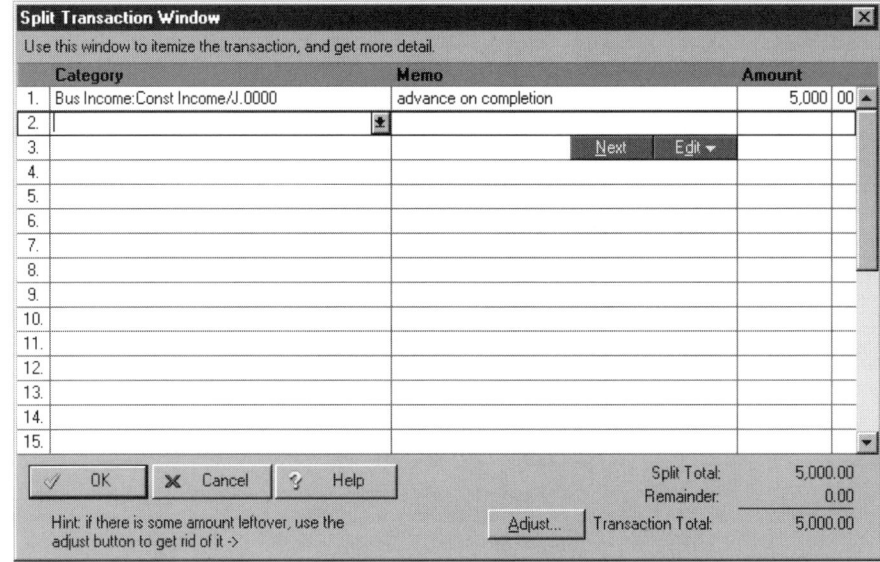

🏠 Invoicing

Quicken is just one element in the software toolbox that contractors use to run their businesses. Chapter 5 explains that you'll need to do your estimating outside of Quicken and then enter the data into Quicken as a budget. Since Quicken (with the exception of the Quicken 98 Home & Business edition) can't create invoices, you may also need to extract data from Quicken and put it into an invoice format.

The diskette that accompanies this book includes a sample set of forms from the book *Construction Forms & Contracts,* available from Craftsman Book Company. If you'd like to order it, we've included an order form in the back of this book. If you don't already have your own invoice format, you may want to start with the JOBINV form provided on the companion diskette and adjust it to your needs.

To help you organize your estimate for entry into Quicken, we have provided an estimate form (filename: CSI-EST) and an estimate checklist form (filename: ESTCHECK) on the companion diskette (see Chapter 1). These forms should make it easier for you to transfer estimated costs to Quicken.

🏠 Entering Payroll Transactions

Most contractors and subcontractors have some payroll expenses. Even builders and contractors who subcontract everything to freelancers usually have a part-time office employee or two. With

Quicken, you have several choices for handling payroll: using a payroll service, using an add-on software product called QuickPay, and/or creating memorized payroll transactions.

Using Payroll Services

The first option, and the one we recommend over all the others, is to use a payroll service to handle your payroll. Then, when you receive reports back from the payroll service, you can enter the payroll checks directly into Quicken.

We recommend the use of payroll services for several reasons:

◆ *Affordability*—Payroll services are cheap and accurate. If you have a small number of employees, the cost is usually only a few dollars per employee per pay period. To justify doing your own payroll, you would have to have several employees and an office assistant with a couple of hours each week to spare.

◆ *Accuracy and familiarity with payroll*—Professional payroll services are specialists.

◆ *Lower audit risk*—Payroll services are less likely than you to be audited by the tax authorities, and in the event of an audit, the tax authorities would examine the payroll service's records before yours. So, if you dread the thought of an external audit, let the payroll service handle it.

Using Intuit's QuickPay Plug-In

Doing your own payroll requires that you handle many tasks and wear many hats. For example, you need to:

◆ Do lots of computations
◆ Write and track many checks with numerous deductions
◆ Keep track of information for payroll taxes
◆ Fill out quarterly payroll tax forms
◆ Pay the taxes in a timely manner
◆ Prepare year-end reports

If our arguments in favor of using payroll services haven't convinced you, and you still want to do your own payroll, then your best choice is to use Intuit's companion payroll program, QuickPay. QuickPay works in conjunction with Quicken. Once you've installed

QuickPay on your computer, Quicken allows you to set it up as a plug-in, creating a button that runs QuickPay from within Quicken.

Entering Payroll Transactions in Quicken

It is possible to use Quicken without QuickPay to track payroll, but we don't recommend it. If you must, however, you can purchase from Intuit the Quicken Business User's Guide, which explains the basics of setting up Quicken for payroll. The process differs according to whether you have salaried or hourly employees.

◆ If you have salaried employees whose gross pay and deductions are the same for each pay period, you can create a separate memorized payroll transaction for each employee. The transaction would contain the correct withholding amounts for that individual. You can then re-use the memorized transaction each time you create a new payroll check for that individual.

◆ If you have hourly employees, you can still create memorized payroll transactions for each employee (see Chapter 6). But you must refer to your state withholding tables for the correct deductions each time you generate a payroll check. You'll also need to edit the memorized transaction each time you use it so it reflects the correct deductions for the current payroll period.

Chapter 6 contains a useful section on how to use the payroll-related memorized transactions that we've included in the Qksample and Company files on the diskette which accompanies this book.

🏠 Using Scheduled Transactions

By scheduling transactions for payment, Quicken will remind you about the regularly scheduled payments you need to make. For example, if you have a truck loan and it is due the fifth of each month, it would be helpful to set up the loan as a scheduled payment.

Creating New Scheduled Transactions

The "Scheduled Transactions for Payroll" sidebar at the end of this chapter contains instructions on how to create a scheduled transaction group. Here, we'll provide information on how to create a single scheduled transaction.

Figure 4-17

This Create Scheduled Transaction dialog box shows sample settings for scheduling a monthly rent payment.

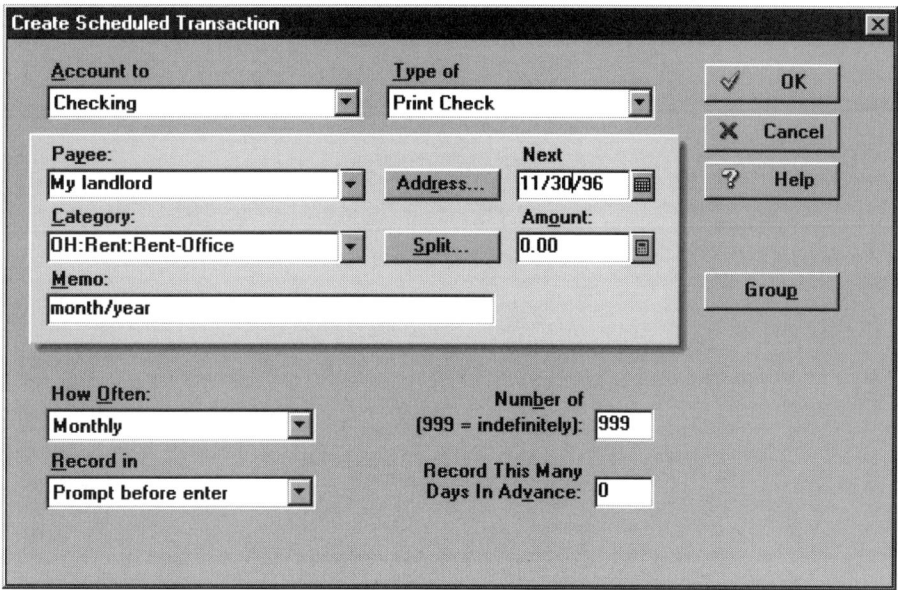

To create a new scheduled transaction:

1. From the menu, select the Lists | Scheduled Transaction command to display the Scheduled Transaction List window. This window will be blank if you haven't created any scheduled transactions previously.

2. In the Scheduled Transaction List window, click the New button to display the Create Scheduled Transaction dialog box. For example, to schedule a monthly rent payment, you would need to enter settings like those shown in Figure 4-17.

3. Start by selecting Checking from the Account to drop-down list.

4. Use the Payee drop-down list to select an existing payee, or enter the name of a new payee in this field.

5. Use the Category drop-down list to assign the desired category to this scheduled transaction.

6. In the Next field, specify the date on which the next payment should be made.

7. Specify an amount for the transaction by entering it into the Amount field. If the amount will vary each time you make a payment, you can either skip this step or enter a default value of 0.00, which you can customize later.

8. Use the How Often drop-down list to choose how often you make the payment.

9. Using the Record in drop-down list, choose whether you want Quicken to prompt you before recording the transaction or whether to let Quicken record it automatically.

10. In the Number of field, enter how many times you want to make this payment. The default value of 999 indicates that the scheduled payment should be made indefinitely.

11. In the Record This Many Days In Advance field, specify whether and how many days in advance you want Quicken to make the payment. Leaving the default value of zero tells Quicken to make the payment on the same day it's due.

12. Click OK to generate the new scheduled transaction. Its name will now appear in the Scheduled Transaction List window.

Modifying an Existing Scheduled Transaction

To modify an existing scheduled transaction:

1. From the menu, select the Lists | Scheduled Transaction command. The Scheduled Transaction List window appears.

2. To highlight the transaction you want to modify, click it once.

3. Click the Edit button to display the Edit Scheduled Transaction dialog box. Modify the information in the fields as needed.

4. Click OK to record your changes.

Deleting an Existing Scheduled Transaction

To delete an existing scheduled transaction:

1. From the menu, select the Lists | Scheduled Transaction command to display the Scheduled Transaction List window.

2. To highlight the transaction you want to modify, click it once.

3. Click the Delete button. You will be prompted with a message that gives you the option not to delete the scheduled transaction. If you are sure you want to delete the scheduled transaction, click OK.

Entering transactions into Quicken is a basic function, but a necessary building block for the "bells and whistles" that Quicken provides in the form of classes, memorized transactions, and memorized reports. The next few chapters give you more in-depth information about how to make the most of these Quicken features.

SCHEDULED TRANSACTIONS FOR PAYROLL

With a bit of extra work, you can create a scheduled transaction group that includes the memorized employee payroll check transactions for all your employees. Using a scheduled transaction group can further streamline your payroll activities. Here's how to create such a group using the Company file from the companion diskette:

1. From the menu, select Lists | Scheduled Transaction to display the Scheduled Transaction List window, and then click the Scheduled tab. This window should be blank if you haven't created any scheduled transactions previously.

2. Click the New button to open the Create Scheduled Transaction dialog box (Figure 4–18).

3. In the Create Scheduled Transaction dialog box, click the Group button. The Create Transaction Group dialog box shown in Figure 4–19 appears.

4. In the Next field, enter the date of the next scheduled payroll.

5. In the Account field, use the drop-down list to select Checking (or another account, if you've set one up).

6. Leave the Group Type set to Regular.

7. In the Group Name field, enter a name that will remind you of the identity of this group, such as "Payroll Checks."

8. Using the Frequency drop-down list, select how often you perform payroll operations. The default value is Monthly.

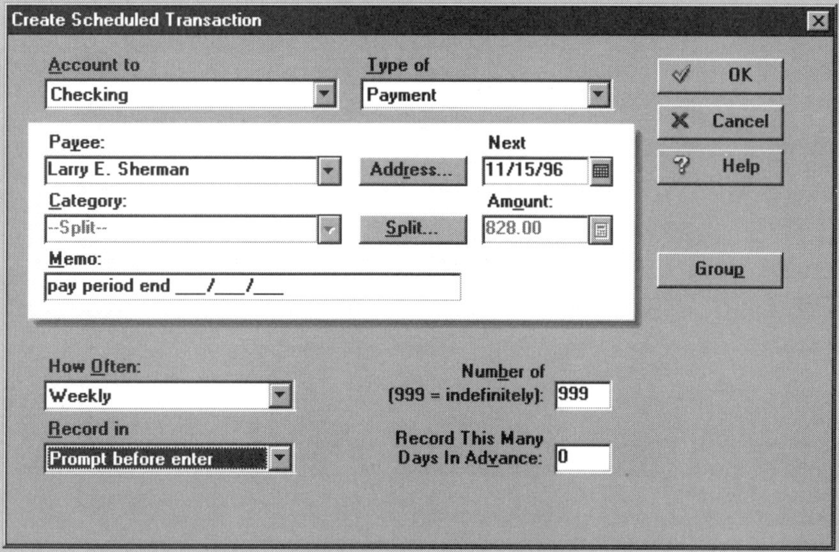

Figure 4–18

To create a scheduled transaction group, click the Group button in the Create Scheduled Transaction dialog box.

SCHEDULED TRANSACTIONS FOR PAYROLL *(continued)*

Figure 4–19

*You enter infor-
mation for your
new scheduled
transaction group
in the Create
Transaction Group
dialog box.*

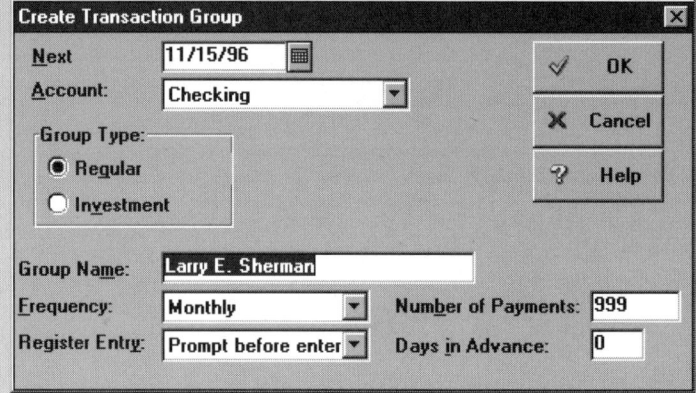

9. Leave Register Entry set to Prompt before entering.

10. Leave Number of Payments set to 999 if you want the scheduled transaction to continue indefinitely. If you want to schedule it for a limited number of uses, enter that number instead.

11. If you'd like Quicken to notify you of the scheduled transaction ahead of the transaction date, enter the number of days in advance in the Days in Advance field. If you don't require notification, leave this value at zero.

12. Click OK. The Assign Transactions to Group window appears as in Figure 4–20. This window allows you to choose which memorized transactions will be included in the scheduled transaction group.

Figure 4–20

*You choose which
memorized transac-
tion will be part of
the group in the
Assign Transactions
to Group window.*

Assign Transactions to Group: 2

Mark   Done

Description	Amount	Type	Memo	Cat	Clr	Grp
Great Living D...		Chk	1099	CS:01Per...		
Hart Excavatio...		Spl	acct. #23...	CS:03Exc...		
Hugo Boss		Spl	P/R job a...	OH:Wage...		1
Jackson Painti...		Chk	1099	CS:24Pnt...		
KD Building S...		Spl	acct. #T...	CS:12Dor...		
Klein & Sons S...		Chk	acct. #23...	CS:06Flo...		
Larry E. Sherm...	-828.00	Spl	pay perio...	OH:Wage...		1
Lewis Brick		Chk	acct. #S...	CS:05Ma...		
Madison Buildi...		Spl	acct. #V...	CS:09R&...		
Mathis Masonr...		Spl	acct. #34...	CS:04Con...		
Northside Con...		Chk	acct. #FL...	CS:04Con...		
P/R Job Cost ...		Spl	P/R job a...	OH:Wage...		
P/R Job Cost ...		Spl	P/R job a...	OH:Wage...		

☐ **View Locked Items Only**

SCHEDULED TRANSACTIONS FOR PAYROLL *(continued)*

13. To include a particular memorized employee payroll transaction in the payroll group, click on it once to highlight it, and then click the Mark button. (We're assuming that you've already created a separate memorized payroll transaction for each employee in your company; instructions for doing so are in Chapter 6.) If you don't see a transaction you want, you'll need to have Quicken memorize it first.

 NOTE: *Create memorized payroll transactions for every current employee and mark all of them in the Assign Transactions to Group window. The steps you're completing will group them together at each pay period and process all of the memorized transactions in one group.*

14. Click the Done button to complete the process of scheduling a group transaction. As the example in Figure 4–21 shows, the new transaction group should appear in the Scheduled Transaction List window.

15. Press Ctrl-F4 to close the Scheduled Transaction List window.

To enter the payroll group into the checking account register and to print the payroll checks, follow this procedure:

1. From the menu, select Lists | Scheduled Transaction to display the Scheduled Transaction List window.

2. Highlight the payroll group by clicking on it once, then click the Pay button to display the Record Transaction Group window (Figure 4–22).

3. In the Due Date field, specify the date on which you want Quicken to enter these transactions in the register. Review the Account field to make certain that the account shown is correct.

4. Click Record to enter the transactions into your account register.

SCHEDULED TRANSACTIONS FOR PAYROLL *(continued).*

Figure 4–21

When you've completed the process, the Scheduled Transaction List window will show the new group payroll transaction you've created.

Figure 4–22

You use the Record Transaction Group window to enter a scheduled group transaction into your account register.

Job Costing and Estimating with Quicken

It has been said that "a contractor who knows where he stands won't stand there very long." And it doesn't take long for a contractor to realize that knowing where he or she stands means comparing estimated costs to actual costs in a timely fashion. Whether you call this task *job costing* or *job cost control,* you're tracking your costs on a job-by-job basis and comparing them to the job's estimate or budget. In this chapter we'll guide you through the two-step process of entering job estimates into Quicken as budgets and creating the appropriate reports to compare actual to estimated job costs.

It's easy to adapt Quicken concepts to the process of job costing and estimating in a construction business. Figure 5–1 shows the correspondence between Quicken functions and their construction-industry equivalents.

The first step is to assign your transactions to specific jobs and job divisions. (Refer to Chapter 2, "Using Quicken Categories, Accounts, and Classes," for more information on how to set up classes to reflect specific jobs.) Let's use an example from the preconfigured Qksample file found on the diskette that accompanies this book. Assume that Nancy Johnson's kitchen remodel is job number 1002. In Quicken, you would enter the job as Class J.1002, with a description such as Johnson Kitchen Remodel. When writing a check in Quicken (see

Construction-industry concept	Quicken concept
Job	Class
Estimate	Budget
Job division/Job subdivision	Category/Subcategory

Chapter 4, "Entering Transactions in Quicken") for a permit for J.1002, you would follow these steps to assign the transaction:

1. Assign the category CS:01Per, which has a description of Plans & Permits.

2. Display the Class List window by choosing the Lists|Class command. Then double-click on the job (class) to which you want to assign the cost. Quicken adds the class after the category and separates them with a forward slash (/). If you already know the name of the job, you can type the forward slash and the class name yourself.

Once you've assigned all your transactions to jobs and job subdivisions this way, you're ready to use the budgeting, reporting, and cost comparison features of Quicken.

Estimating (Budgeting)

One of the most important functions of any construction accounting system is its ability to track a job's actual cost versus its estimated cost. The actual-to-estimate job-cost report is the measuring stick that tells the contractor if he or she is making or losing money on each job. In order to get an actual-to-estimate report, you first must set up a budget in Quicken. The budget amounts you enter will come from the estimate you've generated outside of Quicken.

There is no provision for estimating in Quicken. You will have to create your estimate using other means and transfer the data into Quicken's Budgets feature. Once the estimate (budget) has been entered in Quicken, you can have Quicken create a report that compares the budgeted amount to the actual amount you spent (calculated from the checks you've written and earmarked for that category and subcategory).

You can create an estimate outside of Quicken using notes scratched on a napkin or legal pad, a spreadsheet, or a stand-alone estimating program such as Craftsman's *National Construction Estimator*. Once you have prepared your estimate, you need to summarize and sub-total the estimated amounts so that they parallel the set of subcategories in Quicken. In preparing your summary, it helps to use equivalent or matching names. For example, if one of your planned expenses is for a city permit, use 01Per as the Quicken subcategory, and 01Plans & Permits as your estimate's summary item. Now you're ready to input your estimate summary into Quicken as a Budget.

Setting Up a Budget

The Company file on the diskette that accompanies this book contains a default budget that can serve as a template for creating new budgets for each of your jobs. As you will see in the "Budget Reports" section, you can also use this budget template as the basis of a budget-vs.-actual comparison report that Quicken can memorize for each new job.

To generate a new job-specific budget in your own Company file using the budget template:

1. From the Features menu, select the Planning|Budgets command. Quicken displays the most recently used budget.

2. Click the View button in the upper-left corner of the window, and select the Other Budgets command from the drop-down menu. Highlight the Job Master Budget by clicking on it once, then click the Open button to display the Job Master Budget window (Figure 5–2).

3. Click the New button to display the Create Budget window (Figure 5–3).

4. In the Create Budget window, enter a name and description for the new budget (the figure uses Smith Remodel and Smith Kitchen Remodel as an example), and then activate the Copy Current Budget option. Click the OK button to create the new budget. The new budget window appears, with the name and description at the top.

5. Click into the numerical field on each line and change the amount to match the corresponding amount from your estimate (or to zero if there is no budget amount allotted). The inflow (income) amounts will display as positive numbers and the outflow (expense) amounts will display as negative numbers.

   Pressing the Tab or Enter key after the entry moves you down to the next line.

6. When you have completed your new budget, click the Save button in the upper central area of the window. To exit the Budget window, press Ctrl-F4.

Figure 5–2

*You can generate a
budget for a new job
using the template in
the Job Master
Budget window.*

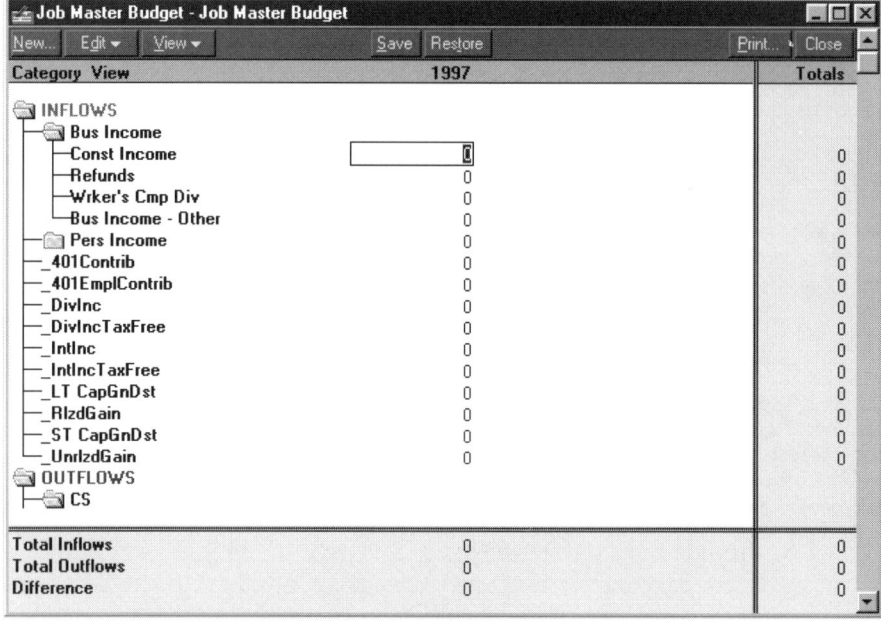

Figure 5–3

*You generate a new
budget based on the
template using the Create
Budget window.*

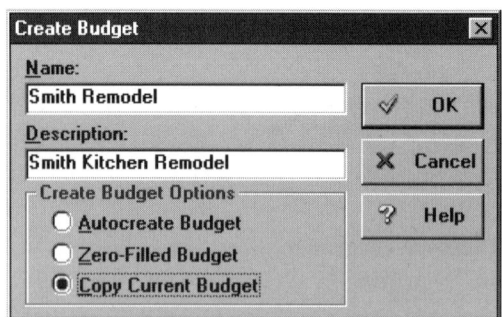

The more detail you include in your job-costing reports, the better. For example, it helps to know (and should make you happy) that you actually spent $500 on framing when you budgeted (estimated) the Framing category to cost $600. But the lump sum $500 doesn't tell you what portion of the total was spent on labor, material, subcontractors, or some other subcategory such as equipment rental. And if you happen to have spent more money on a given category than you budgeted for, you'll want to find out why. Therefore, to keep your costs in line, you need to know the breakdown of your costs for each category. That's why we've created two levels of subcategories in the Quicken data files found on the companion diskette.

In the Qksample and Company files, the Cost of goods sold (CS) categories are broken down into subcategories. For each subcategory, there is a further sub-subcategory breakdown into Lab (Labor), Mat (Material), and Sub (Subcontractor). If you want to expand a given budget subcategory to show these sub-subcategories, click the folder icon to the left of the parent category once. This action causes Quicken to display the sub-subcategories, where you can enter the sub-subcategory amounts. The parent category then displays the total of the amounts you've entered in the sub-subcategories. Conversely, if you want to collapse (hide) the sub-subcategories of a parent category when they are visible, click the folder icon of the parent category once.

Job-Cost and Budget Reports

The core of job costing is the budget-vs.-actual report. In the Quicken data files on the companion diskette, the Budget-vs-Actual report, broken down by category, has been set up as a memorized report for your reference. (For more information, look ahead to Chapter 7, "Using Memorized Reports.")

When you assign categories and classes to transactions, you are giving Quicken the means to sort your information and present it in a line-by-line comparison to the budget you have entered. When you ask Quicken for a Budget-vs-Actual report, Quicken first looks for the *most recently used* budget (which may or may not be the one you want a report for) and then prints a report showing that budget compared to matching categories. So it's extremely important that you make sure the budget you are comparing is in fact the budget for the job on which you want to report. We suggest you double-check the budget title before you run the Budget-vs-Actual report—that way you won't mistakenly match the J.1001 budget to the J.1005 costs.

Job-Cost Reports

The Company file on the companion diskette contains three memorized job-cost reports: Jobs Summary (Activity by Job), Job Summary Report-Job____ (Activity by Month), and Job Detail Report-Job____(Job Income_Expense). You can use these as templates for creating your own job-cost reports. We'll describe each report template briefly and then guide you through the process of creating a job-cost report of your own. For more information about using memorized reports, see Chapter 7.

Jobs Summary (Activity by Job)

This report template shows you the totals for each of your cost categories and subcategories for income and expenses. Using the Customize

Figure 5–4

The Jobs Summary window shows you a report based on activity by job.

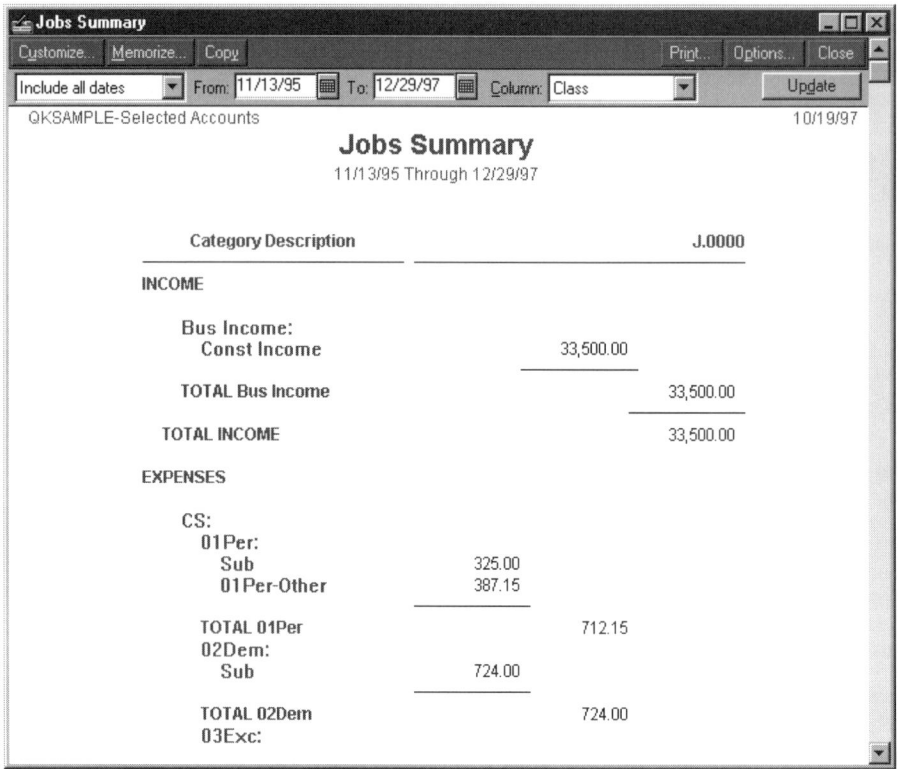

Report dialog boxes, you can define the specific job (class) and the date range to report on. Figure 5–4 shows how a sample Jobs Summary report might look.

Job Summary Report-Job_____(Activity by Month)

This report template is similar in format to the Jobs Summary report, except that it breaks down the amounts by calendar month. Figure 5–5 shows a sample report based on this template.

Job Detail Report-Job_____ (Job Income_Expense)

This report template shows you a listing of each job-related transaction, with a category subtotal based on the job (class) that you select and the date range that you define in the Customize Report dialog boxes. Figure 5–6 shows a sample report based on this template.

Creating a Job-Cost Report Based on the Sample Memorized Reports

To create your own job-cost report:

1. Select the Reports | Memorized Reports command to display the Memorized Reports list.

Figure 5–5

The Job Summary Report-Job_____ window shows you a report based on activity by month.

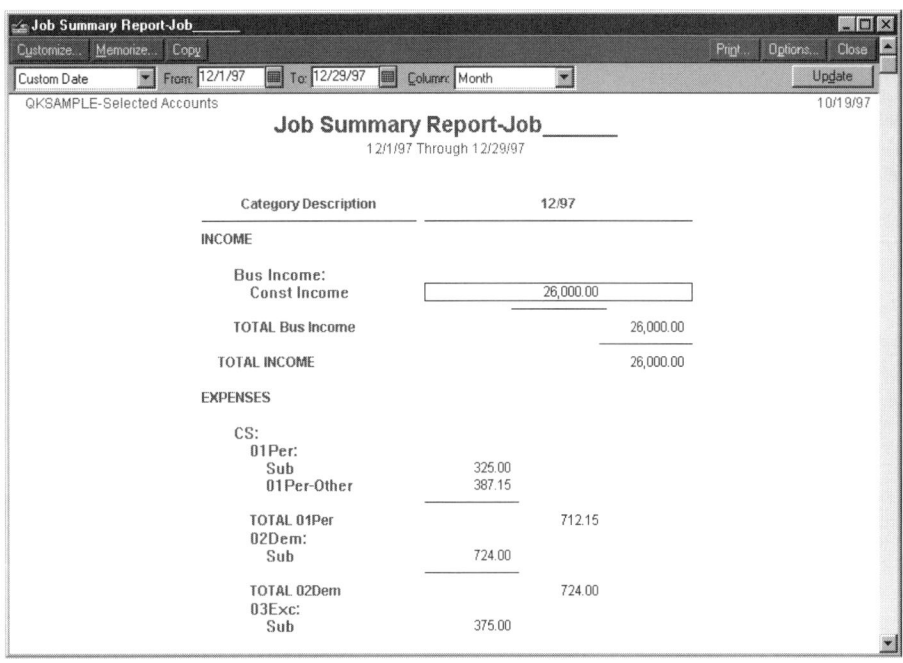

Figure 5–6

The Job Detail Report-Job_____ window shows a report based on job-related transactions.

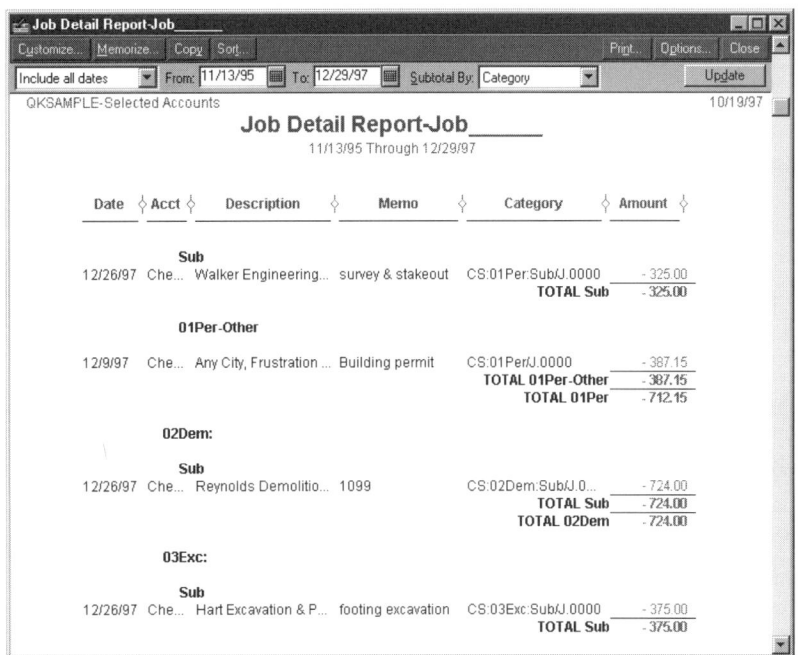

2. Select the desired job-cost report from the list. Check the date range and make any changes if necessary, then click the Customize button to display the Customize Report dialog box. The dialog box first appears showing the Display tab. Figure 5–7 shows the Display tab for the Customize Job Detail Report-Job_____ dialog box.

Figure 5–7

*Use the Display tab of the
Customize Job Detail
Report-Job ____ dialog
box to edit the title of the
report so that it reflects
the correct job number.*

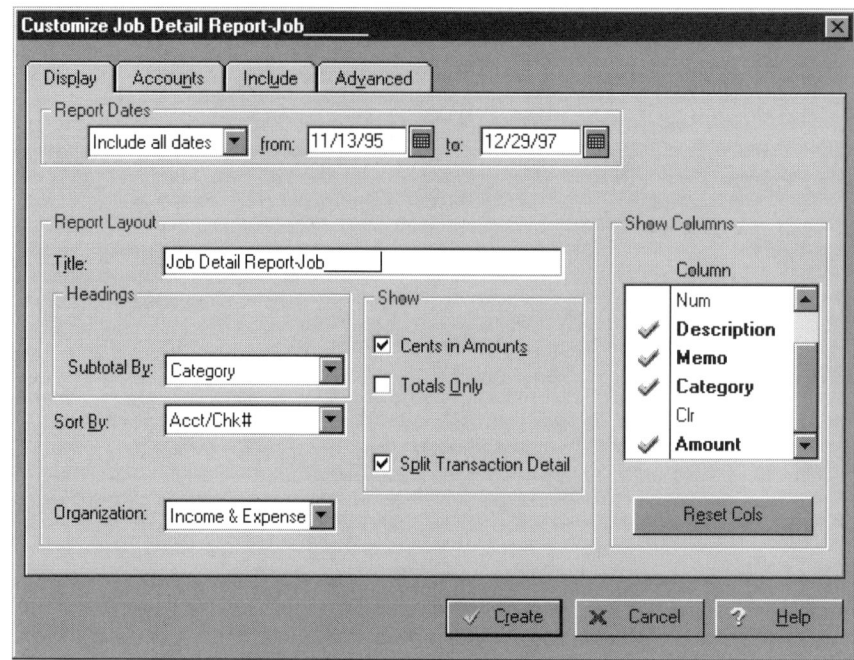

3. In the Display tab, edit the Title field to reflect the correct job number for your customized report.

4. Click on the Include tab. Once there, click the Classes option to display the list of available jobs. Figure 5–8 shows the Include tab in the Customize Job Detail Report-Job____ dialog box.

5. Select the job (or jobs, if you're creating a Jobs Summary report) that you want summarized in the report. More than one job can be selected if you want a report to cover a group of jobs in a particular project or development.

6. Click the Create button at the bottom of the dialog box to generate the report.

Once a report is on the screen, you can have Quicken memorize it so it can be used as a template for future reports. Here's how to create a memorized report (see Chapter 7 for further information and examples):

1. Click the Memorize button at the top of the report window. The Memorize Report dialog box will open.

2. Choose how Quicken should memorize the dates for this report template. For example, if you choose a fixed date range, such as Month to date, the default report will always cover the period from the beginning of the current month to the day

Figure 5–8

With the Classes option selected, the Include tab of the Customize Job Detail Report-Job _____ dialog box displays all available classes (jobs).

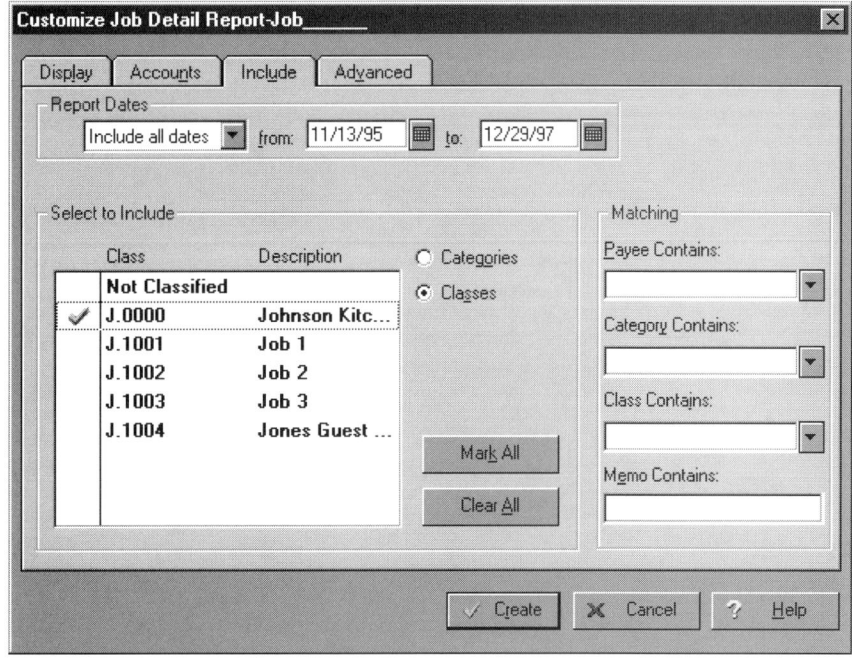

when you run the report. If you choose Custom Dates, those original dates will appear each time you run the report.

3. To avoid overwriting the previous memorized report, be sure to use a new name. We recommend that you use the job number (for example, Job J.1002) in the name of the memorized report.

Budget Reports

The default budget in the Company file on the companion diskette can be used not only as a template to create new budgets for each of your jobs, but also as the basis for an individual budget-vs.-actual comparison report that can be memorized for each new job.

To create a budget-vs.-actual job-cost report using your new budget:

1. From the menu, select the Reports | Memorized Reports command. Highlight the report Budget Report-Job _____ (Budget vs Actual) by clicking on it once.

2. Click the Customize button to display the Customize Report dialog box. In the Display tab, set the Report Dates date range to Current Year by using the drop-down list, as shown in Figure 5–9.

3. Click into the Title field and give the report a name that contains the job number or name.

Figure 5–9

Use the Display tab of the Customize Budget Report-Job_____ dialog box to enter the date range and title for your report.

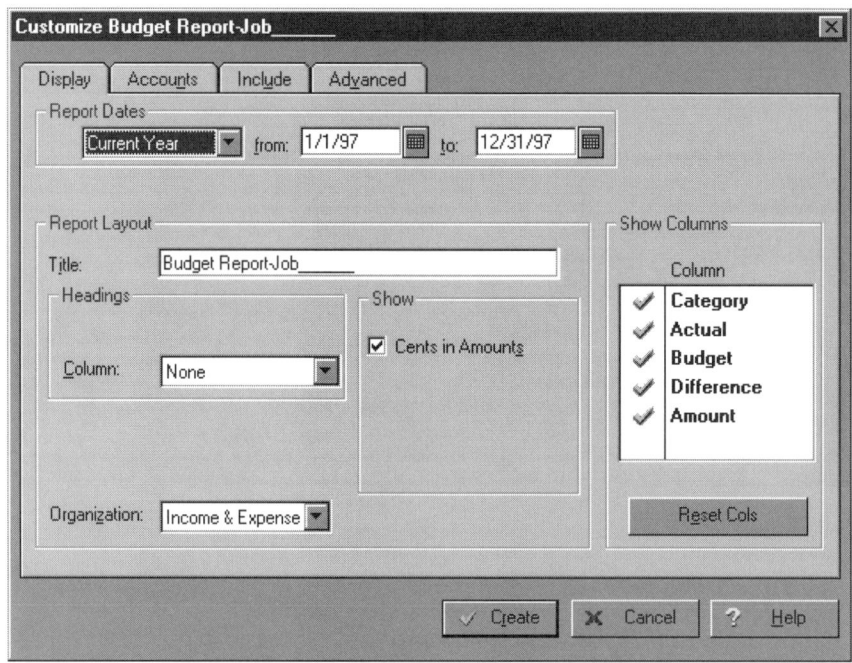

Figure 5–9

Use the Display tab of the Customize Budget Report-Job_____ dialog box to enter the date range and title for your report.

Figure 5–10

Use the Include tab of the Customize Budget Report-Job_____ dialog box to choose the job that matches the budget you have selected.

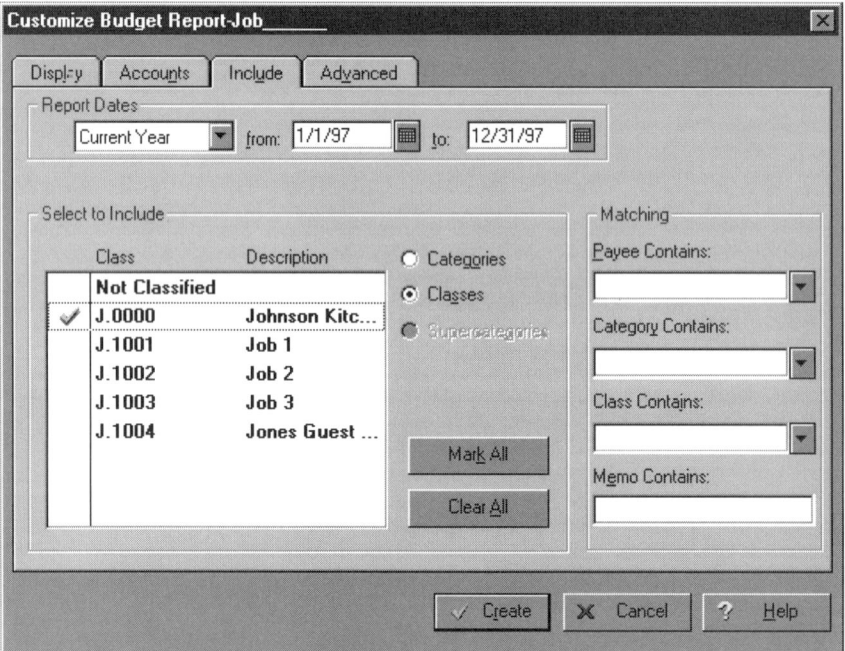

4. Click on the Include tab, then click the Classes option and select only the single job that matches the selected budget (Figure 5–10).

5. Click the Create button to generate the report.

Figure 5–11

The Budget Report-Job J.0000 shows actual vs. budgeted amounts for sample data.

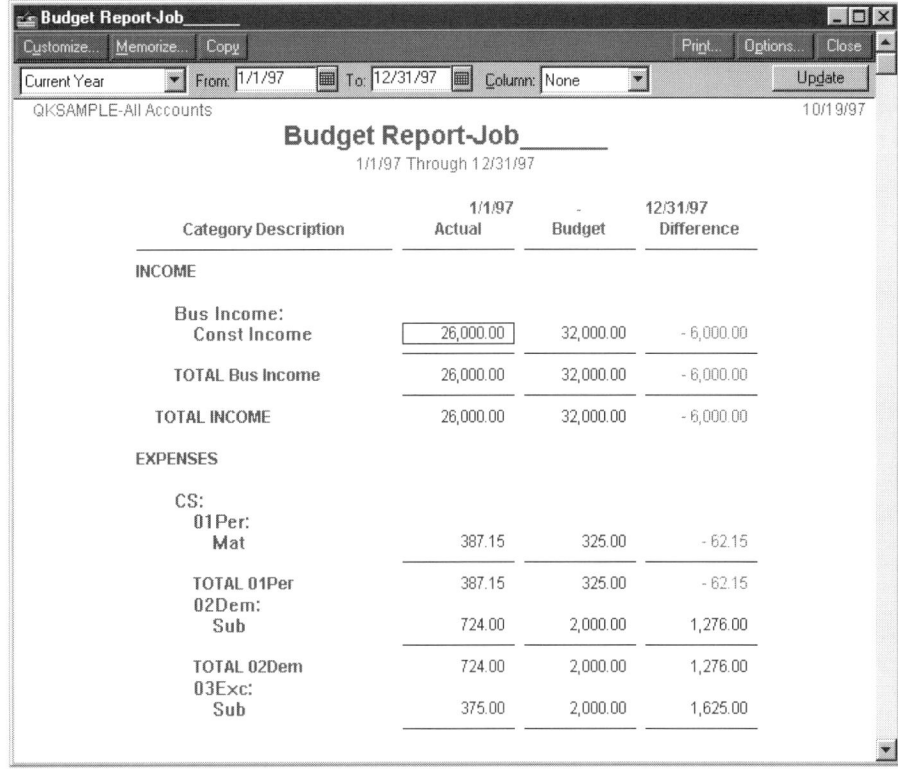

Figure 5–12

Use the Memorize Report dialog box to store a report format and to specify a report name and date range.

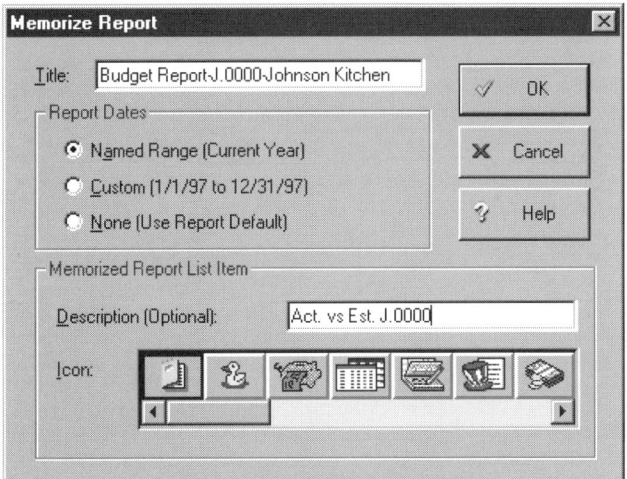

6. Review the displayed report (see the example in Figure 5–11). If it's to your satisfaction, click the Memorize button to display the Memorize Report dialog box shown in Figure 5–12. Name it Budget Report-J.*xxxx* (where J.*xxxx* represents your job number) and then click the OK button.

The memorized report for that job will now appear in the Memorized Reports list that you access whenever you select the Reports | Memorized Reports command. Each time you display the report, the actual job-cost data will reflect the current costs for each of the cost categories within the selected date range.

 NOTE: *Remember, you should first enter the name of the budget you want to report on before you attempt to display a memorized budget report. Otherwise, Quicken will not be able to generate a report on the screen.*

Using Memorized Transactions

In Quicken, memorized transactions are simply check or deposit transactions that have been created and then saved (memorized) for future re-use in an account Register window. Quicken makes it very easy for you to create a memorized transaction and then save it so it appears in the Memorized Transaction List.

To be able to use memorized transactions, you'll need to activate the following settings when customizing Quicken (refer to Chapter 3, "Customizing Quicken"):

- Register Options dialog box, QuickFill tab: Auto Memorize New Transactions
- Write Checks Options dialog box, QuickFill tab: Auto Memorize New Transactions

These settings tell Quicken to automatically memorize new transactions for you whenever you work in the Register or Write Checks window. To make Quicken's memorization feature even more efficient, you should also activate the following settings in both the Register Options and Write Checks Options dialog boxes:

- Complete Fields Using Previous Entries
- Recall Memorized Transactions

These options configure Quicken to automatically complete the entire transaction when you type in the first few letters of the payee's name in the Payee field of the register. This can save you a great deal of data-entry time because, for many transactions, you won't have to enter class or category information—it will already be entered for you.

NOTE*: When Complete Fields Using Previous Entries is turned on, Quicken matches all the details of the last transaction entered for the payee. That includes category, class, amount, and splits, if any. If any of these details are different for the current transaction, you must change them before you record (save) the new transaction, or it will not be accurate.*

Another way to enter memorized transactions in the currently open register is to display the Memorized Transaction List (Lists | Memorized Transaction) and double-click on the transaction you want to enter. You can also save any existing completed transaction to the Memorized Transaction List by selecting the transaction in the register and then choosing the Edit | Transaction | Memorize command.

We'll spend the first part of this chapter examining the four basic types of memorized transactions provided with the Quicken data files on the diskette that accompanies this book: entry adjustments, customer deposits, overhead expenses, and payments to job vendors. Then, we'll take a closer look at how you can use the sample memorized transactions to streamline payroll functions. Finally, we'll provide information on how to create your own memorized transactions.

Why Use or Create Memorized Transactions?

Using memorized transactions saves you keystrokes and valuable time. It can also reduce record-entry mistakes by ensuring that names are properly spelled and that the correct category is selected for the payee (assuming that the category is supposed to be the same for each transaction with that payee). Consistent spelling of names and use of the correct category and class are a must for obtaining accurate reports. For instance, memorized transactions will keep you from identifying a payee as "A-4 Construction" in one transaction and "A-Four Construction" in a different transaction. That way, when it comes time to sort your transactions by subcontractor, you won't have two different entries for the same company.

🔯 Working in the Memorized Transaction List Window

The Quicken data files on the diskette that comes with this book contain many memorized transactions already set up for you. We'll take a look at these files to help you become familiar with the Memorized Transaction List window. You can access this window by selecting Lists | Memorized Transaction from the menu. Figure 6–1 shows some of the memorized transactions available in the Company file.

The Memorized Transaction List window displays all the memorized transactions in your data file. You can use this window to create new memorized transactions, to edit existing memorized transactions, and to delete memorized transactions that you no longer need. For each memorized transaction you can record a standardized description, amount, type, category, and memo information. You can also lock a memorized transaction to prevent any of the standardized information in it from being altered or customized, and you can set up any memorized transaction as a calendar item. Each of these fields is described below.

- ◆ The Description field indicates the purpose of the transaction.
- ◆ The Amount field can be filled in if the amount is always the same for this transaction; if the amount varies each time you use the transaction, you should leave the Amount field blank.
- ◆ The Type field describes whether the memorized transaction is a payment, deposit, or split transaction.

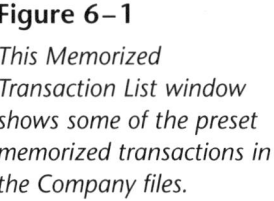

Figure 6–1

This Memorized Transaction List window shows some of the preset memorized transactions in the Company files.

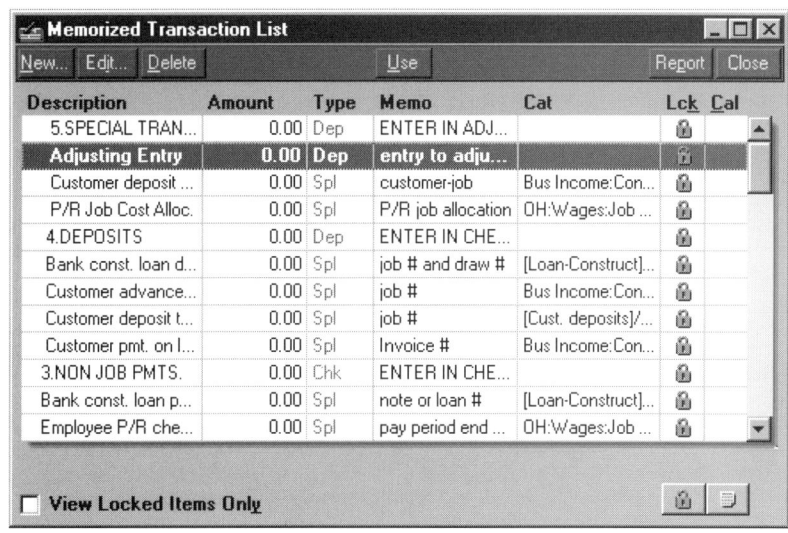

◆ The Memo field can provide a more detailed description of the memorized transaction.

◆ The Cat (Category) field is useful when you always want to apply the same category for job-costing purposes.

◆ The Lck field indicates (by the presence or absence of a padlock icon) whether a given memorized transaction is locked or unlocked. This is a subtle distinction. You can always change the information for any *specific* transaction that you create based on a memorized transaction. The locked or unlocked status simply determines what Quicken memorizes. When a memorized transaction is locked, all its data remains the same as when it was originally locked; this is the default information that appears in the Register window whenever you use the transaction. When a memorized transaction is *un*locked, Quicken's QuickFill feature (see Chapter 3) simply memorizes the transaction again using the new information you entered the last time you used the transaction. With unlocked transactions, the memorized information is constantly changing. To toggle the locked status of a memorized transaction on or off, just click once in the Lck field.

◆ The Cal (Calendar) field lets you place a memorized transaction on Quicken's Financial Calendar so that you'll always receive a reminder about when to use the transaction. Click into this field to toggle the Financial Calendar icon on or off.

🏠 Using a Memorized Transaction

As Figure 6–1 shows, there are five categories of preset memorized transactions in the Company file: SPECIAL TRANSACTIONS, DEPOSITS, NON JOB PMTS., JOB VENDOR PAYMENTS, and MY VENDOR PMNTS. This last category is one you will want to customize based on the needs of your own business.

Before you examine specific memorized transactions hands-on, it's important to gain an understanding of how to apply and use them in Quicken. One of the most common transactions you'll encounter is writing a check to pay a subcontractor, so we'll use it as an instructive example. In the Company file on the companion diskette, one of the memorized transactions under 2.JOB VENDOR PAYMENTS is set up to write a check to a 1099 vendor (such as a subcontractor or materials supplier) and record it in the checking account register. Entering a memorized Job Vendor Payment into the register takes only two clicks once the Memorized Transaction List and Checking Register windows are open. To enter a Job Vendor "1099" or other Job Vendor Payment transaction:

1. Open the Register window of the Checking account in the Company file.

2. Position the cursor in the Date field of a new transaction line and adjust the date if required.

3. From the menu, select Lists | Memorized Transaction to open the Memorized Transaction List window. Click the memorized transaction Job Vendor "1099" once to highlight it. (This memorized transaction is located in group 2.)

4. Click the Use button in the upper central area of the Memorized Transaction List window (or double-click the name of the transaction) to automatically enter this transaction into the check register as a new transaction.

With this, as with all memorized transactions, you'll want to check the transaction for accuracy. You may want to change some of the information, such as the amount, date, and category or subcategory.

🏠 Memorized Transactions Included on the Companion Diskette

The Company file included on the diskette that accompanies this book contains a number of preset memorized transactions. You can find these transactions in the Memorized Transaction List, which you can access by choosing the Lists | Memorized Transaction command. They are grouped in the list by transaction type.

To make the most effective use of these preset transactions, you should customize your Company file using the following settings in the QuickFill tab of the Register Options dialog box:

◆   Complete Fields Using Previous Entries turned *on*

◆   Recall Memorized Transactions turned *on*

◆   Drop Down Lists on Field Entry turned *on*

◆   Auto Memorize New Transactions turned *on*

In addition, the Show Buttons on QuickFill Fields option found in the Display tab of the Register Options dialog box should be turned on.

The memorized transactions in the Quicken data files on the companion diskette are grouped numerically in the list according to their type. This organization keeps similar transaction types together and makes it easier to find the one you need. The memorized transactions in groups 2 through 5 are set up to help you properly enter special types of transactions. When you use the Company file for your own business data, the memorized transactions that you create for your own vendors will be in the bottom group, group 1.

Some of the preset memorized transactions, such as groups 3 through 5, are intended for use exactly as they are in the list. Others, such as group 2, are provided as templates for you to use in creating other memorized transactions, substituting your own specific vendor/payee name for the generic vendor/payee that is in the supplied transaction.

Some of these memorized transactions will be appropriate for your business and some may not. You may find yourself using some quite often and others only on occasion. If you're sure you'll never want to use a given memorized transaction, you can delete it by highlighting it in the Memorized Transaction List window and then clicking the Delete button. Quicken will give you a warning message to make sure you don't delete a memorized transaction inadvertently.

An overview of each of the memorized transaction groups provided in the Company file follows.

Special Transactions

The top group in the Memorized Transaction List window is shown under the heading 5.SPECIAL TRANSACTIONS. These adjusting transactions are intended to be entered only in the Adjustments register and usually involve accounts other than your Checking account. The Adjustments register is set up in our Quicken data files as an Asset account. You can display it on your screen by highlighting it in the Account List window and then clicking the Open button (Figure 6–2).

The Adjustments register provides some of the functions of a General Journal in traditional accounting systems. The purpose of adjusting entries is not to enter new transaction amounts into the accounting system, but to adjust or re-distribute amounts from prior transactions.

In a traditional double-entry accounting system, when you make a journal entry the total debits must exactly equal the total credits in the transaction balance. In Quicken, your Adjustments account is balanced when the total of the amounts on all the transaction Split lines is equal to zero. If each transaction in the register is balanced, then

Figure 6–2

You can display the Adjustments register by highlighting the Adjustments account in the Account List window and then double-clicking.

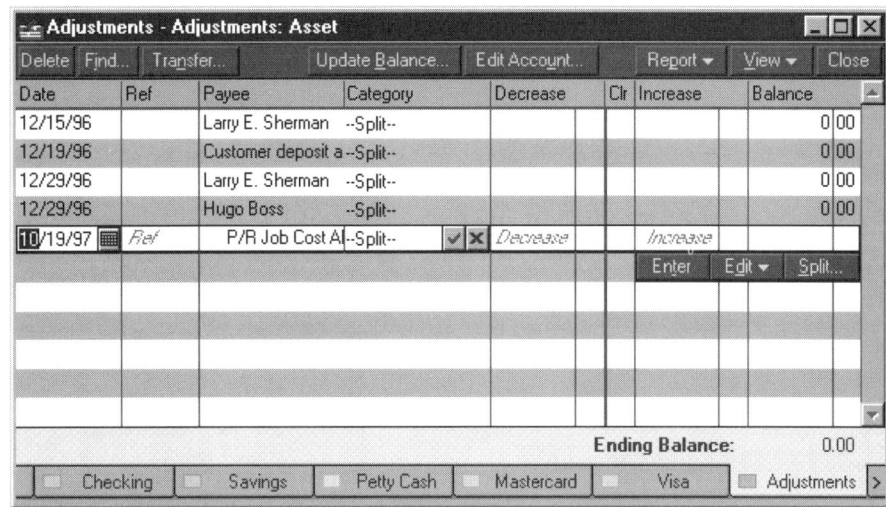

the balance in the Adjustments account (as shown at the bottom of the register and beside the account name in the Account List) should always be zero. The Adjustments register will provide your accountant with a convenient method of reviewing adjustments that have been made to your account—more convenient than having to find these transactions in all your other accounts.

Figure 6–3 shows the names and descriptions of the preset memorized transactions in the Special Transactions category.

Deposits

The second group of preset memorized transactions in our Company file appears under the heading 4.DEPOSITS. These transactions are intended for use in the Check register. Different types of checking-account deposits require that you assign different categories in order

Figure 6–3

The Company file on the companion diskette provides you with three types of memorized Special Transactions.

5. Special Transactions	Description
Adjusting Entry	An entry (usually supplied by your accountant) used to adjust account balances, such as loans, or to record depreciation
Customer deposit applied	An entry used to transfer a job deposit amount from the liability account Customer deposits to the income account Construction Income
P/R Job Cost Alloc.	An entry used to allocate payroll and burden to your job-cost categories

to properly distribute the amounts. Using the appropriate memorized transaction for a new record entry will ensure that you assign the correct category to your deposit.

If a customer gives you a deposit, it is technically the customer's money you are holding. It can later be applied to the first or last invoice, but until then it should be treated as a liability rather than as income. Here's how to record a typical customer deposit using the memorized transaction, Customer deposit taken, from our Quicken data files:

1. To enter the amount received from the customer, begin by opening the Register window of the account to which you deposited the money (for example, Checking or Savings).

2. Open the Memorized Transaction List window and select the memorized transaction Customer deposit taken (it's listed under 4.DEPOSITS).

3. Fill in the data for this transaction. Enter the date of the deposit in the Date field and the customer's check number in the Num field. Be sure to leave the default "Customer deposit" in the Payee field to avoid changing the memorized transaction. To identify the payee, enter the customer's name in the Memo field so you can trace the deposit later if necessary.

4. Tab over to the Deposit field and enter the amount of the actual deposit.

5. Click the Split button to open the Split Transaction Window. It will appear as shown in Figure 6–4.

6. In the Category field of the Split Transaction Window, change the job number to the actual job number for your transaction.

7. In the Amount field of the Split Transaction Window, enter the amount of the deposit again.

8. Click the OK button and press Enter to record the transaction.

Later, when it's time to apply the deposit to the job and recognize the money as income (no longer a liability), you'd proceed like this:

1. Open the Register for the Adjustments account.

2. Open the Memorized Transaction List window and double-click the memorized transaction Customer deposit applied, which is listed under 5.SPECIAL TRANSACTIONS. This action enters the transaction into the Adjustments register.

3. In the Date field of the Adjustments register, enter the date on which the deposit should be recognized as income.

Figure 6–4

This is how the default information for the memorized transaction Customer deposit taken appears in the Split Transaction Window before you enter data pertaining to a specific transaction.

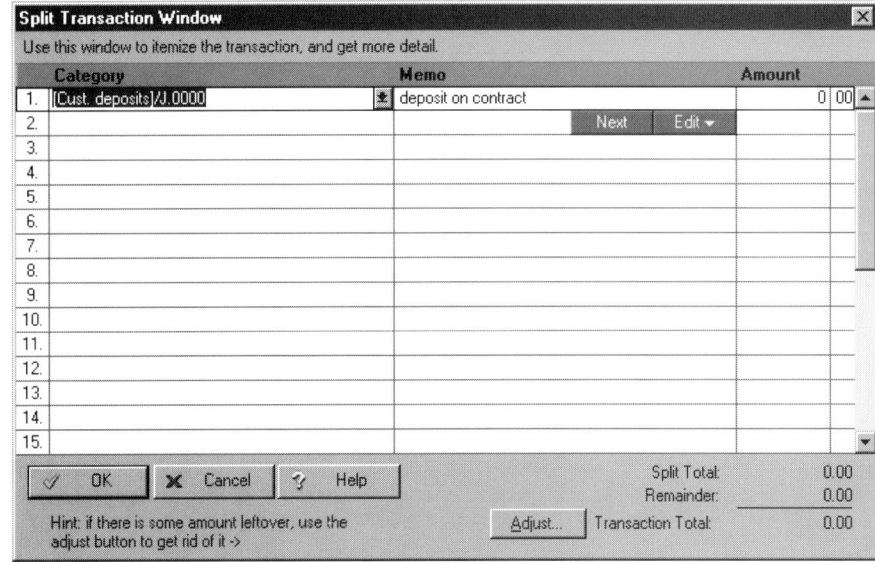

4. Leave the default information, "Customer deposit applied," in the Payee field to preserve the original memorized transaction information.

5. Click the Split button to open the Split Transaction Window.

6. In the Category field of the Split Transaction Window, change the job number to reflect the actual job that pertains to this transaction.

7. Enter the amount of the deposit now being recognized as income on the *first* line of the Amount field of the Split Transaction Window.

8. On the *second* line of the Split Transaction Window, enter the same amount as a *negative* number in the Amount field. Figure 6–5 shows how this action moves the deposit from a liability account to an income account.

9. Click the OK button, and then press Enter to record the transaction.

 NOTE: *Although Quicken uses the Category field of the Split Transaction Window to assign both the category and the class (job), you must use a forward slash (/) to separate the category from the class when making the entry.*

Figure 6–6 shows the names and descriptions of the preset memorized transactions in the Deposits category.

Figure 6–5

*This is how the default
information for the
memorized transaction
Customer deposit applied
appears in the Split
Transaction Window
before you enter data.*

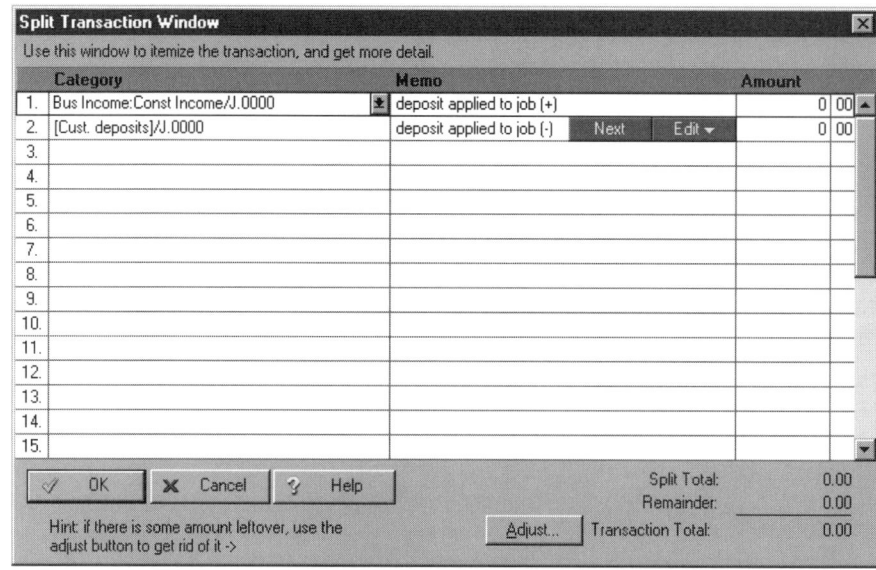

Figure 6–6

*The Company file on the
companion diskette
provides you with four
types of memorized
deposit transactions.*

4. Deposits	Description
Bank const. loan draw	An entry used to assign a loan draw deposit to the Const. Loan liability account
Customer advance on job	An entry used to assign the deposit of a job advance to the Const. Income category
Customer deposit taken	An entry used to assign a job deposit to the Cust. Deposits liability account
Customer pmt. on Invoice	An entry used to assign a job payment received to the Const. Income Category and Sales Tax liability account

Non Job Payments (NON JOB PMTS.)

The third group of preset memorized transactions in the Quicken data files on the companion diskette to this book appears under the heading 3.NON JOB PMTS. These are memorized check transactions that are intended for use in the Check register. The memorized transactions in this group are typical of your overhead and management expenses.

You may choose to use most of these transactions as templates to create another memorized transaction with your own specific vendor/payee name and address entered. You can also change the name of each transaction. For example, you might want to change the name of the My landlord transaction to reflect the name of your actual land-lord—let's call him Mr. Block. Here's how you'd proceed:

1. Open the Memorized Transaction List window, if it isn't open already.

2. Click once on the memorized transaction you want to change (in this case, My landlord).

3. Click the Edit button to bring up the Edit Memorized Transaction dialog box (Figure 6–7).

4. In the Payee field, change the name of the payee from "My landlord" to "Mr. Block" (or whatever your landlord's actual name is).

5. Click the OK button. The new payee name now appears as the name of the memorized transaction in the Memorized Transaction List window.

Of course, you can go beyond editing our memorized transactions and create new memorized transactions of your own (see the section "Creating a New Memorized Transaction" later in this chapter for details).

Figure 6–8 shows the names and descriptions of the preset memorized transactions in the NON JOB PMTS. category.

Job Vendor Payments

The fourth group of preset memorized transactions in the Company file is shown in the Memorized Transaction List under the heading 2.JOB VENDOR PAYMENTS. These are memorized check transactions that are intended for use in the Check register. The memorized

Figure 6–7

You can change the name of a memorized transaction from the Company files by using the Edit Memorized Transaction dialog box.

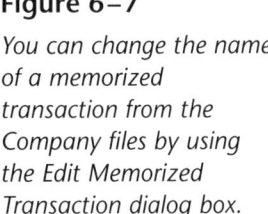

3. Non Job Pmts.	Description
Bank const. loan pmt.	A check entry used to split a construction loan payment, assigning the principal portion of the payment to the Const. Loan liability account and the interest portion of the payment to the Cost of Sales category for the job
Employee P/R check	A check entry used to assign an employee's payroll amount to the Wages category, and the withholding amounts to the Payroll Tax category and the individual liability account
Fed. W/H tax Depository	A check entry used to assign the Federal Withholding tax deposit to the individual P/R federal tax liability accounts FWH, FICA (Social Security), and MEDI
Internal Revenue Service	A check entry used to assign the Federal Unemployment Tax to a liability account such as Payroll-FUTA
My gas-elec utility co.	A check template that should be used to create a memorized transaction (using your own utility company's name) in the transaction group 1.MY VENDOR PMNTS. The payment amount will be assigned to the expense category OH:Utilities-Gas & Electric.
My landlord	A check template that should be used to create a memorized transaction (using your landlord's name) in the transaction group 1.MY VENDOR PMNTS. The payment amount will be assigned to the expense category OH:Rent:Rent-Office.
My Phone Company	A check template that should be used to create a memorized transaction (using your telephone company's name) in the transaction group 1.MY VENDOR PMNTS. The payment amount will be assigned to the expense categories OH:Tel:Main line, Mobile Phone, Fax Line, and Pager.
	NOTE: *If you make a payment to more than one vendor, create a memorized transaction for each vendor and include only the categories that apply to payments made to that vendor.*
My water company	A check template that should be used to create a memorized transaction (using your water company's name) in the transaction group 1.MY VENDOR PMNTS. The payment amount will be assigned to the expense category OH:Utilities:Water.
Sales tax payment	A check entry used to assign the state sales tax payment to the Sales Tax liability account
State tax department	A check entry used to assign the State Withholding tax payment to the Payroll-SWH state withholding tax liability account
State unempl. tax	A check entry used to assign the State Unemployment insurance payment to the Payroll-SUI state unemployment insurance liability account

Figure 6–8

The Company files on the companion diskette provide eleven types of memorized Non Job Payment transactions.

Figure 6–9

To enter a check to a vendor in the Write Checks window, use the memorized transaction Job Vendor "1099."

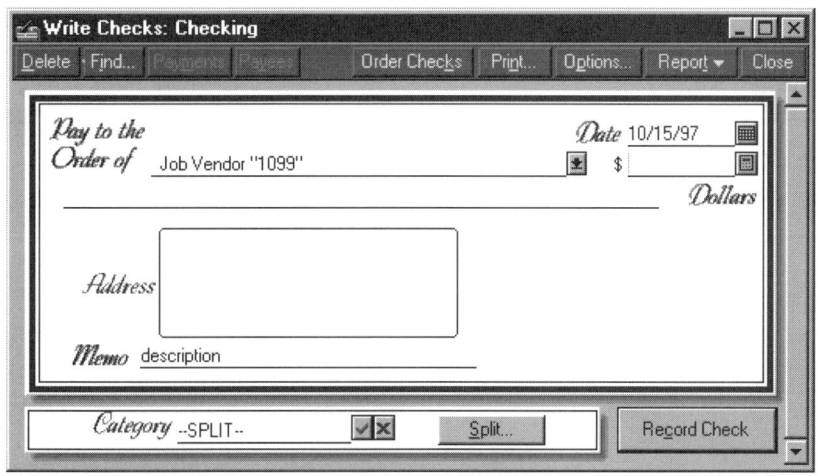

Figure 6–10

This Write Checks window shows a customized memorized transaction that uses an actual vendor name and actual dollar amount.

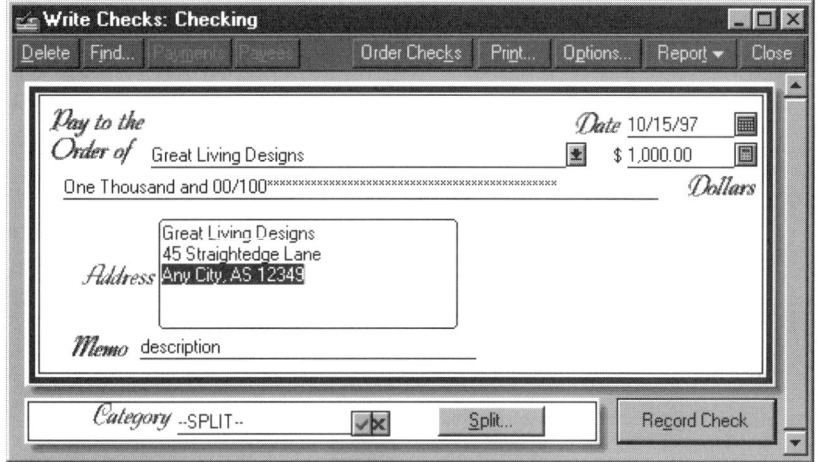

transactions in this group are generic transactions (see Figure 6–9) for two different types of vendors:

◆ Either a 1099-type vendor (service providers who are sole proprietors, partnerships, or dba's that require 1099 notices for their earnings from your company) or

◆ A corporate vendor (service providers who are incorporated and/or only provide materials and do not require 1099 notices)

Use these transactions as templates to generate new memorized transactions with your own specific vendor/payee name and address (see Figure 6–10). The basic procedure is similar to the one described in the "Creating a New Memorized Transaction" section later in this chapter.

Figure 6–11

When you enter data in the Split Transaction Window for an actual job based on the memorized 1099 transaction, assign the actual job number and leave the 1099 notation in the Memo field.

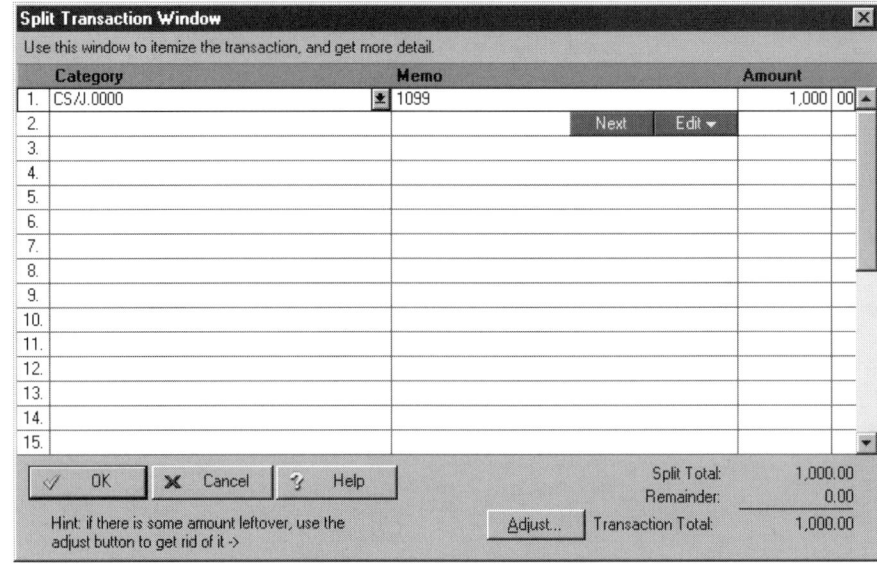

Whenever you create a new Job Vendor Payment memorized transaction, you will also need to select the appropriate expense category for that vendor. In most cases, this will be one of the CS (cost of goods sold) subcategories. To assign a specific cost-of-sales subcategory rather than the default CS parent category, click in the Category field of the Register window (or Split Transaction Window if you'll be using more than one category) and select the appropriate cost-of-sales subcategory from the drop-down list.

These memorized job transactions all have a generic entry J.0000 for the Class/Job. Whenever you generate a new memorized transaction, start with this generic class (job) number. The time to change it is when you are entering an actual job transaction and want to assign the transaction to a particular job (Figure 6–11). For your 1099 vendors, do not remove the 1099 notation that appears in the Memo field of the Register window or Split Transaction Window. This number identifies the record for inclusion in the memorized 1099 Detail Report.

 NOTE: *Be sure to lock each newly memorized transaction when you generate it. This will prevent Quicken from overwriting the default information for it.*

Figure 6–12 shows the names and descriptions of the preset memorized transactions in the 2.JOB VENDOR PAYMENTS category.

Figure 6–12

The Company files on the companion diskette provide you with two types of memorized Job Vendor Payments transactions.

2.Job Vendor Payments	Description
Job vendor "1099"	A check template that should be used to create a memorized transaction (substituting your own subcontractor's name) in the transaction group 1.MY VENDOR PMNTS. When substituting your subcontractor's name, you will also need to change the category to the specific Cost of Sales (CS) subcategory that matches the service provided.
Job vendor "Corp"	A check template that should be used to create a memorized transaction (substituting your own supplier's name) in the transaction group 1.MY VENDOR PMNTS. When substituting your supplier's name, you will also need to change the category to the specific Cost of Sales (CS) subcategory that matches the goods or services provided.

Memorized Transactions for Payroll Functions

The Company file included on the diskette that accompanies this book has the necessary payroll accounts already set up for you. In addition, the file contains four memorized transactions that you can use to enter your payroll and payroll tax transactions: Employee P/R check, P/R Job Cost Alloc., Fed. W/H tax Depository, and Internal Revenue Service.

Employee P/R check

The Employee P/R check memorized transaction included in the Company file is intended for use in either the Check Register window or the Write Checks window. Use it to assign an employee's payroll amount to the Wages category and to assign the withholding and employer contributions to the individual payroll liability accounts and to the Payroll Tax category. Here's how to tailor the memorized transaction to your own company's needs:

1. Open the Company file, if you haven't done so already. From the menu, select Lists | Account and double-click on Checking to open the Check Register window.

2. From the menu, select Lists | Memorized Transaction and then double-click the Employee P/R check transaction, found in the group 3.NON JOB PMTS. (See Figure 6–13.) Double-clicking the memorized transaction causes Quicken to enter it automatically into the Check Register window as the active transaction.

Figure 6–13

*To customize the
Employee P/R check
memorized transaction
for your company,
double-click its entry
in the Memorized
Transaction List window.*

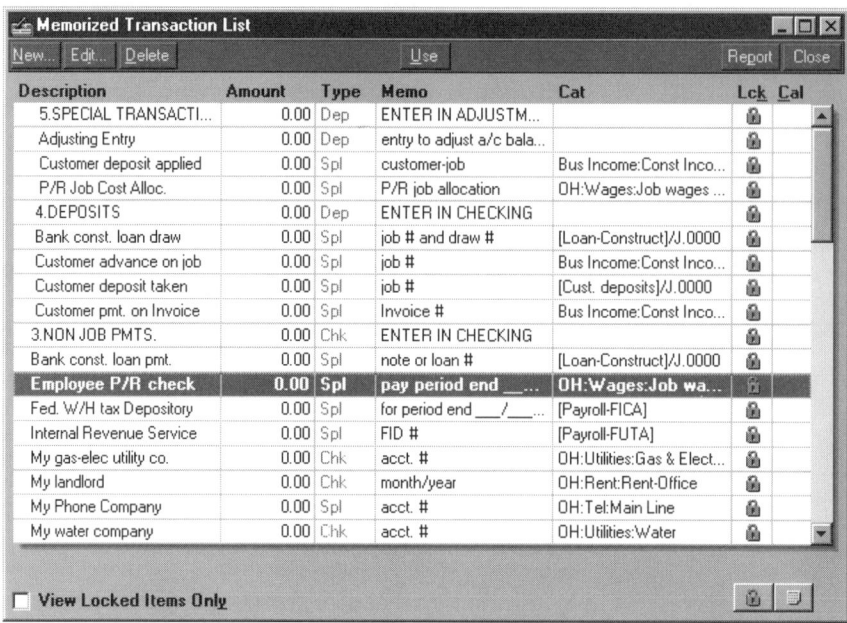

Figure 6–14

*The default amounts for
the Employee P/R check
memorized transaction are
all set to zero in the Split
Transaction Window.*

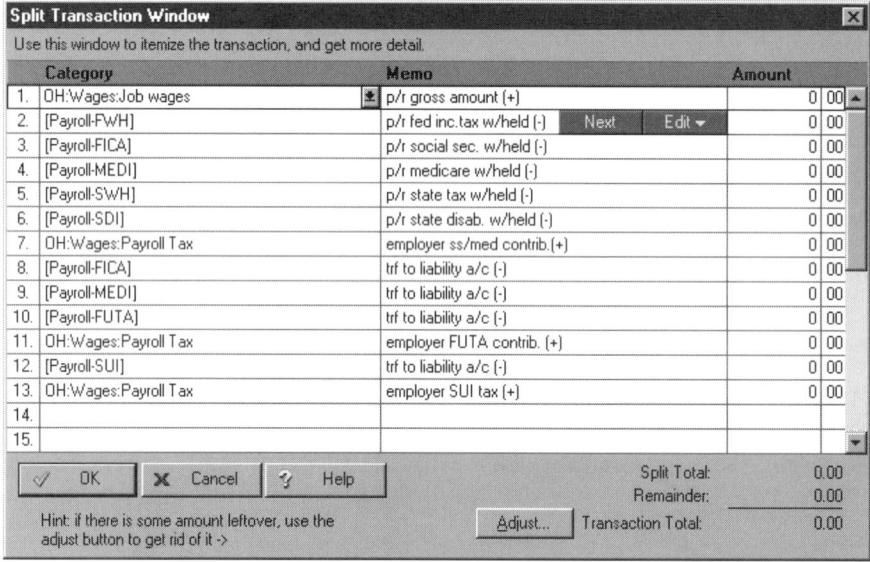

3. In the Check Register window, click into the Payee field and type the name of an actual employee.

4. Click the Split button to open the Split Transaction Window. Notice that the default amounts for each category are all set to zero as shown in Figure 6–14. This allows you to customize amounts when creating variations on this memorized transaction for your own employees.

5. Click into the Amount field of the first line and enter the gross payroll amount for the current employee.

6. Click into the Amount field of the second line and enter the amount of federal income tax (FWH) withheld for the current employee. *Enter the amount preceded by a minus (–) sign* to indicate that this amount is being withheld from the paycheck for federal taxes.

7. Click into the Amount field of the third line and enter the amount of Social Security (FICA) withheld for the current employee. *Enter the amount preceded by a minus (–) sign.*

8. Click into the Amount field of the fourth line and enter the amount of Medicare (MEDI) withheld for the current employee. *Enter the amount preceded by a minus (–) sign.*

9. Click into the Amount field of the fifth line and enter the amount of state income tax (SWH) withheld for the current employee. *Enter the amount preceded by a minus (–) sign.*

10. Click into the Amount field of the sixth line and enter the amount of state disability (SDI) withheld for the current employee. *Enter the amount preceded by a minus (–) sign.*

11. Click into the Amount field of the seventh line and enter the amount of the employer contribution for combined Social Security and Medicare (OH:Wages:Payroll Tax subcategory). Enter the amount *without* a minus (–) sign to record employer payroll taxes for Social Security and Medicare.

12. Click into the Amount field of the eighth line and enter the amount to be contributed by the employer for Social Security (FICA). *Enter the amount preceded by a minus (–) sign.* This action causes employer Social Security taxes to accrue as a liability.

13. Click into the Amount field of the ninth line and enter the amount to be contributed by the employer for Medicare (MEDI). *Enter the amount preceded by a minus (–) sign.* This action causes employer Medicare taxes to accrue as a liability.

14. Click into the Amount field of the tenth line and enter the amount to be paid by the employer for federal unemployment tax (FUTA). *Enter the amount preceded by a minus (–) sign.* This action causes FUTA taxes to accrue as a liability.

15. Click into the Amount field of the eleventh line and enter the amount to be paid by the employer for federal unemployment tax (FUTA). In this case, enter the amount *without* a minus (–) sign to record a payroll tax expense for FUTA.

16. Click into the Amount field of the twelfth line and enter the amount to be paid by the employer for state unemployment insurance (SUI). *Enter the amount preceded by a minus (–) sign* to record SUI taxes as an expense.

17. Click into the Amount field of the thirteenth line and enter the amount to be paid by the employer for state unemployment insurance (SUI). In this case, enter the amount *without* a minus (–) sign to cause SUI taxes to accrue as a liability.

18. Click the Adjust button at the bottom of the Split Transaction Window. The split total amount should match the net amount of the payroll check.

19. Click the OK button to close the Split Transaction Window. When the Payment/Deposit selection window appears, select Payment and click the OK button.

20. Click the Enter button to record the transaction.

Another option is to generate a group of transactions that includes memorized payroll transactions for all the employees in your company. See the "Scheduled Transactions for Payroll" sidebar in Chapter 4, "Entering Transactions in Quicken," for more information.

P/R Job Cost Allocation

The P/R Job Cost Alloc. memorized transaction is a split adjustments entry that adds and subtracts category amounts in order to allocate payroll and burden to your job-cost categories. The net sum of this transaction should always be zero, and the net effect is to move money amounts from one job-cost category to another.

Burden is the mandated costs of payroll in addition to wages that are a valid cost of the job. Burden includes items such as worker's compensation; disability; and employer's contribution of Social Security, Medicare, and federal and state unemployment taxes. Burden is usually calculated as a percentage of the gross wages of the employee for the period. The P/R Job Cost Alloc. transaction takes your payroll and burden costs out of your operating expense categories and assigns them to your job-cost categories.

To use the memorized transaction for payroll job cost allocation:

1. From the menu, select Lists|Account to display the Account List window.

2. Double-click the Adjustments account in the list to display the Adjustments–Adjustments: Asset register.

Figure 6–15

Double-clicking the P/R Job Cost Alloc. memorized transaction enters it into the Adjustments register automatically.

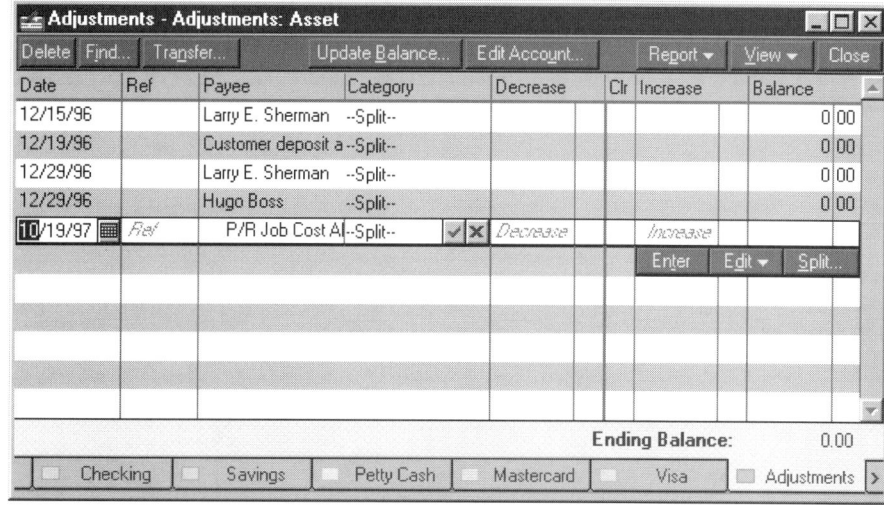

3. From the menu, select Lists | Memorized Transaction, and then double-click the P/R Job Cost Alloc. transaction, found under 5.SPECIAL TRANSACTIONS. Double-clicking the transaction enters it into the Adjustments register automatically as the active transaction, as shown in Figure 6–15.

4. Click into the Ref field and type the check number of the original payroll check for the employee.

5. Tab to the Payee field and change the default name to the name of the employee. The first four lines in Figure 6–15 show examples of the P/R Job Cost Alloc. transaction that have been customized for individual employees.

6. Click the Split button to display the Split Transaction Window (Figure 6–16).

7. Click into the Amount field of the first line in the Split Transaction Window and enter the gross payroll amount to be allocated for the current employee.

8. Click into the Category field of the first line. Press Ctrl-L to display the Class List window. Select the job to allocate the amount to and click the Use button. The selected job number automatically replaces the default J.0000 entry.

9. Click into the Amount field of the second line and enter the burden amount that you want to allocate to the job.

10. Click into the Category field of the second line and press Ctrl-L to display the class list. Select the job to allocate the amount to and click the Use button. The selected job number replaces the default J.0000 entry.

Figure 6-16

This Split Transaction Window shows itemized amounts for a particular employee for the P/R Job Cost Alloc. memorized transaction. When you have finished itemizing the payroll allocations, the totals should balance to zero.

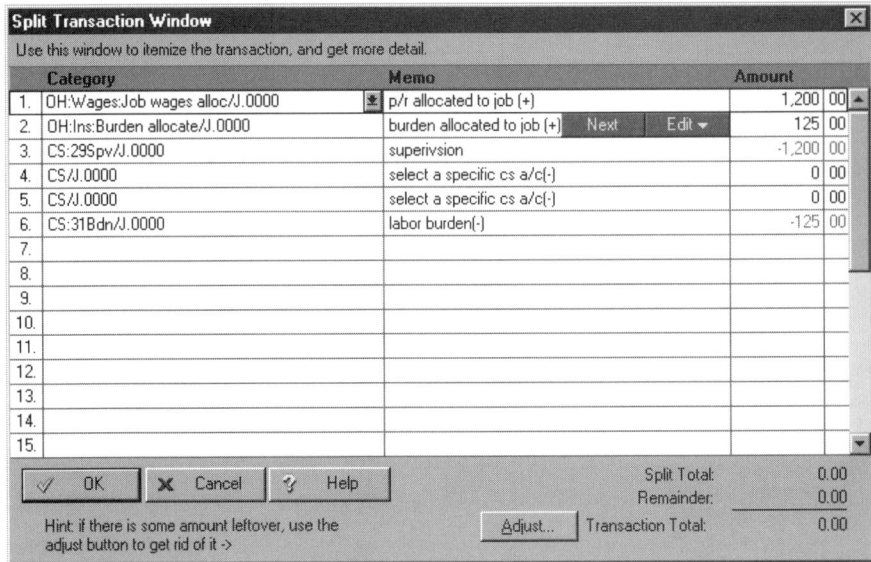

11. The next three lines in the memorized transaction can be related to specific job costs. Click into the Amount field of the third line and enter the payroll amount that you want to allocate to the first job-cost category. *Enter the amount preceded by a minus (–) sign.*

12. Click into the Category field of the third line and click the down arrow at the right side of the field to display the drop-down Category list. Click on the appropriate job-cost category to enter it automatically into this field.

13. Keeping your cursor in the same (Category) field, press Ctrl-L to display the Class List window. Select the job to which you want to allocate the payroll item and click the Use button. The selected job number replaces the default J.0000 entry.

14. Edit the Memo field as needed to reflect the changes you've made to the default Category entry.

15. Repeat steps 11 through 14 for the other two job-cost splits on lines 4 and 5. (If you need additional split lines for your own transactions, up to 30 lines are available in the Split Transaction Window.)

16. Click into the Amount field of the sixth line and enter the burden amount that you entered on the second line (step 9). *Enter the amount preceded by a minus (–) sign.*

17. Click into the Category field of the sixth line and press Ctrl-L to display the class list. Select the job to allocate the amount to and click the Use button. The selected job number replaces the default J.0000 entry.

18. When you have completed allocating the transaction in the Split Transaction Window, the transaction total at the bottom should be 0.00. If it is not 0.00, then one of two human errors has occurred:

 ◆ Either the negative total of the allocated job costs on lines 3, 4, and 5 does not equal the total P/R amount on line 1, or

 ◆ The burden amount on line 2 does not equal the negative burden amount on line 6.

 Make any necessary adjustments to balance the total to 0.00, as shown in the example in Figure 6–16.

19. Click the OK button to close the Split Transaction Window.

20. Click the Enter button to record the transaction.

Fed. W/H tax Depository

The Fed. W/H tax Depository memorized transaction in the Company file is a check register entry. Its purpose is to assign the Federal withholding tax deposit to the payroll federal tax liability accounts FICA, FWH, & MEDI. Before customizing this transaction, print the memorized report "Payroll Tax Report" to determine the amounts to include in the transaction. Refer to Chapter 7, "Using Memorized Reports," for more information about using this and other memorized reports.

When you're ready to work with this memorized transaction:

1. From the menu, select Lists|Account and double-click on Checking to open the Check Register window.

2. From the menu, select Lists|Memorized Transaction to display the Memorized Transaction List window.

3. Double-click the Fed. W/H tax Depository memorized transaction, found under 3.NON JOB PMTS. The transaction is automatically entered into the Check Register as the active transaction.

4. Click into the Payee field and type the name of the bank or institution that will receive the payment.

5. Click the Split button to display the Split Transaction Window, shown in Figure 6–17.

6. Enter the appropriate payment amount in the Amount field of each of the three split lines for Social Security (FICA), federal withholding (FWH), and Medicare (MEDI).

7. When you have completed allocating the transaction, click the Adjust button. This step customizes the total amount on the check so that it no longer defaults to zero.

Figure 6–17

This Split Transaction Window shows the default amounts for the Fed. W/H tax Depository memorized transaction.

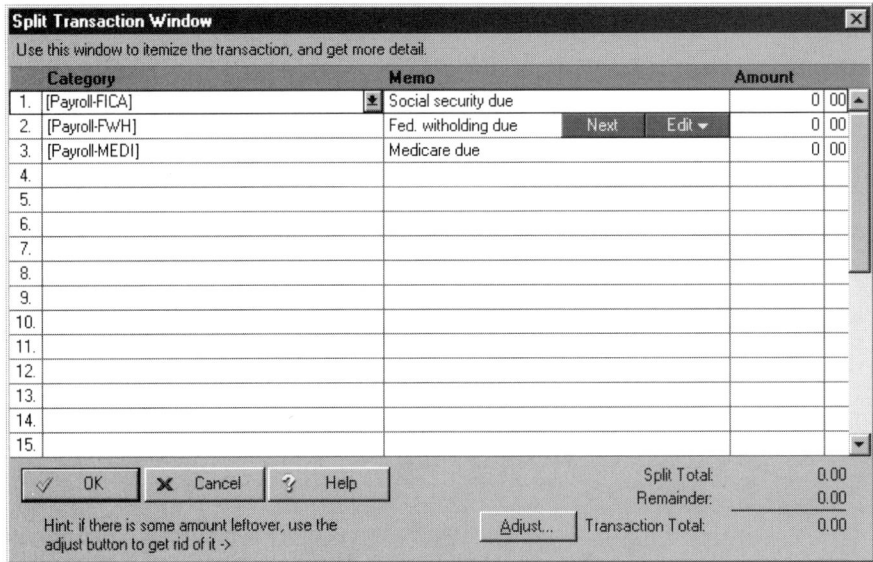

8. Click the OK button to close the Split Transaction Window and return to the main entry in the Check Register window. (If you see a dialog box asking you to choose either payment or deposit, select Payment and click the OK button.)

9. Click the Enter button to record the transaction.

Internal Revenue Service

The Internal Revenue Service memorized transaction is a check register entry. Its purpose is to assign the Federal unemployment tax deposit to the payroll federal tax liability account (FUTA). Before using this memorized transaction, create a payroll tax report to use in determining the amounts to include in the transaction. See the section on "Payroll Tax Reports" in Chapter 7 for more information.

To use the Internal Revenue Service memorized transaction:

1. From the menu, select Lists | Account to open the Account List window.

2. Double-click the Checking account to bring up the Check Register window.

3. From the menu, select Lists | Memorized Transaction and double-click the Internal Revenue Service memorized transaction. It can be found under the heading 3.NON JOB PMTS. Quicken enters the transaction into the Check register as the active transaction.

4. Click the Split button to display the Split Transaction Window, as shown in Figure 6–18.

Figure 6-18

This Split Transaction Window shows the default entries for the Internal Revenue Service memorized payroll transaction.

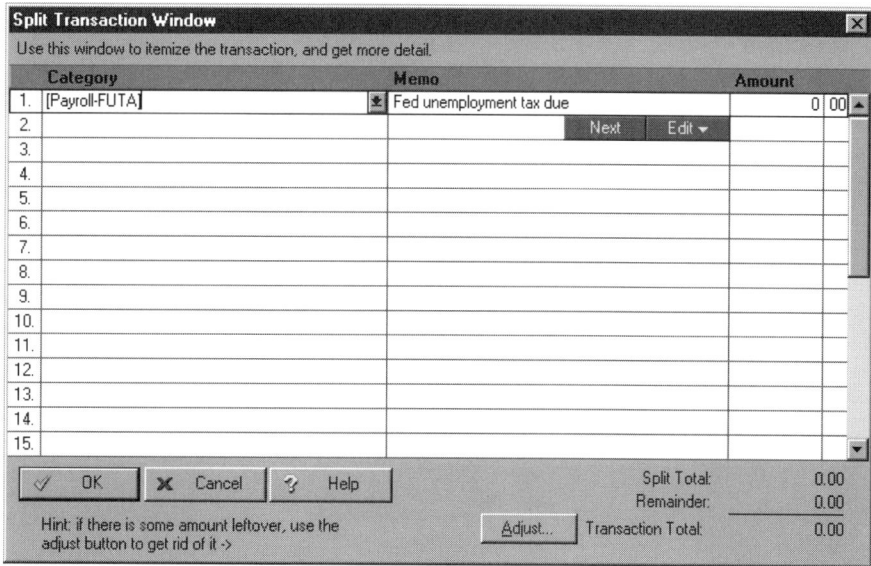

5. Enter the appropriate payment in the Amount field of the first line.

6. Click the Adjust button, then the OK button in the Split Transaction Window. (If you see a dialog box asking you to choose either payment or deposit, select Payment and click the OK button.)

7. To record the transaction in the Check register, press Enter or click the Enter button.

🏠 Creating a New Memorized Transaction

The Quicken data files on the diskette that accompanies this book include many memorized transactions created with the needs of construction professionals in mind. However, every business is unique. Sooner or later, you may want to generate additional memorized transactions of your own to fit your business's unique requirements.

One way to do this is to use one of our preconfigured memorized transactions as a template that you can modify and save under another name. To create a new memorized transaction using a supplied transaction as a template:

1. From the menu, select the Features | Bills | Write Checks command to display the Write Checks: Checking window.

2. Click the down-facing arrow to the right of the Pay to the Order of field to display the drop-down list of memorized transactions.

3. Scroll through the list and click on the name of the generic transaction that matches the type of new memorized transaction that you want to create. The details of the generic transaction fill into the screen, as shown in the example in Figure 6–19.

 NOTE: *In Quicken's drop-down lists, the names of the memorized transactions appear in alphabetical order rather than in the order that they appear in the Memorized Transaction List window.*

4. Change the name, address, and other general information to fit your new vendor/payee. The category is already selected for you and the amount should remain blank unless the payment amount will be exactly the same every time you enter the transaction.

5. When you have completed making the necessary changes on the screen, select Edit | Transaction | Memorize and the transaction (without a specific dollar amount) will be saved to the Memorized Transactions List under the group heading 1.MY VENDOR PMNTS., as shown in Figure 6–20.

 NOTE: *The Category field in the memorized transactions supplied in the Company file on our companion diskette needs to remain unchanged. The Category description is vital for correct job costing; it determines which group the memorized transaction belongs to and has been set so that the transactions will create the correct category entries for accounting purposes.*

Figure 6–19

To create a new memorized transaction using a supplied memorized transaction as a template, start by writing a check in the Write Checks: Checking window.

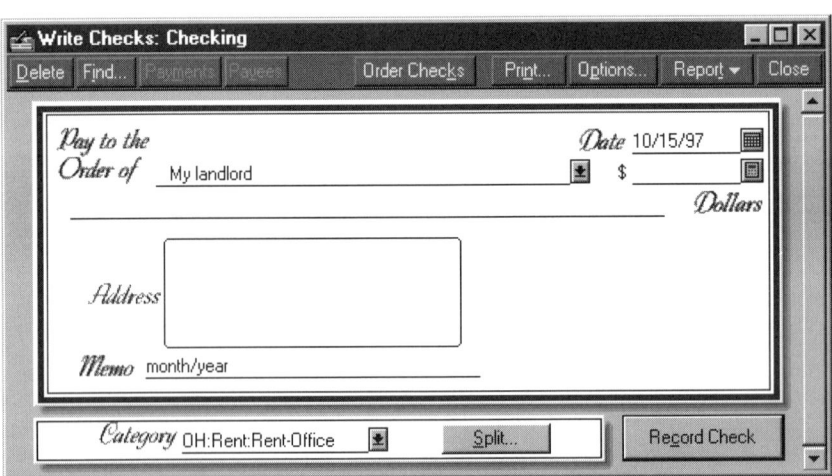

Figure 6–20

After customizing and resaving the generic memorized transaction, the new memorized transaction appears under category 1.MY VENDOR PMNTS. in the Memorized Transaction List window.

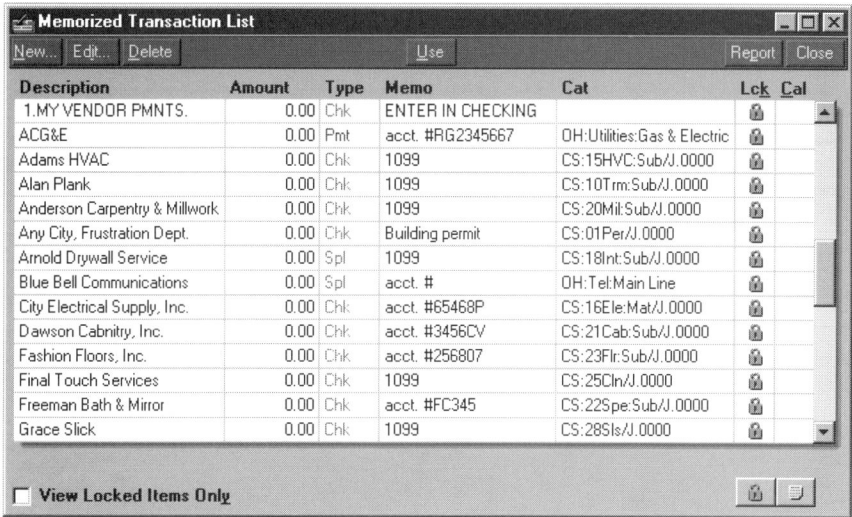

NOTE: *All of your new memorized transactions in the list should be locked to prevent them from being accidentally overwritten. You can tell if your memorized transaction is locked by viewing the Memorized Transaction List window. In the sixth column, labeled Lck, you will see a small padlock if the transaction is locked. To unlock a given transaction, click on the padlock. Likewise, if the transaction is unlocked, click in the Lck column of the transaction to lock it. The padlock icon then appears in this field.*

Once you've created a custom memorized transaction, using it in the Check Register or Write Checks window is easy. Assume, for example, that you want to create a check for the vendor/payee using the memorized transaction you have created:

1. In the Pay to the Order of field of the Write Checks window, just type the first few letters of the payee's name (or select the vendor/payee from the drop-down list). Quicken enters the rest of the record automatically.

2. Change the dollar amount.

3. Record the transaction by clicking the Record Check button.

When you first set up your account file, consider using the generic memorized transactions (the ones supplied with the Quicken data files on the companion diskette) to create new, custom memorized transactions for all of your vendors. Taking this initial step will streamline your future sessions in Quicken.

Memorized transactions save you time and make your business accounting process more accurate and efficient. They also form the cornerstones of memorized reports, which give you up-to-the-minute summaries of how your business is functioning in key areas. In the next chapter, we'll discuss the use of memorized reports in greater detail.

Using Memorized Reports

emorized transactions are about standardizing your day-to-day accounting procedures to make them more accurate and efficient. But as any construction professional knows, there are times when you want to see the forest rather than the trees—times when you need a "big-picture" overview of how much money you're making on a particular job, how high your payroll expenditures are, and so on. That's when you need to use Quicken's report features.

In Quicken, reports, like transactions, can be memorized. Memorized reports let you standardize and streamline the data-gathering process so you always get the exact "big picture" you want. In this chapter, we'll examine how memorized reports work and how they can be helpful in construction-related businesses. You'll see how to make the most of the predefined memorized reports we've supplied with the Quicken data files on the diskette that accompanies this book. You'll also see how to customize these and other memorized reports that you may choose to create for yourself.

🏠 Memorized Report Basics

In Quicken, you can create a report at any time based on any combination of accounts, categories, classes, dates, and other settings. But if you need to use exactly the same report format over and over again—say, for your monthly or quarterly financial reporting—then it's to your advantage to let Quicken *memorize* that report. With memorized reports, you can store an exact combination of report settings so that important data is never left out and remains consistent from one reporting period to another

You specify the conditions that determine which records will be included in a report. You, the user, define the accounts, categories, classes, transaction types, payee, date, transaction amounts, and memo contents that must be matched in order for Quicken to include the record in the report.

Determining exactly what combination of conditions will produce the desired report can be a bit of a brain twister. When you have determined just the right settings to create the report, you will want to save those settings as a memorized report. Memorized reports save you time because you don't have to re-establish all the report conditions every time you want to generate a new report.

The easiest way to memorize a report is to display an existing report and then click the Memorize button at the top of the report window. Your Quicken software provides a number of predefined report formats in four categories: Home, Investment, Business, and Other. For business purposes, the best built-in reports to use as starting points for creating your own memorized reports are the ones found in the Business and Other categories. To view their names, select the Reports|Business or Reports|Other command as shown in Figure 7–1. To display the default report format for any of these reports, click on the report name in the menu.

Customizing a report format in preparation for memorizing it is the hard part. We want to simplify that process for you. That's why the Company file on the companion diskette for this book contains 16 memorized business reports that cover most of your additional reporting requirements as a construction-industry businessperson (see the next section). You may find that these memorized reports meet your business needs exactly. If not, you can make changes to the setup, then review the changes you made to make sure you are getting the information you want in the report. If not, you will need to modify the report and re-memorize it, either using the same name or a different name. Using the same name overwrites the original memorized report; using a different report name creates a new memorized report and leaves the previous one in the file as well. The section "Creating a New Memorized Report" later in this chapter walks you step-by-step through the process of creating a new memorized report by customizing an existing one.

Figure 7–1

These predefined report formats that come standard with Quicken can be useful jumping-off points for creating your own memorized reports.

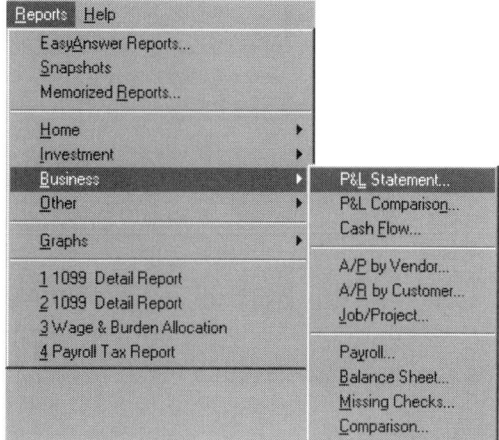

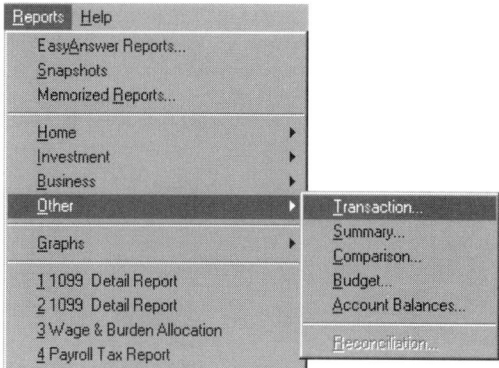

To ensure that your memorized reports always give you the information you seek, you must pay close attention to two things:

◆ Be certain that you specify exactly the set of report conditions that you require. Information that doesn't match those conditions won't be included in the report.

◆ Be consistent and accurate with the entry of your day-to-day transactions. If you enter a record incorrectly—for example, if you leave out the category that pertains to a given transaction—that transaction won't be included in reports, even reports for which it is suited. This is one reason why using memorized transactions is so important (see Chapter 6, "Using Memorized Transactions"). Incorrect data entry can undermine the decision-making process on which you base your reports.

Memorized Reports Included in the Quicken Data Files

As mentioned, the Company file provided on the diskette in the back of this book contains 16 memorized reports appropriate to business needs in the construction industry. To view the names of these reports, select the Memorized Reports command from the Reports menu. This displays the Create Report window with the Memorized tab on top, as shown in Figure 7–2.

To display a memorized report, just click the icon to the left of the report title in the Create Report window. If you want to filter the report for a specific date range, for a specific job or selected jobs, or for a selected vendor or employee, click once on the report title and then click the Customize button at the bottom of the window. The four tabs in the Customize [Report Name] window—Display, Accounts, Include, and Advanced—allow you to set up the specific filters (report conditions) you want.

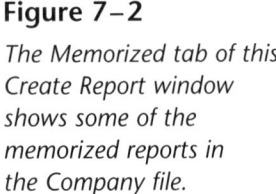 **NOTE:** *Quicken generates a report only if the file with which you are working contains actual data. If your data file is blank, Quicken displays a message indicating that no matching transactions were found.*

Figure 7–2

The Memorized tab of this Create Report window shows some of the memorized reports in the Company file.

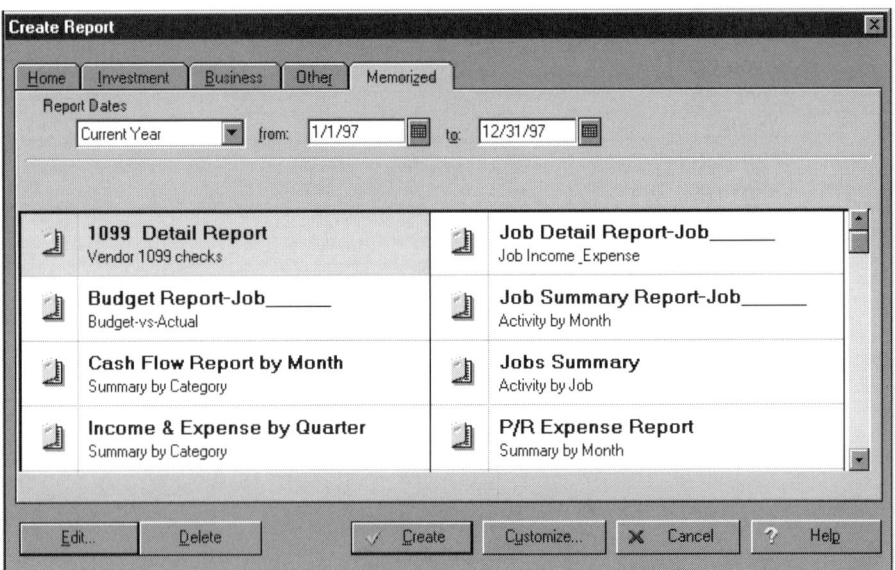

To give you a better hands-on understanding of how the tabs work in the Customize Report window, open the 1099 Detail Report from our Qksample file (choose Reports | Memorized Reports and then click *once* on the title of this report in the Create Report window). Then click the Customize button. When the Customize Report window opens, click the Advanced tab. Notice that we've preset the Amounts field to greater than 0 and the Transaction Types field to Payments (look ahead to Figure 7–6). A bit of logic makes it clear that we wouldn't want the Transaction Types to be Deposits when we're trying to determine how much we've paid out to 1099 vendors.

Here's an overview of the types of settings you can change in each tab of the Customize Report window:

◆ *Display tab*—Use the controls in this tab (Figure 7–3) to change the report dates, alter the title that appears at the top of the report, define column headings and which columns to display, change the report organization, and determine how to display cents in the Amount category.

◆ *Accounts tab*—Use the controls in this tab (Figure 7–4) to select the accounts from which you want to pull data for the report. You can change the report dates from this tab, too.

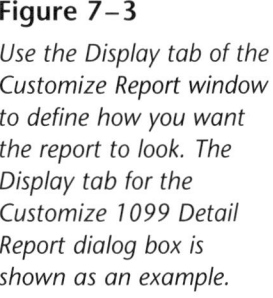

Figure 7–3

Use the Display tab of the Customize Report window to define how you want the report to look. The Display tab for the Customize 1099 Detail Report dialog box is shown as an example.

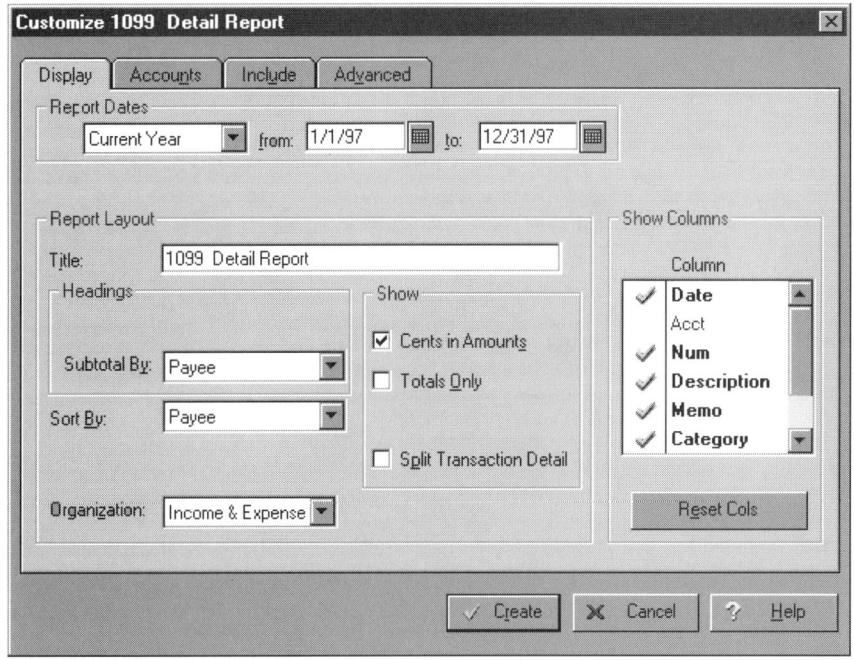

Figure 7–4

Use the Accounts tab of the Customize Report window to select the type of accounts for the report. The Accounts tab for the Customize 1099 Detail Report dialog box is shown as an example.

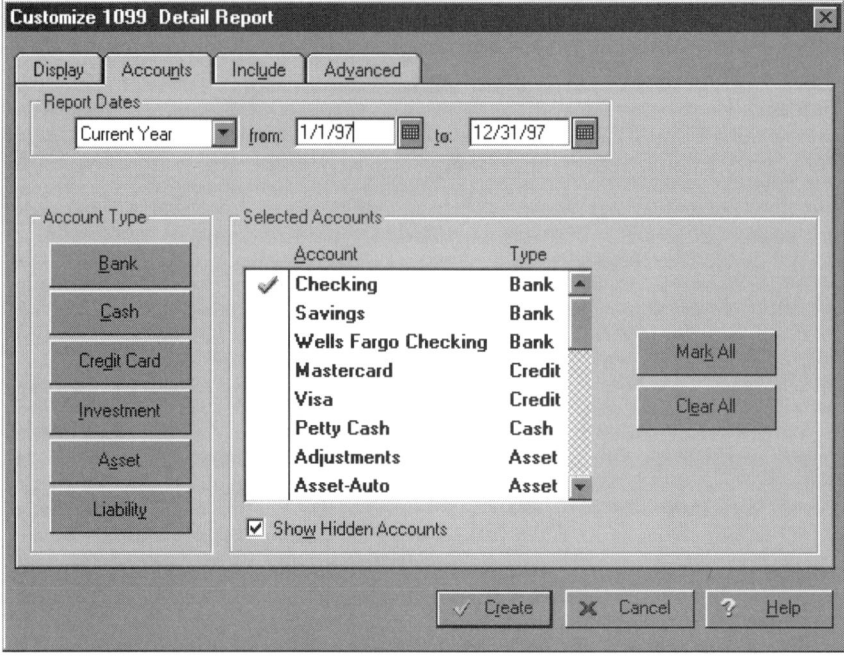

Figure 7–5

Use the Include tab of the Customize Report window to select which categories and/or classes to include in the report. The Include tab for the Customize 1099 Detail Report dialog box is shown as an example.

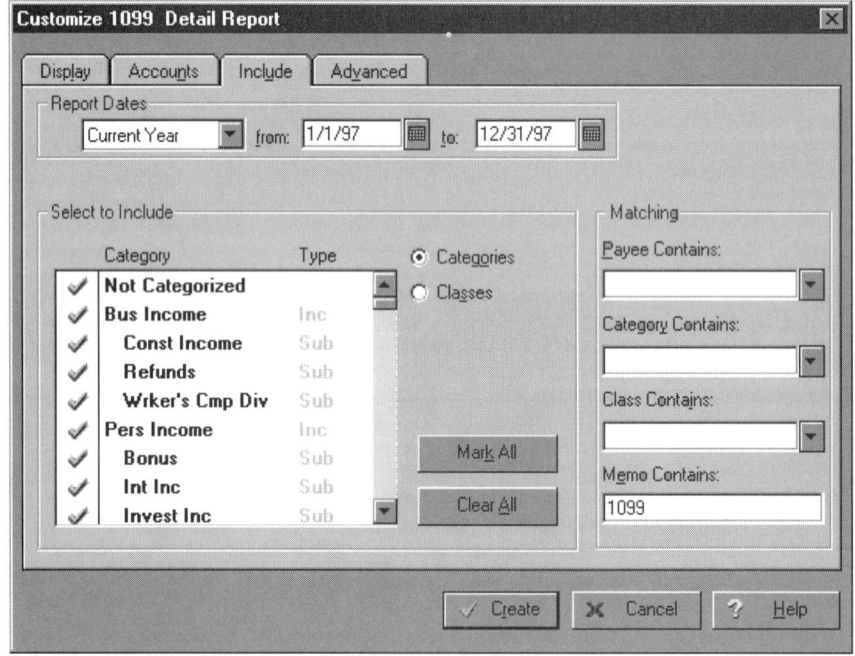

◆ *Include tab*—The controls in this tab (Figure 7–5) let you specify which categories and/or classes to include in the report. You can filter the information even more narrowly by requiring that data in the Payee, Category, Class, or Memo field contain a certain word, name, or number in order to be included.

Figure 7–6

Use the Advanced tab of the Customize Report window to include or exclude certain types of data from the report. The Advanced tab for the 1099 Detail Report is shown as an example.

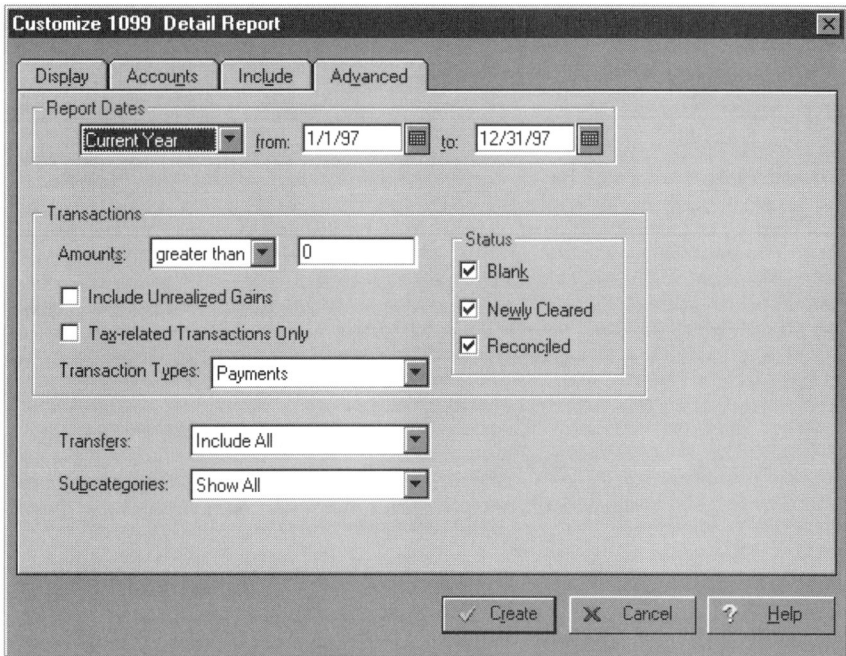

◆ *Advanced tab*—Use the controls in this tab (Figure 7–6) to exclude certain amount ranges, exclude non-tax-related transactions, exclude transactions by type, include or exclude subcategories, or include only budgeted data. You can also exclude transactions according to the status of a check—Blank, Newly Cleared, or Reconciled.

The following pages describe each of the memorized reports in the Company file and the settings that define them. Also included is a sample illustration of each report using the default settings. We will leave it up to you to determine whether the information in the report might be helpful in managing your own business.

1099 Detail Report (Vendor 1099 checks)

The Internal Revenue Service (IRS) requires businesses to furnish a 1099 form to any individual, sole proprietorship, or partnership that receives more than $600 for labor in a calendar year; a copy of the 1099 form is also sent to the IRS. For example, if you paid a subcontractor $610 for labor and $125 for materials during 1997, you must report the $610 to the IRS using a 1099 form. Vendors who are incorporated are excluded from this requirement.

Figure 7-7

This example of a 1099 Detail Report was generated from the memorized 1099 Detail Report.

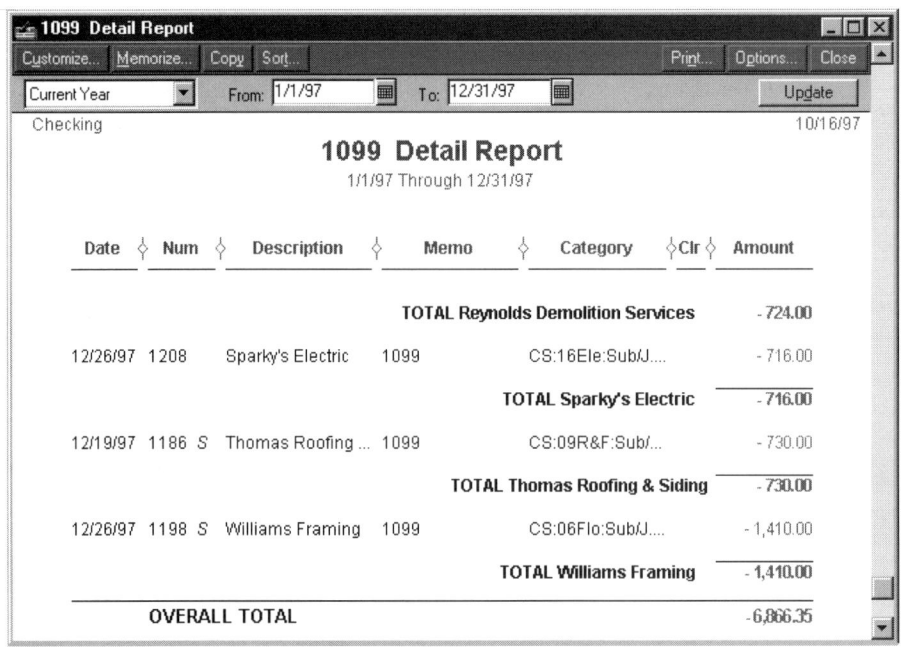

The 1099 Detail Report included in our Quicken data files lets you see all payments to vendors at a glance for the current year. Figure 7-7 shows a sample report generated from this memorized report based on the default settings.

Display tab

Report Dates:	Current Year
Report Layout:	Sort By: Payee
	Organization: Income & Expense
Headings:	Subtotal: Payee
Show:	Cents in Amounts
Show Columns:	Column: All but Account

Accounts tab

Selected Accounts:	Checking only

Include tab

Select to Include:	Categories: All
	Classes: All
Matching:	Memo Contains: 1099

Advanced tab

Transactions:	Amounts: Greater than 0
	Transaction Types: Payments
Status:	Blank, Newly Cleared, Reconciled
Transfers:	Include All
Subcategories:	Show All

Budget Report-Job____ (Budget-vs-Actual)

Perhaps we're being redundant, but the Budget Report-Job____ is probably the most useful report a contractor can generate. It tells you at a glance whether you're building a specific project within the constraints of your estimate (budget). Figure 7–8 shows an example of this report generated for a hypothetical job J.1002.

Display tab

Report Dates:	Current Year
Report Layout:	Organization: Income & Expense
Headings:	Column: None
Show:	Cents in Amounts
Show Columns:	Column: All

Accounts tab

Selected Accounts:	All

Include tab

Select to Include:	Categories: Not Categorized, Bus Income, CS (Cost of Sales) subcategories
	Classes: Single selected class (job) only; default is job J.0000

Advanced tab

Transactions:	Amounts: All
	Transaction Types: All Transactions
Status:	Blank, Newly Cleared, Reconciled
Transfers:	Include All
Subcategories:	Show All
Categories:	Non-Zero Actual/Budgeted

Figure 7–8

This sample report for job J.1002 was generated from the memorized Budget Report-Job____ report.

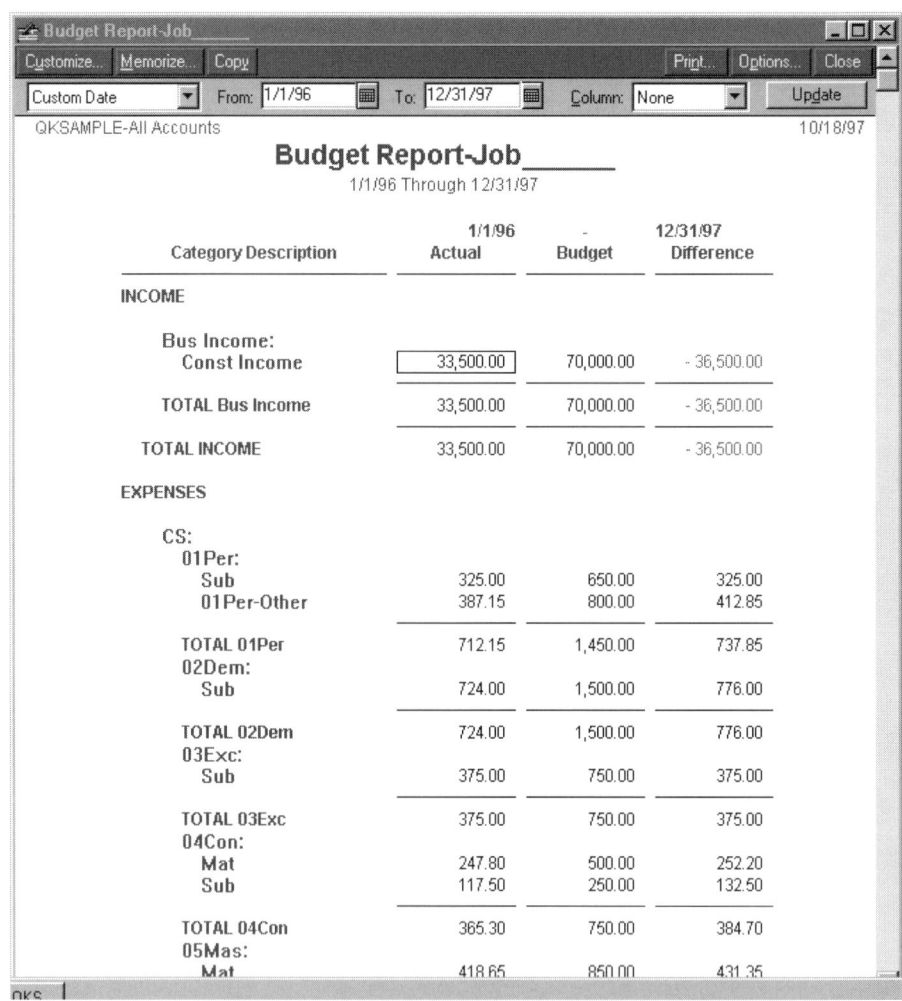

Cash Flow Report by Month (Summary by Category)

This memorized report lets you review your cash flow for a given month, subtotaled by category. Figure 7–9 shows a sample report generated using the default settings.

Display tab

Report Dates:	Can be for any defined date range
Report Layout:	Organization: Cash Flow Basis
Headings:	Row: Category
	Column: Month
Show:	Cents in Amounts
Show Columns	Column: All

Figure 7–9

This example of a cash flow report was generated from the memorized Cash Flow Report by Month report.

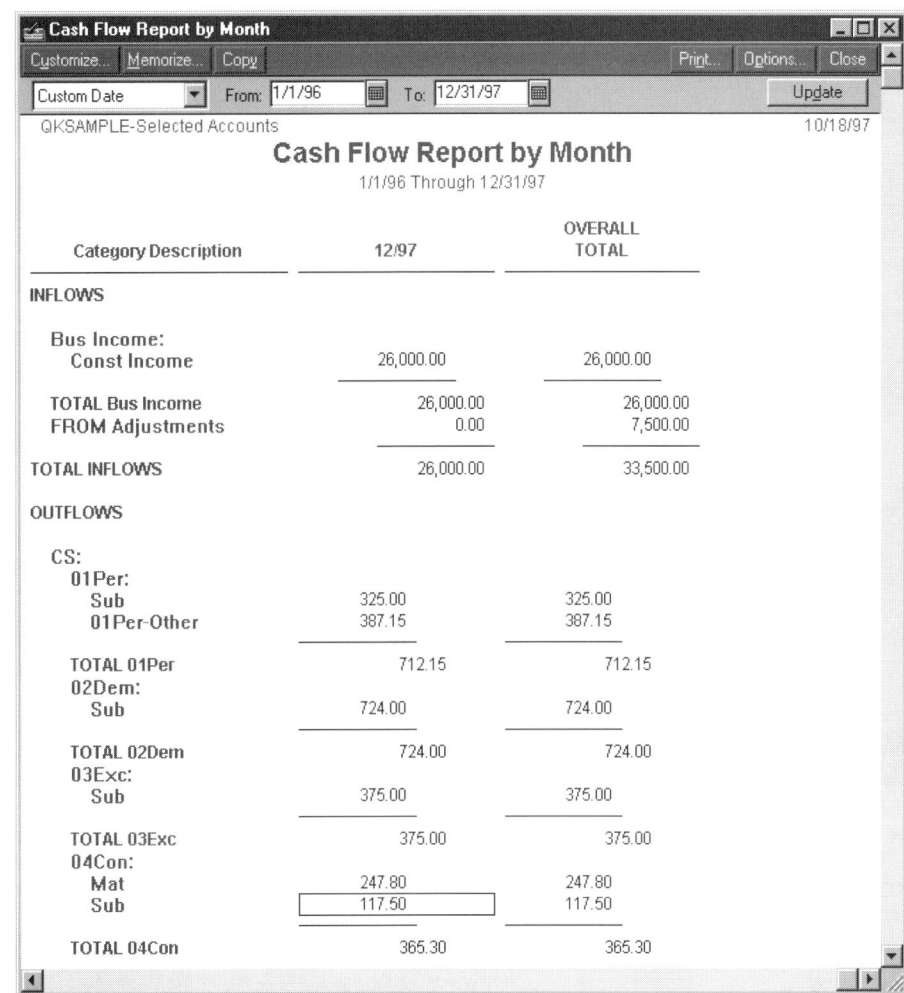

Accounts tab

Selected Accounts: All Cash accounts
All Credit Card accounts
All Bank accounts
Customer Deposits
All Payroll Liability accounts
Sales Tax account

Include tab

Select to Include: Categories: All
Classes: All

Advanced tab

Transactions: Amounts: Greater than 0
Transaction Types: All Transactions

Advanced tab *(continued)*

Status:	Blank, Newly Cleared, Reconciled
Transfers:	Exclude Internal
Subcategories:	Show All

Income & Expense by Quarter (Summary by Category)

The memorized report Income & Expense by Quarter lets you review business income and expenses for any fiscal quarter you designate. This report subtotals all amounts by category. Figure 7–10 shows a sample report generated from this format.

Figure 7–10

This sample report, showing quarterly income and expenses, was generated from the memorized Income & Expense by Quarter report.

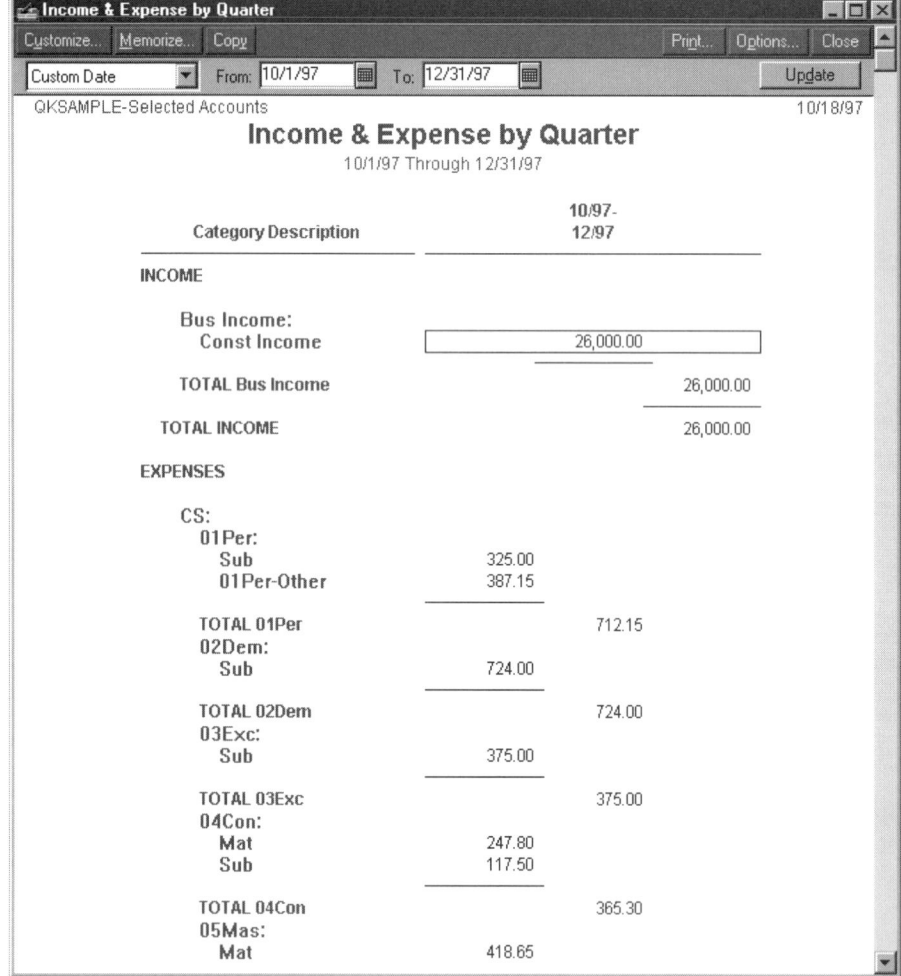

Display tab

Report Dates:	Quarter beginning and ending dates (user customizable)
Report Layout:	Organization: Income & Expense
Headings:	Row: Category
	Column: Quarter
Show:	Cents in Amounts
Show Columns:	Column: Category, Amount

Accounts tab

Selected Accounts:	All Cash accounts
	All Credit Card accounts
	All Bank accounts
	Customer Deposits
	All Payroll Liability accounts
	Sales Tax account

Include tab

Select to Include:	Categories: All
	Classes: All

Advanced tab

Transactions:	Amounts: Greater than 0
	Transaction Types: All Transactions
Status:	Blank, Newly Cleared, Reconciled
Transfers:	Exclude Internal
Subcategories:	Show All

Job Detail Report-Job____ (Job Income_Expense)

This memorized report lets you review all income and expenses related to a specific job for any date range you define. The default job is J.0000, but you can substitute your own job numbers as you set up the classes for them. See Chapter 2, "Using Quicken Categories, Accounts, and Classes," and Chapter 5, "Budgeting with Quicken," for more information about working with classes. Figure 7–11 shows a sample report generated from this memorized report.

Figure 7–11

This sample job detail report was generated from the memorized Job Detail Report-Job____ report.

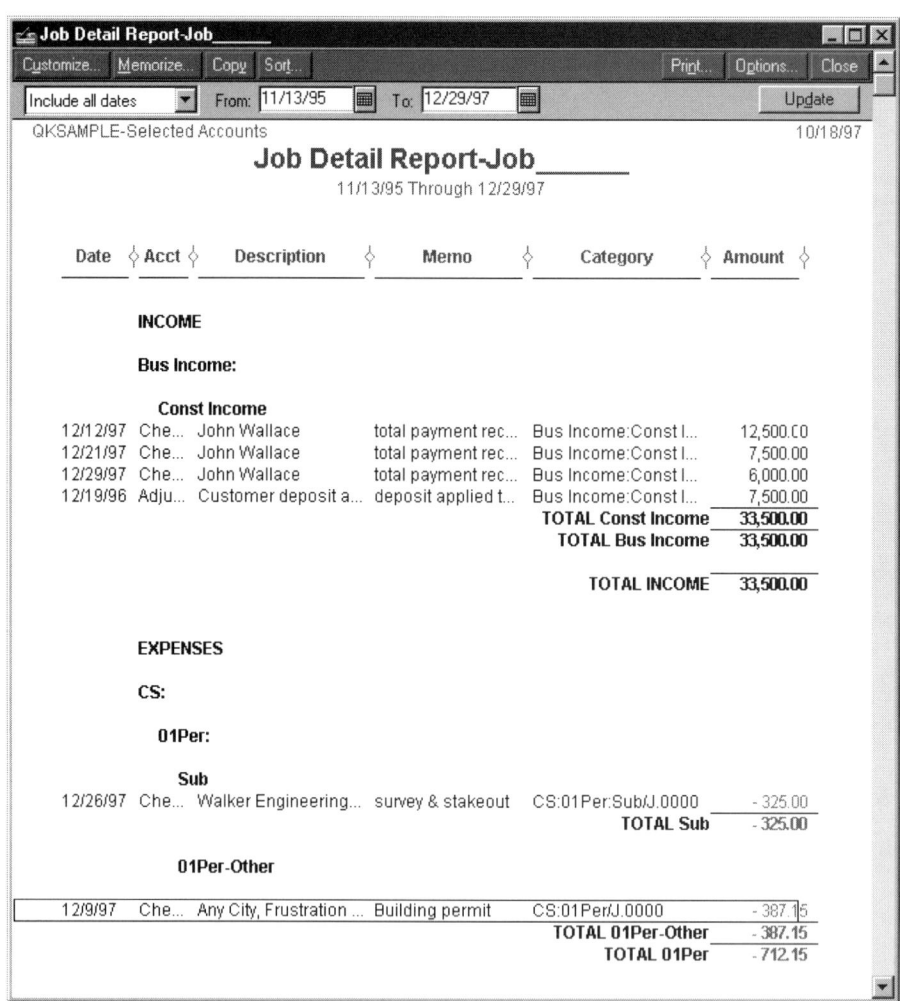

Display tab

Report Dates:	Can be for any defined date range
Report Layout:	Sort By: Acct/Chk#
	Organization: Income & Expense
Headings:	Subtotal: Category
Show:	Cents in Amounts
	Split Transaction Detail
Show Columns:	Column: Date, Acct., Description, Memo, Category, Amount

Accounts tab

Selected Accounts: Checking, Mastercard, Visa, Petty Cash, Adjustments

Include tab

Select to Include: Categories: All business income categories
except Wrker's Cmp Div
All Cost of Sale (CS) categories
Burden allocate
Job wages, Job wages alloc
Cust. deposits

Classes: Single selected class (job) only;
default is job J.0000

Advanced tab

Transactions: Amounts: Greater than 0

Transaction Types: All Transactions

Status: Blank, Newly Cleared, Reconciled

Transfers: Include All

Subcategories: Show All

Job Summary Report-Job_____ (Activity by Month)

The memorized report Job Summary Report-Job____ lists monthly income and expenses for the class (job) you specify. You can generate this report for any number of sequential months. Figure 7–12 shows a sample report generated using this report format.

Display tab

Report Dates: Can be for any defined date range

Report Layout: Organization: Income & Expense

Headings: Row: Category

Column: Month

Show: Cents in Amounts

Show Columns: Column: All

Figure 7–12

This sample report, listing monthly job-related income and expenses, was generated from the memorized Job Summary Report-Job____ report.

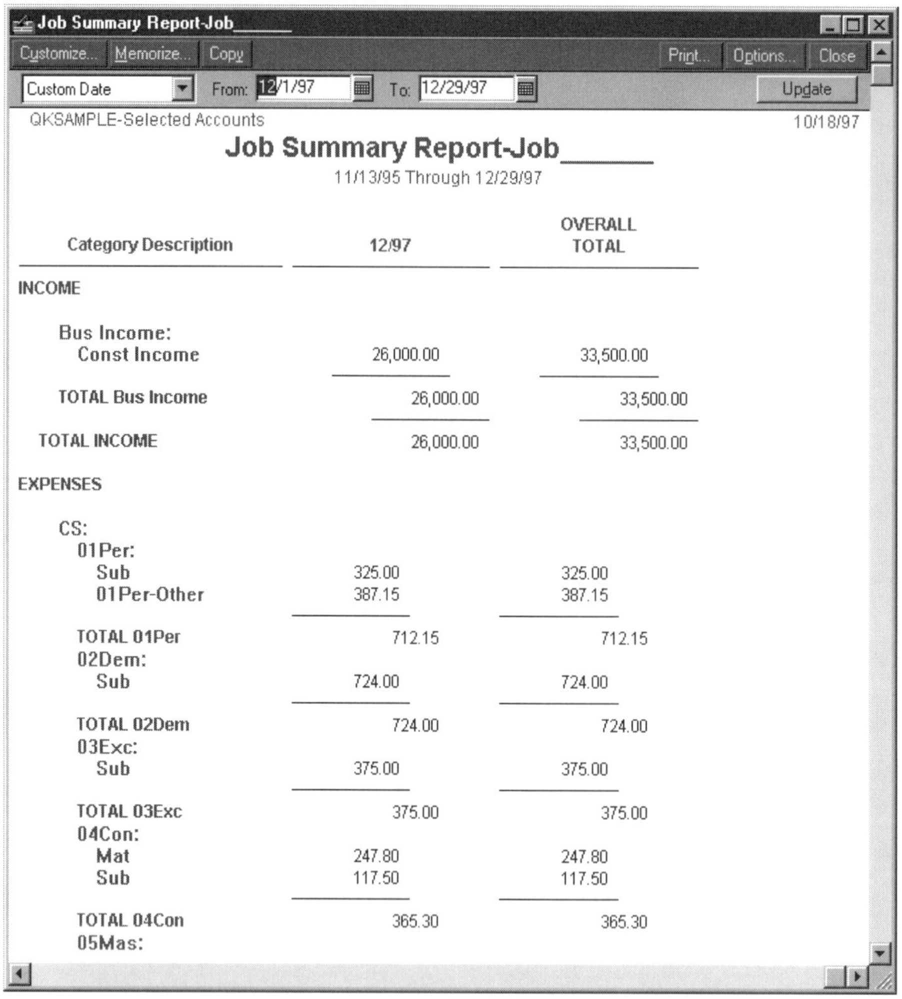

QKSAMPLE-Selected Accounts 10/18/97

Job Summary Report-Job_____

11/13/95 Through 12/29/97

Category Description	12/97	OVERALL TOTAL
INCOME		
Bus Income:		
Const Income	26,000.00	33,500.00
TOTAL Bus Income	26,000.00	33,500.00
TOTAL INCOME	26,000.00	33,500.00
EXPENSES		
CS:		
01Per:		
Sub	325.00	325.00
01Per-Other	387.15	387.15
TOTAL 01Per	712.15	712.15
02Dem:		
Sub	724.00	724.00
TOTAL 02Dem	724.00	724.00
03Exc:		
Sub	375.00	375.00
TOTAL 03Exc	375.00	375.00
04Con:		
Mat	247.80	247.80
Sub	117.50	117.50
TOTAL 04Con	365.30	365.30
05Mas:		

Accounts tab

Selected Accounts: Checking, Mastercard, Visa, Petty Cash, Adjustments

Include tab

Select to Include: Categories: All business income categories except Wrker's Cmp Div
All Cost of Sale (CS) categories
Burden allocate
Job wages, Job wages alloc
Cust. deposits

Classes: Single selected class (job) only; default is job J.0000

Advanced tab

Transactions:	Amounts: Greater than 0
	Transaction Types: All Transactions
Status:	Blank, Newly Cleared, Reconciled
Transfers:	Include All
Subcategories:	Show All

Jobs Summary (Activity by Job)

Use the Jobs Summary memorized report to compare income and expenses for current jobs (classes) over the period you specify. Figure 7–13 shows a sample report generated from this report format.

Figure 7–13

This sample report, comparing income and expenses for current jobs, was generated from the memorized Jobs Summary report.

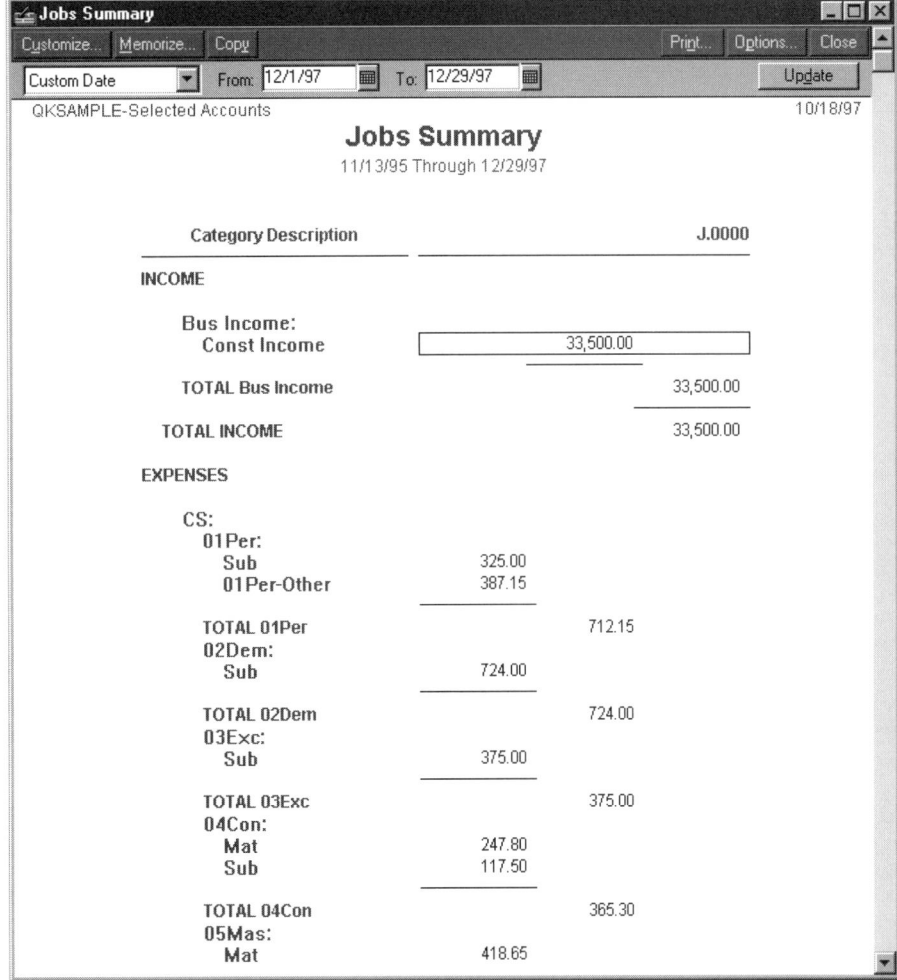

Display tab

Report Dates:	Can be for any defined date range
Report Layout:	Organization: Income & Expense
Headings:	Row: Category
	Column: Class
Show:	Cents in Amounts
Show Columns:	Column: All

Accounts tab

Selected Accounts:	Checking, Mastercard, Visa, Petty Cash, Adjustments

Include tab

Select to Include:	Categories: All business income categories except Wrker's Cmp Div All Cost of Sale (CS) categories Burden allocate Job wages, Job wages alloc Cust. deposits
	Classes: Single selected class (job); one job per report

Advanced tab

Transactions:	Amounts: Greater than 0
	Transaction Types: All Transactions
Status:	Blank, Newly Cleared, Reconciled
Transfers:	Include All
Subcategories:	Show All

P/R Expense Report (Summary by month)

Use the P/R Expense Report to review payroll expenses (wages, payroll taxes, and allocated payroll expenses) for all current jobs, summarized by month. The report uses the Checking and Adjustments accounts, together with the subcategories of the Wages category (Job Wages, Job wages alloc, Office Wages, and Payroll Tax). The default date range for this report is for the entire current year. Figure 7–14 shows a sample report generated from this memorized report for payroll expenses during the months of November and December.

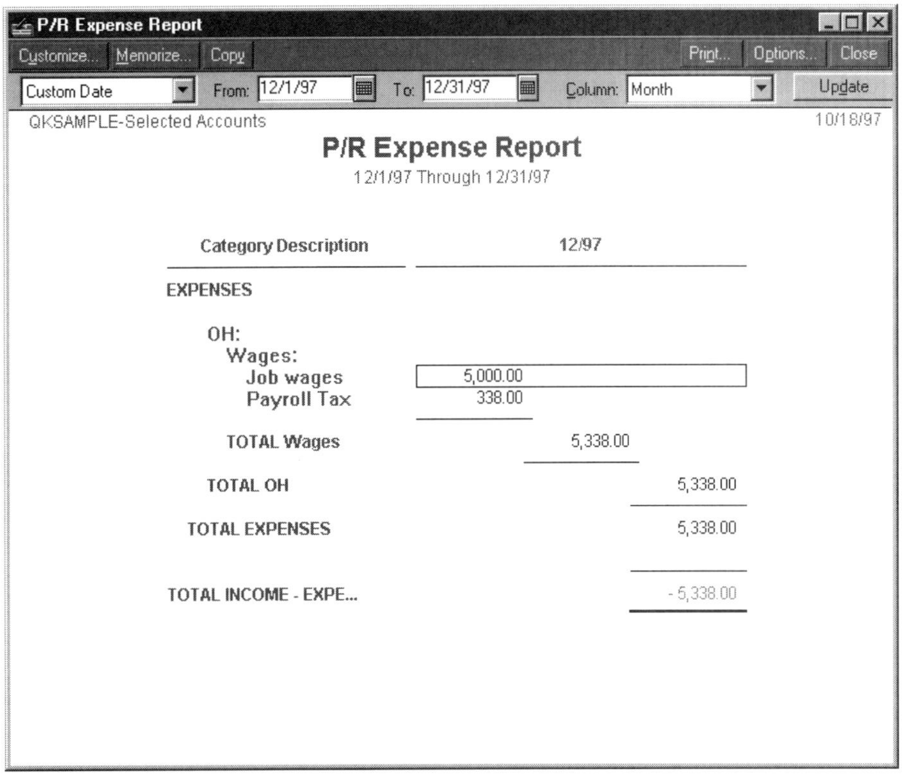

Figure 7–14

This sample payroll expense report was generated using the memorized P/R Expense Report.

Display tab

Report Dates:	Can be for any range of months (default range is the current year)
Report Layout:	Organization: Income & Expense
Headings:	Row: Category
	Column: Month
Show:	Cents in Amounts

Accounts tab

Selected Accounts:	Checking, Adjustments

Include tab

Select to Include:	Categories: Wages and all its subcategories
	Classes: All
Matching:	Category contains: Payroll

Advanced tab

Transactions:	Amounts: All
	Transaction Types: All Transactions

Advanced tab *(continued)*

Status:	Blank, Newly Cleared, Reconciled
Transfers:	Include All
Subcategories:	Show All

P/R Withholding Report (Summary by Month)

Use the P/R Withholding Report to obtain a month-by-month summary of categorized payroll withholding amounts for all your current jobs. This report draws data from the Checking account and the P/R Liability accounts (Payroll-FICA, Payroll-FUTA, Payroll-FWH, Payroll-MEDI, Payroll-SDI, Payroll-SUI, and Payroll-SWA). The default date range of the report is the current year. Figure 7–15 shows a sample report generated using this format.

Display tab

Report Dates:	Can be for any defined range of months (default is the current year)
Report Layout:	Organization: Income & Expense

Figure 7–15

This sample payroll withholdings report was generated using the memorized P/R Withholding Report.

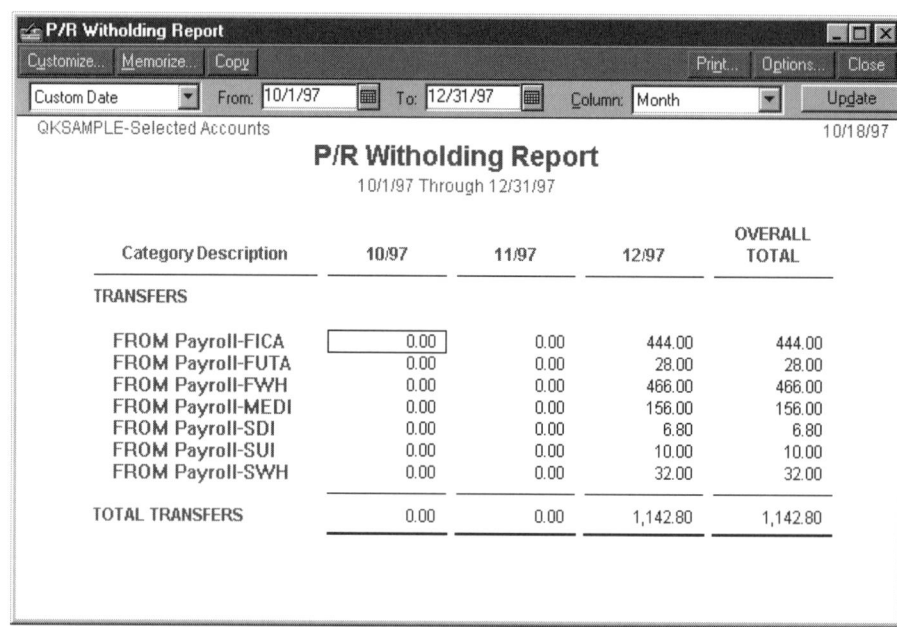

Headings:	Row: Category
	Column: Month
Show:	Cents in Amounts

Accounts tab

Selected Accounts:	Checking, all Payroll Liability accounts

Include tab

Select to Include:	Categories: All
	Classes: All
Matching:	Category Contains: Payroll

Advanced tab

Transactions:	Amounts: All
	Transaction Types: All Transactions
Status:	Blank, Newly Cleared, Reconciled
Transfers:	Include All
Subcategories:	Show All

Payroll Employee Report (Wages_withholding)

The Payroll Employee Report lets you view wages and withholding amounts broken down by employee, for any date range you select (the default period is the current year). Figure 7–16 shows a sample report derived from the memorized Payroll Employee Report format.

 NOTE: *To ensure that the Payroll Employee Report gathers data from all of your payroll transactions, be sure to include the text "**p/r**" in the Memo field of all such transactions. Transactions that do not include this will not be included in your reports.*

Display tab

Report Dates:	Can be for any defined date range (default range is the current year)
Report Layout:	Organization: Income & Expense
Headings:	Row: Category
	Column: Payee
Show:	Cents in Amounts

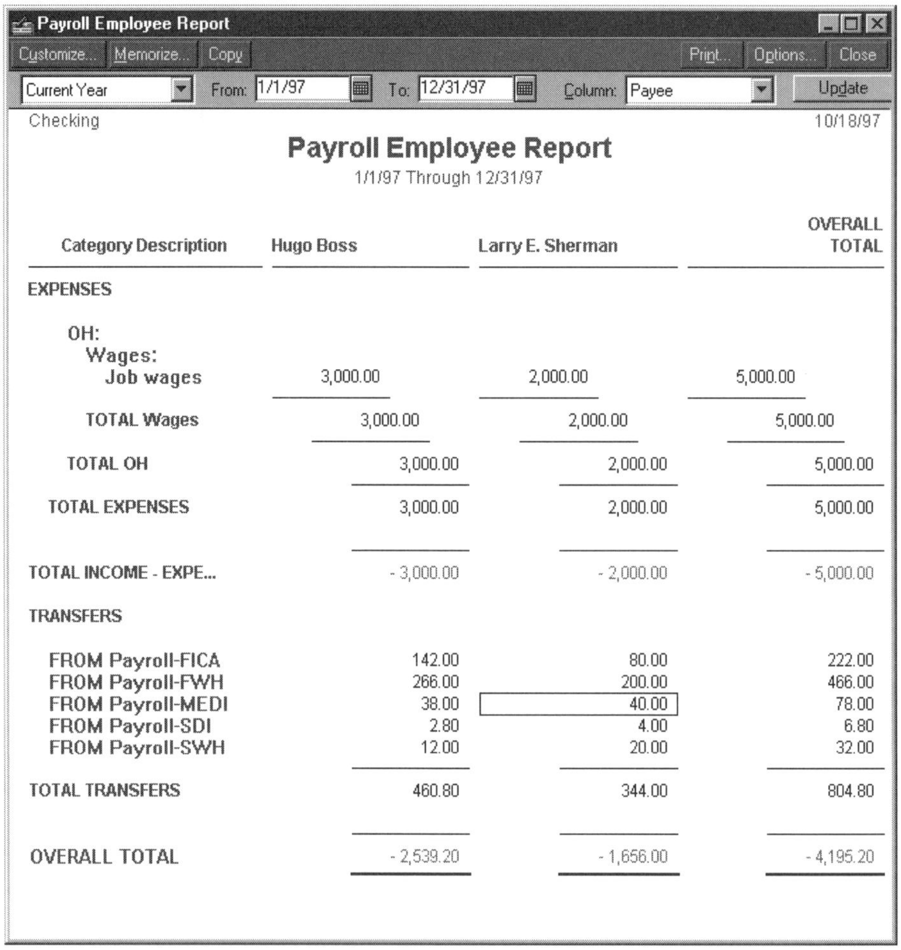

Figure 7-16

This sample report, showing payroll information broken down by employee, was generated using the memorized Payroll Employee Report.

Category Description	Hugo Boss	Larry E. Sherman	OVERALL TOTAL
EXPENSES			
OH:			
Wages:			
Job wages	3,000.00	2,000.00	5,000.00
TOTAL Wages	3,000.00	2,000.00	5,000.00
TOTAL OH	3,000.00	2,000.00	5,000.00
TOTAL EXPENSES	3,000.00	2,000.00	5,000.00
TOTAL INCOME - EXPE...	- 3,000.00	- 2,000.00	- 5,000.00
TRANSFERS			
FROM Payroll-FICA	142.00	80.00	222.00
FROM Payroll-FWH	266.00	200.00	466.00
FROM Payroll-MEDI	38.00	40.00	78.00
FROM Payroll-SDI	2.80	4.00	6.80
FROM Payroll-SWH	12.00	20.00	32.00
TOTAL TRANSFERS	460.80	344.00	804.80
OVERALL TOTAL	- 2,539.20	- 1,656.00	- 4,195.20

Payroll Employee Report
1/1/97 Through 12/31/97

Accounts tab

Selected Accounts: Checking only

Include tab

Select to Include: Categories: All

                            Classes: All

Matching: Memo Contains: p/r

Advanced tab

Transactions: Amounts: Greater than 0

                            Transaction Types: All Transactions

Status: Blank, Newly Cleared, Reconciled

Transfers: Include All

Subcategories: Show All

Payroll Expense Report (Summary by Employee)

Whereas the P/R Expense Report summarizes payroll expenses by month, the Payroll Expense Report summarizes these expenses by employee. The report uses the Checking and Adjustments accounts, together with the subcategories of the Wages category (Job Wages, Job wages alloc, Office Wages, and Payroll Tax). The default date range for this report is for the entire current year. See Figure 7–17 for a look at a sample report based on this memorized format.

Display tab

Report Dates:	Can be for any defined date range (default is the current year)
Report Layout:	Organization: Income & Expense
Headings:	Row: Category
	Column: Payee
Show:	Cents in Amounts

Figure 7–17

This sample report, generated using the memorized Payroll Expense Report, shows payroll expenses broken down by employee.

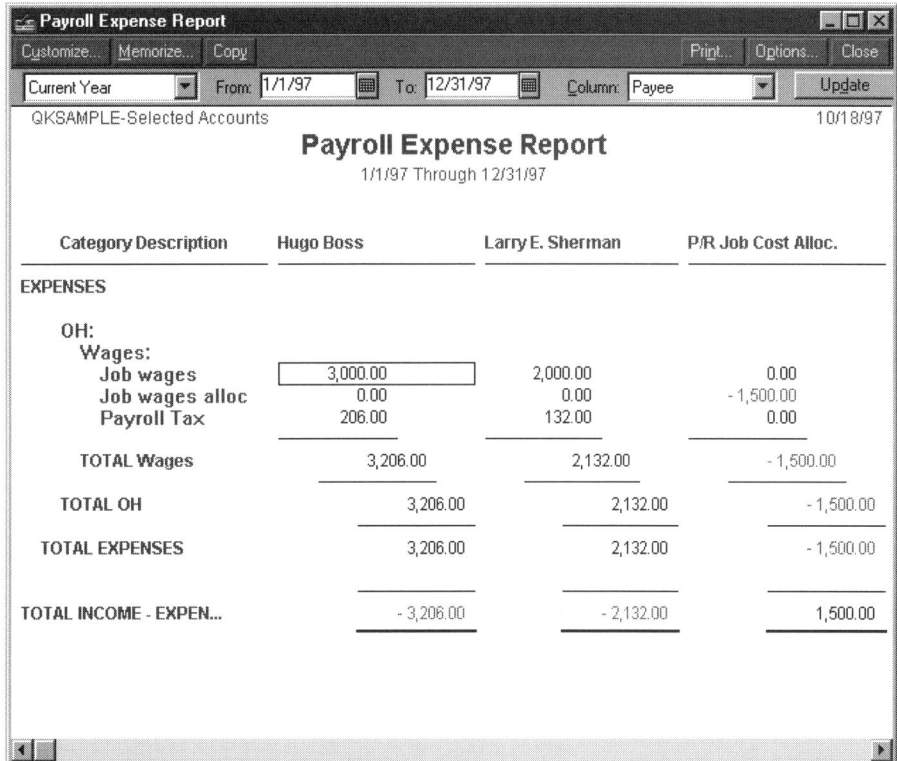

Accounts tab

Selected Accounts: Checking, Adjustments

Include tab

Select to Include: Categories: Wages and all its subcategories

                            Classes: All

Advanced tab

Transactions: Amounts: All

                            Transaction Types: All Transactions

Status: Blank, Newly Cleared, Reconciled

Transfers: Include All

Subcategories: Show All

Payroll Tax Report

The Payroll Tax Report is essentially the same report as the Payroll Report that comes standard with Quicken (see "Quicken's Payroll Report" on page 193). It summarizes all the standard state and federal payroll taxes by category and by employee. The default date range for this report is for the current year to date. Figure 7–18 shows a sample report generated using the Payroll Tax Report format.

Display tab

Report Dates: Can be for any defined date range (default
                            is Year to date)

Report Layout: Organization: Income & Expense

Headings: Row: Category

                            Column: Payee

Show: Cents in Amounts

Accounts tab

Selected Accounts: All

Include tab

Select to Include: Categories: All

                            Classes: All

Matching: Category Contains: Payroll

QUICKEN'S PAYROLL REPORT

You can use Quicken's built-in Payroll report by selecting Reports | Business | Payroll from the menu. This report summarizes wages and taxes by category, with a separate column for each payee. It is limited to transactions with category or transfer information containing the word "payroll." In other words, if the Category field contains the word "payroll," or if the transaction is a transfer to another account that has the word "payroll" as part of its name, the transaction will be summarized in the payroll report. You can, of course, customize this report to include other categories and transfer accounts, just as you can with any report in Quicken.

Quicken's built-in Payroll report looks similar to the memorized Payroll Tax Report from the Quicken data files on the companion diskette (see Figure 7–18). Here's a brief explanation of other aspects of the built-in payroll report format:

◆ The TRANSFERS TO rows show decreases in your accrued payroll liabilities. For example, each time you record a FICA payment in your checking account, Quicken automatically transfers the amount to the Payroll-FICA account, where it decreases the balance you owe.

◆ The TRANSFERS FROM rows show increases in your accrued payroll liabilities. For example, each time you record a paycheck, Quicken automatically transfers the FICA contribution amount from your checking account to the Payroll-FICA account, where it increases the balance you owe. In the same way, the report can track your liability for other tax-related items like FUTA, SUI, and Federal Withholding.

Advanced tab

Transactions:	Amounts: All
	Transaction Types: All Transactions
Status:	Blank, Newly Cleared, Reconciled
Transfers:	Include All
Subcategories:	Show All

Figure 7–18

This sample report, showing payroll taxes broken down by category and employee, was generated using the memorized Payroll Tax Report.

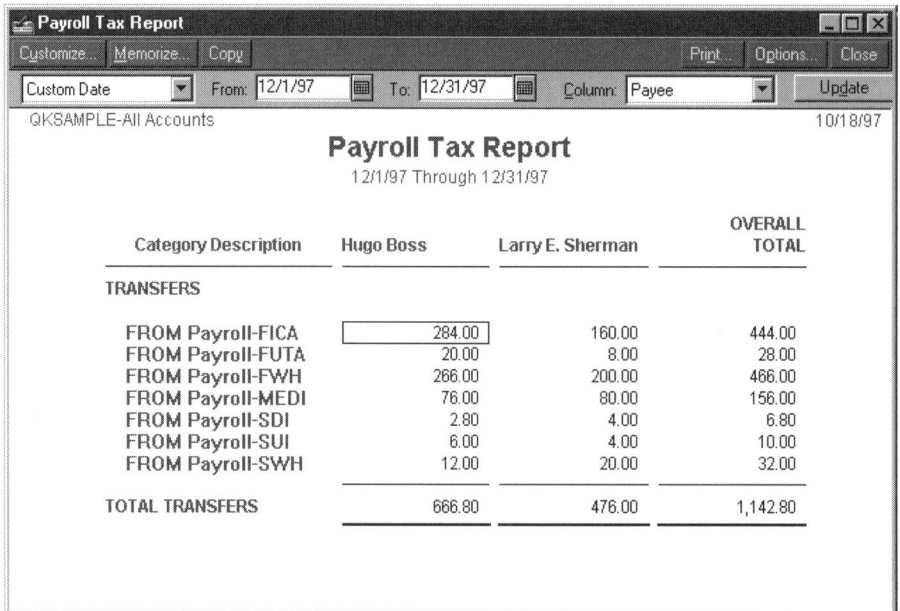

Transaction History by Name (All transactions)

This memorized report lets you view all transactions from all accounts in chronological order, subtotaled by payee. Figure 7–19 shows a sample report generated using the memorized Transaction History by Name format.

Display tab

Report Dates:	Can be for any defined date range
Report Layout:	Sort By: Date/Acct
	Organization: Income & Expense
Headings:	Subtotal: Payee
Show:	Cents in Amounts
Show Columns:	Column: All but Clr

Accounts tab

Selected Accounts:	All

Include tab

Select to Include:	Categories: All
	Classes: All

Figure 7–19

This sample report, generated using the memorized Transaction History by Name report, shows all your transactions in chronological order.

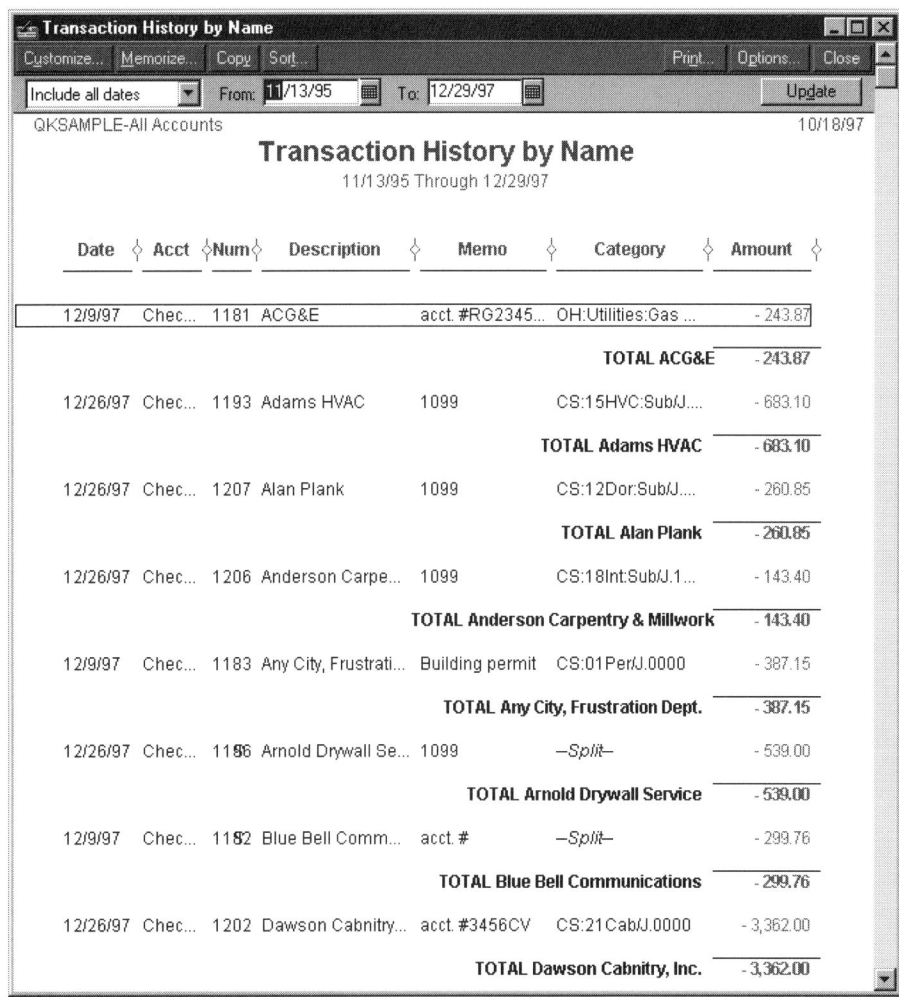

Advanced tab

Transactions:	Amounts: Greater than 0
	Transaction Types: All Transactions
Status:	Blank, Newly Cleared, Reconciled
Transfers:	Include All
Subcategories:	Show All

Unprinted Checks-Detail by Job (Job unprinted checks)

This memorized report lets you view a list of checks that are scheduled to be printed, broken down by job (class). Figure 7–20 shows a sample report generated using the Unprinted Checks-Detail by Job format.

Figure 7–20

This sample report was generated using the memorized Unprinted Checks-Detail by Job report. It lists checks that are scheduled to be printed for each of your jobs (classes).

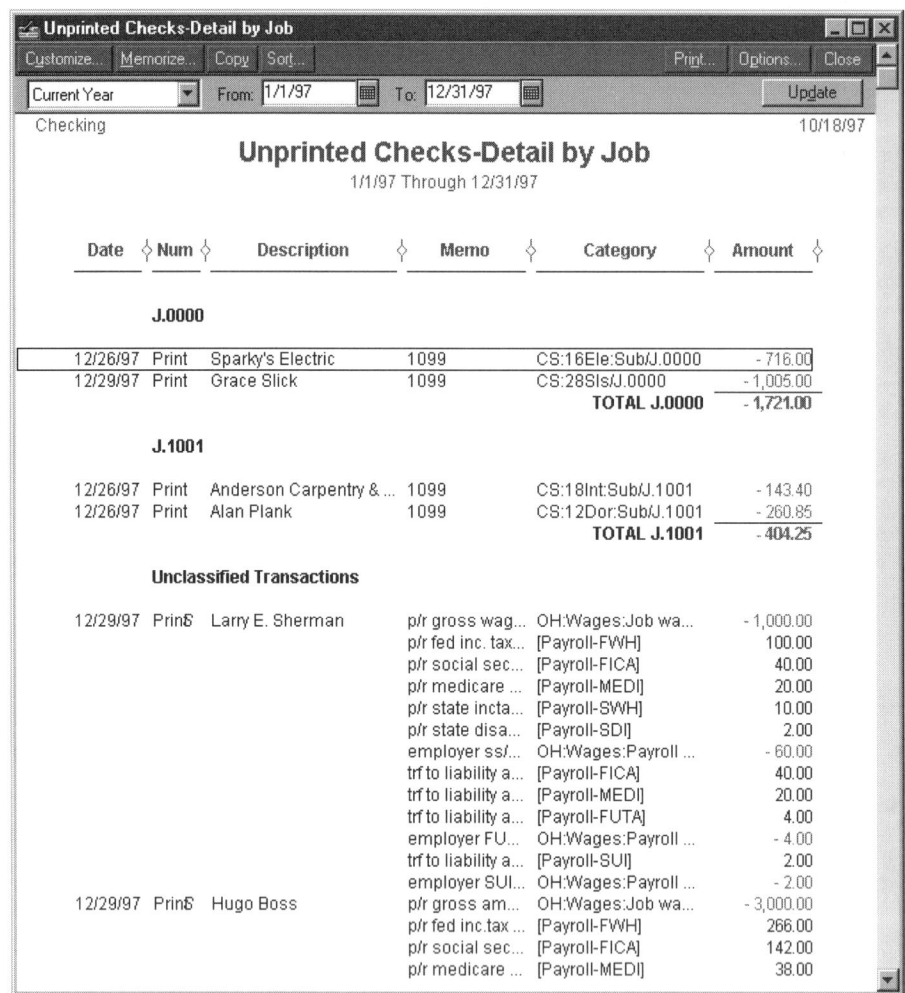

Display tab

Report Dates:	Can be for any defined date range (default is the current year)
Report Layout:	Sort By: Acct/Chk#
	Organization: Income & Expense
Headings:	Subtotal: Class
Show:	Cents in Amounts, Split Transaction Detail
Show Columns:	Column: Date, Num, Description, Memo, Category, Amount

Accounts tab

Selected Accounts:	Checking only

Include tab

Select to Include: Categories: All

                           Classes: All

Advanced tab

Transactions: Amounts: Greater than 0

                           Transaction Types: Unprinted Checks

Status: Blank, Newly Cleared, Reconciled

Transfers: Include All

Subcategories: Show All

Unprinted Checks-Detail by Vendor (All unprinted checks)

This memorized report allows you to see a list of all currently unprinted checks, subtotaled by the name of the vendor. Figure 7–21 shows a sample report generated using this memorized report format.

Display tab

Report Dates: Can be for any defined date range (default is the current year)

Report Layout: Sort By: Acct/Chk#

                           Organization: Income & Expense

Headings: Subtotal: Payee

Show: Cents in Amounts, Split Transaction Detail

Show Columns: Column: Date, Num, Description, Memo, Category, Amount

Accounts tab

Selected Accounts: Checking only

Include tab

Select to Include: Categories: All

                           Classes: All

Advanced tab

Transactions: Amounts: Greater than 0

                           Transaction Types: Unprinted Checks

Figure 7–21

This sample report listing unprinted checks by vendor was generated using the memorized Unprinted Checks-Detail by Vendor report.

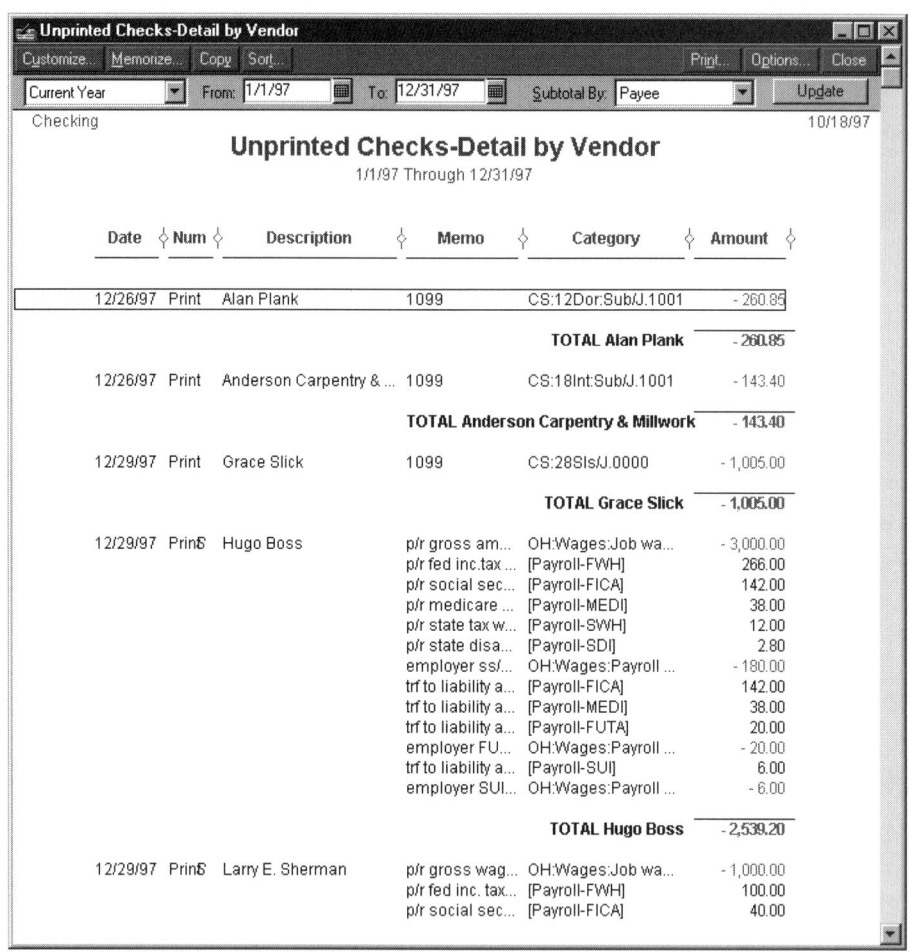

Advanced tab *(continued)*

Status:	Blank, Newly Cleared, Reconciled
Transfers:	Include All
Subcategories:	Show All

Unprinted Checks-Summary by Vendor (All unprinted checks)

The memorized report Unprinted Checks-Summary by Vendor lets you view a month-by-month summary of unprinted checks, broken down by vendor name. Figure 7–22 shows a sample report generated using this format.

Display tab

Report Dates:	Can be for any defined date range (default is the current year)

Figure 7–22

This month-by-month unprinted-check summary report was generated using the Unprinted Checks-Summary by Vendor format.

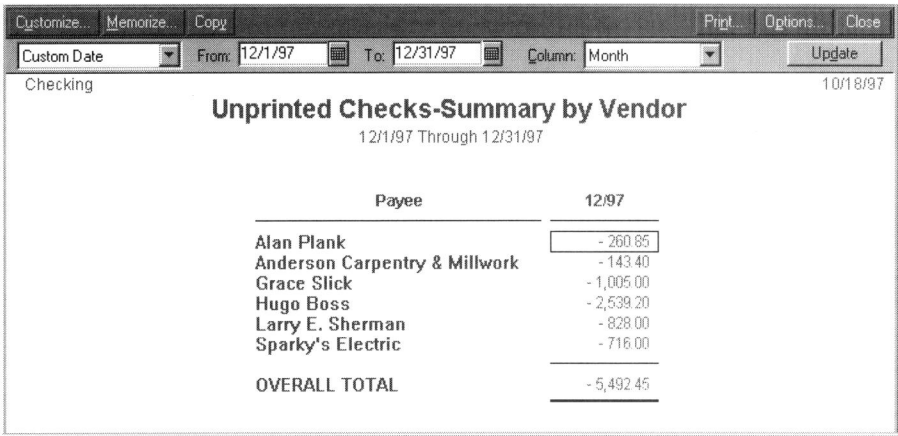

Report Layout:	Organization: Income & Expense
Headings:	Row: Payee
	Column: Month
Show:	Cents in Amounts

Accounts tab

Selected Accounts:	Checking only

Include tab

Select to Include:	Categories: All
	Classes: All

Advanced tab

Transactions:	Amounts: All
	Transaction Types: Unprinted Checks
Status:	Blank, Newly Cleared, Reconciled
Transfers:	Include All
Subcategories:	Show All

Wage & Burden Allocation (Detail by Category)

There are two components to the cost of having employees: their actual payroll, and the additional costs such as Workers' Compensation Insurance. These additional costs are known as *labor burden.* The Wage & Burden Allocation memorized report processes this data. It draws upon data from the Adjustments account and generates a listing of all labor burden expenses, broken down by category. The default date range for this report is for the current year. Figure 7–23 shows a sample report generated using this report format.

Display tab

Report Dates:	Can be for any defined date range (default is the current year)
Report Layout:	Sort By: None
	Organization: Income & Expense
Headings:	Subtotal: Category
Show:	Cents in Amounts
Show Columns:	Column: Date, Num, Description, Memo, Category, Clr, Amount

Figure 7–23

This sample report listing burden expenses by category was generated using the memorized Wage & Burden Allocation report.

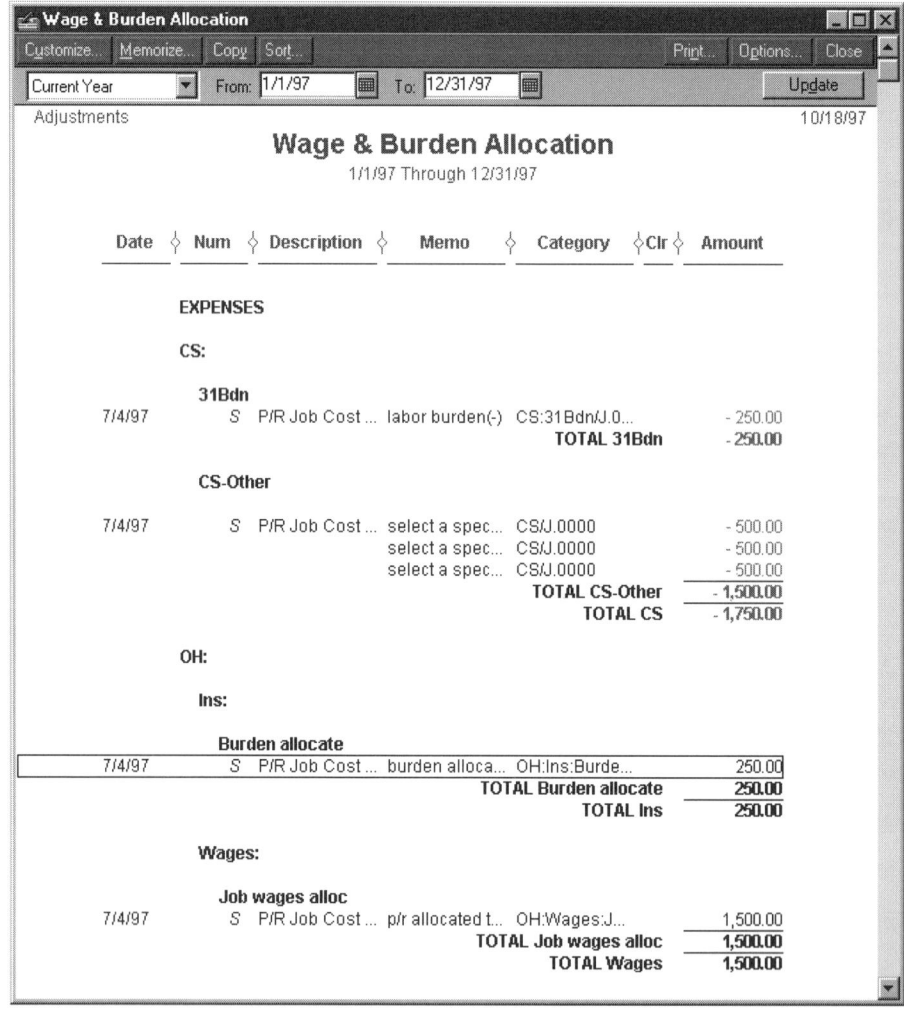

Accounts tab

Selected Accounts: Adjustments only

Include tab

Select to Include: Categories: CS (Cost of Sales) and all its
subcategories
Wages and all its subcategories
Ins (insurance) and all its
subcategories

Classes: All

Advanced tab

Transactions: Amounts: All

Transaction Types: All Transactions

Status: Blank, Newly Cleared, Reconciled

Transfers: Exclude All

Subcategories: Show All

💲 Creating a New Memorized Report

As you become more familiar with the preconfigured memorized
reports on the companion diskette, you may wish to modify some of
them to better suit the unique needs of your business. One way to
modify a memorized report is to customize the settings each time you
run the report. However, this can become tiresome if you run the
same report frequently.

Another, and more efficient, alternative is to create a new memorized report specific to your business, using one of our preconfigured
reports as a template. For example, the memorized report Job Detail
Report-Job_____ requires that you input a specific job number (class)
before it will give you information for a specific job. If you run many
short-term jobs simultaneously and they're always changing, you can
simply input a job number each time you run this report, making no
other changes. But if you have a small number of jobs or tend to have
longer-term jobs, you might prefer to run different variations of this
report for each job, accessible with a single click. The best way to do
that would be to set up multiple memorized reports, each with a separate job (class) number.

Here's how you might proceed, using the memorized report Job
Detail Report-Job_____ as an example:

1. Select the Reports | Memorized Reports command from the menu.

2. When the Create Report window appears (refer back to Figure 7–2), *don't* click on the icon next to the report title. Clicking on the icon immediately runs the default report without changing any settings. Instead, click once on the title of the report itself to select it.

3. Click the Customize button at the bottom of the window. This brings up the Customize Report window with its four tabs—Display, Accounts, Include, Advanced—that we discussed earlier in the chapter (refer to Figure 7–3).

4. For your new customized report, you'll want to change the Job (Class) designation to a specific job number. Click on the Include Tab and then use the drop-down menu in the Class Contains field to select the specific job you want to report on.

5. Click the Create button at the bottom of the Customize Report window to generate a sample report based on this new setting.

6. If the report includes all the types of details you would like to set as a new default, click the Memorize button at the top of the report window. The Memorize Report dialog box will appear, as shown in Figure 7–24.

7. Change the name of the report to indicate the new job number and click OK. Quicken saves this new report separate from the original memorized report you used as a template.

Each of the tabs in the Customize Report window has different options that you can include or exclude in your reports, but the concept behind creating a customized memorized report is exactly the same as changing the class (job) in the example just given.

Figure 7–24

You enter the new title of your customized report in the Memorize Report dialog box.

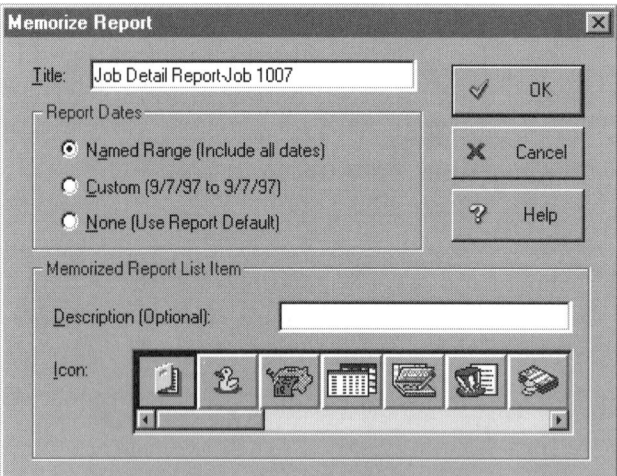

End-of-Month Procedures

For the sake of good financial record keeping, it's important to print certain reports and complete other financial procedures at the end of every month. By following the steps outlined in this section, you will verify the accuracy of your data entry. This will ensure that the reports you produce are accurate, as well as give you the correct information you need to make decisions in managing your jobs and your company.

In Quicken, end-of-the-month procedures are a simple process:

◆ Reconcile your checkbook
◆ Ensure accuracy of data entry
◆ Print reports and back up the data file

Reconcile the Checkbook(s)

To reconcile your checkbook in Quicken:

1. From the menu, select Lists|Account. Double-click on the checking account you want to reconcile. This will bring up the register, as shown in Figure 8–1.

Figure 8–1

This sample Checking register is for the Company Checking account.

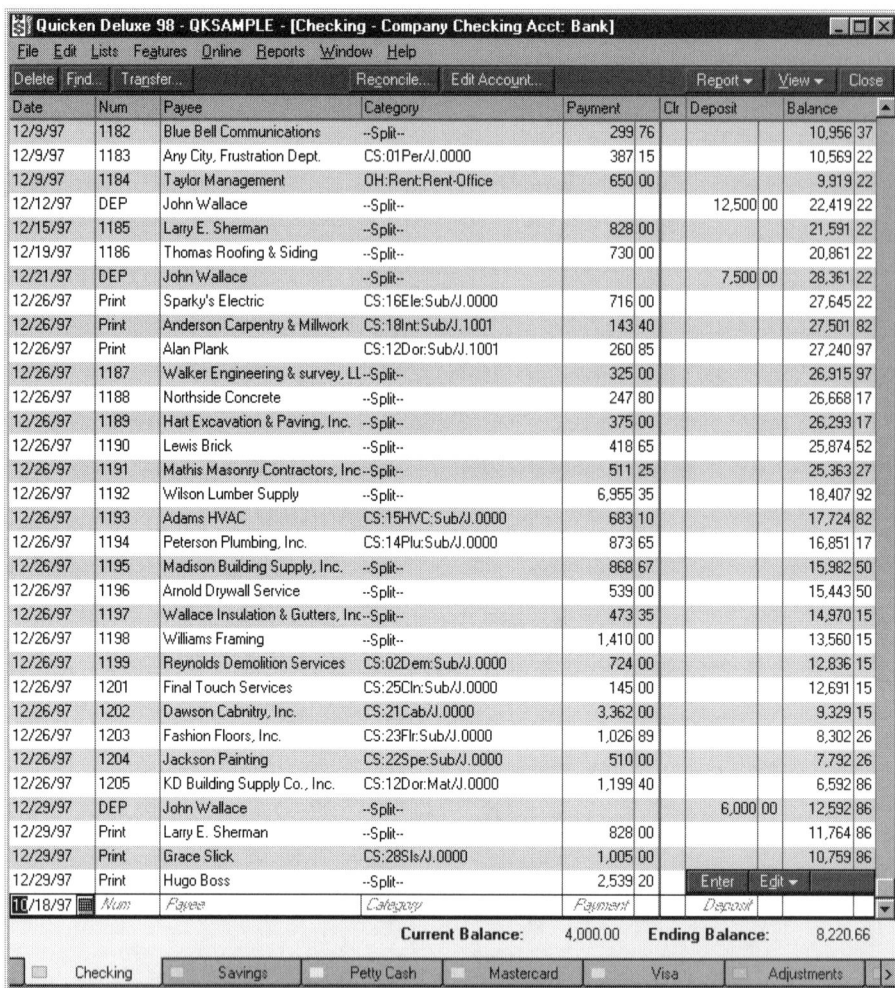

2. Click the Reconcile button to display the Reconcile Bank Statement: Checking window, as shown in Figure 8–2.

3. If this is the first time you are reconciling the account using Quicken, fill in the Opening Balance field based on your bank statement. If you've reconciled this account previously, Quicken automatically supplies the Ending Balance amount from the last reconciliation period.

4. From your bank statement, enter your ending balance in the Ending Balance field. You may see it listed as "Ending bank balance" or "New balance" on your paper-based bank statement.

5. In the Service Charge field, enter the amount of the service charges listed on your bank statement (if any). Enter the date on which these charges were posted to your account in the Date field.

Figure 8–2

The Reconcile Bank Statement: Checking dialog box opens when you click Reconcile in the Checking register window.

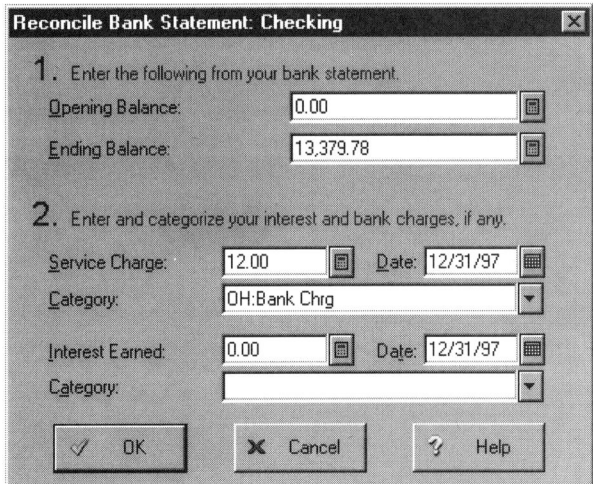

Figure 8–3

The first time you reconcile your checkbook in Quicken, you have to fill in all the fields in the Reconcile Bank Statement: Checking dialog box, as this completed sample shows.

6. For the Category field, use the subcategory OH:Bank Chrg (listed simply as Bank Chrg in the Category & Transfer List window).

7. If your account earned any interest, enter the amount in the Interest Earned field. In the Date field next to it, enter the date on which the interest was posted from the bank statement.

8. For the Category field, use the category Int Inc (interest income). See Figure 8–3 for an example of data that has already been entered into this dialog box.

9. When you've finished entering your data, click the OK button. A list of your currently uncleared Payments and Checks, as well as any uncleared Deposits, now appears.

10. In the Payments and Checks area of the window, click once in the Clr column for each check that has cleared according to

Figure 8–4

You clear checks and deposits according to your bank statement in the Reconcile Bank Statement: Checking window.

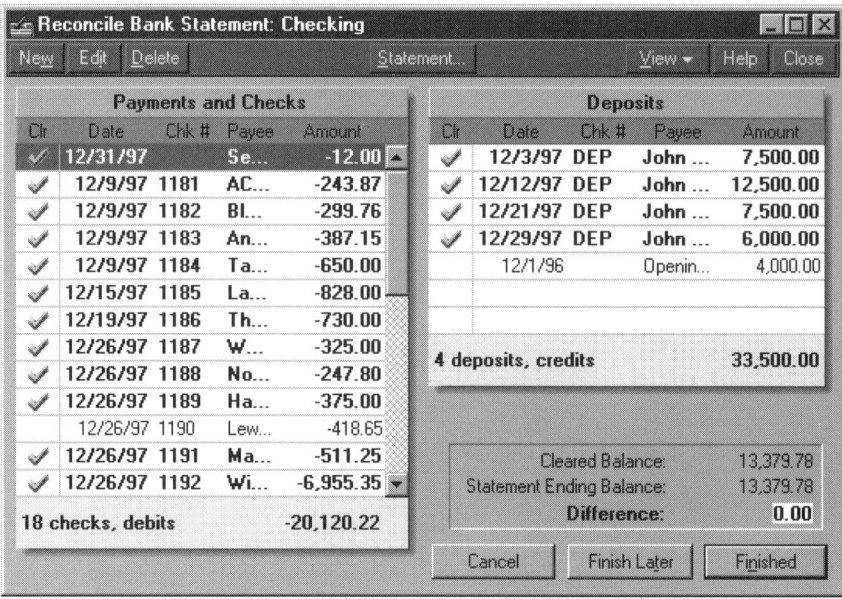

your bank statement. Clicking in this column marks the check on that line as cleared. Continue marking each cleared check until no more remain on your bank statement.

11. In the Deposits area of the window, click once in the Clr column for each deposit that has cleared according to your bank statement. Continue marking each cleared deposit until no more remain on your bank statement. Figure 8–4 shows an example of how the reconciliation window might appear at this point.

12. If you've marked all the checks and deposits that appear on your bank statement, the Difference amount in the Reconcile Bank Statement: Checking window should be zero. If so, click the Finished button to complete the reconciliation process. Quicken presents you with a Reconciliation Complete message like the one in Figure 8–5.

If you have marked all your cleared checks and cleared deposits according to your bank statement, but the Difference amount is still not zero, there are several possible reasons. Review the following points to retrace your steps:

◆ Look at the bottom row in the Payments and Checks area of the reconciliation window. Does the total number of checks match what is listed on your bank statement? If not, review the checks you've marked and make certain you haven't marked too many or too few.

Figure 8–5

When you have successfully balanced your checking account, the Reconciliation Complete dialog box appears.

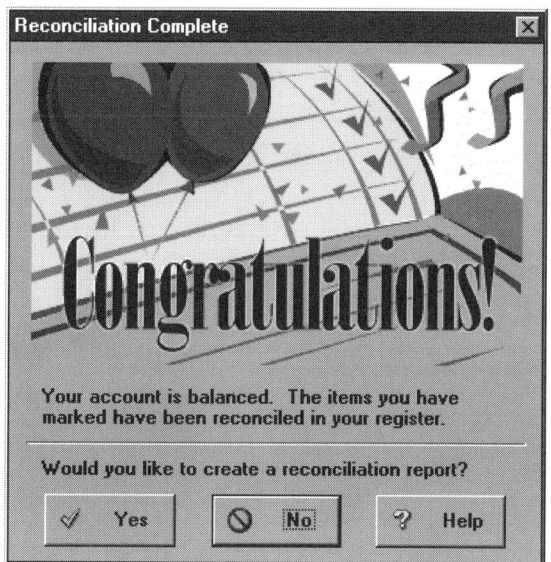

- ◆ Does the total amount in the bottom row of the Payments and Checks area match what is listed on your bank statement? If not, look carefully at the amounts for each check on your screen. It's possible that you've entered an amount incorrectly or that the bank has cleared an incorrect amount.

- ◆ Look at the bottom row in the Deposits area of the window. Does the total number of deposits match your bank statement? If not, review the deposits you've marked and make certain you haven't marked too many or too few.

- ◆ Does the total amount of deposits and credits equal what the bank statement shows? If not, review your electronic entries to see if there are any differences from their counterparts on the bank statement. It's possible that you've entered a deposit amount incorrectly or that the bank has cleared an incorrect deposit amount.

- ◆ Is the difference caused by a service charge or interest payment that you haven't entered electronically? If so, click the Statement button at the top of the Reconcile Bank Statement window and verify or enter the amount of the service charge or interest paid that appears on your bank statement.

Once you've completed reconciling your monthly bank statement, Quicken asks you if you'd like to generate and print a reconciliation report. We suggest that you print this report every time you reconcile your checkbook and store it in a three-ring binder for reference.

💲 Ensure Accuracy of Data Entry

An important step in your end-of-month procedure is to review all the data you've entered electronically during that month. This involves double-checking not only the amounts, but also the payee names and categories you've assigned to each transaction. If you're using Quicken's automated entry features (see Chapter 3, "Customizing Quicken"), Quicken will ensure that items are spelled correctly.

Quicken includes a built-in report format to help you review the accuracy of your data entry each month. Here's how to use it:

1. From the menu, select the Reports | Home | Itemized Categories command to display the Create Report window.

2. In the Report Dates area of the window, specify the month being closed or the month you've just reconciled. Then click the Create button to generate the report. A sample report is shown in Figure 8–6.

 NOTE: *If you are wondering why you are running a Home report for business purposes, it is because this report is classified as a Home report by Intuit, but it is traditionally a business report known as a General Ledger Detail Report.*

---

3. Review the report on screen to ensure everything has been accurately recorded to the correct category. For example, verify that all transactions under 14Plu:Sub are from plumbing subcontractors. If you see an error, such as a Roofing Sub bill entered as a Plumbing bill, double-click on the transaction and make the correction to the category.

💲 Printing Financial Reports

It doesn't matter which program you are using or what industry you are in, it is critical that you understand your company's financial statements if you plan on staying in business. Unfortunately, even the best craftsperson cannot rely completely on his or her excellent handiwork to stay in business. That person will still have to learn how to bill for services, pay bills, collect money, and keep control of overhead expenses. In other words, acquire some business skills. Although

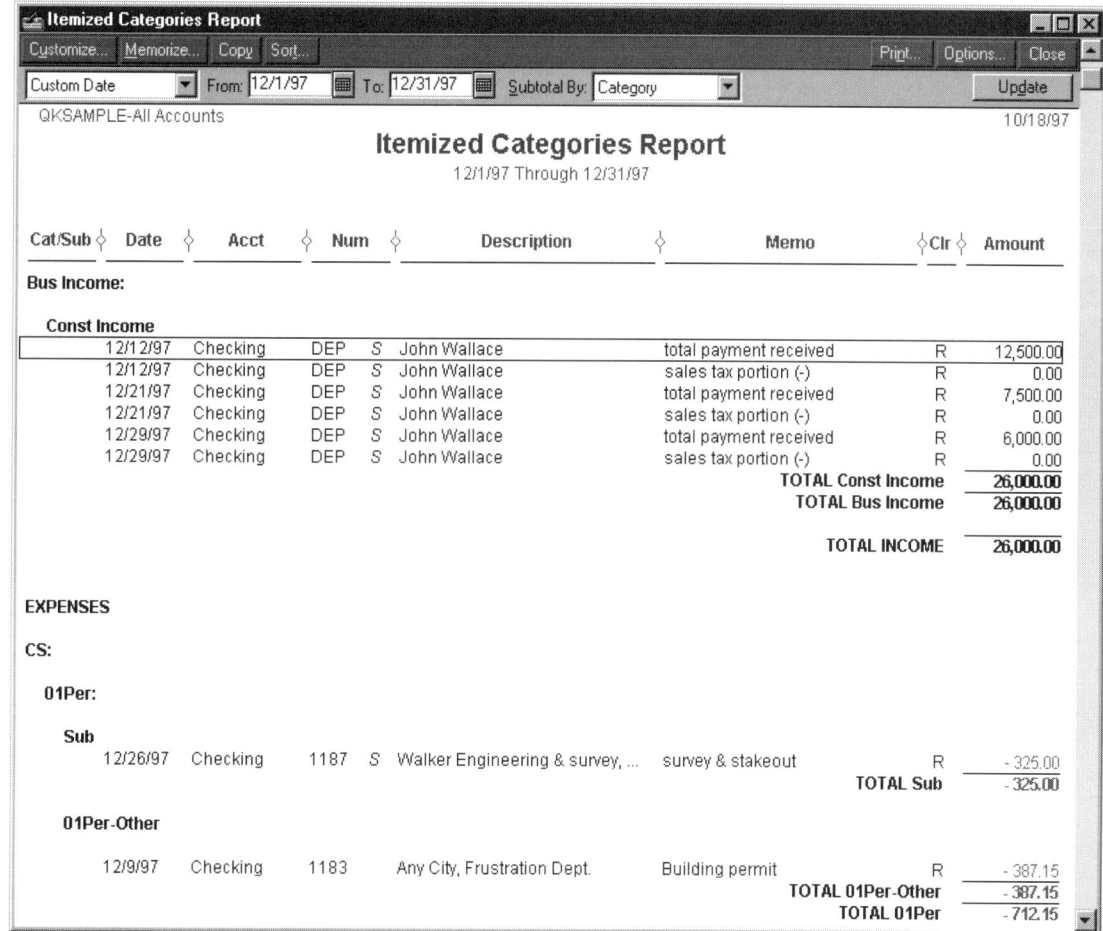

Figure 8–6

Creating an Itemized Categories Report helps you check the accuracy of your data entry at the end of each month.

we can't teach a business class in the course of this book, we can teach you how to read and understand the importance of your financial statements, a big step toward sharpening your business skills.

The Quicken standard financial reports you should print every month and become familiar with are:

◆ Profit & Loss Statement

◆ Profit & Loss Comparison

◆ Balance Sheet

We'll review each of these in this section.

Profit & Loss Statement

In accounting terms, a Profit & Loss (P&L) Statement is synonymous with an Income Statement. You will often hear it referred to as simply a "P&L." The P&L is important because it gives you insight into how well your company is doing over a given time period. The most common time periods are a month or the year-to-date. Your Profit & Loss Statement is calculated as follows:

> Total Income
> − Total Cost of Goods Sold (Job-Related Costs)
> = Gross Profit

> Gross Profit
> − Overhead Expenses
> = Net Profit

Quicken includes a standard report format for Profit & Loss Statements. To create a P&L report:

1. From the menu, select Reports | Business | Profit & Loss Statement.

2. Click the Customize button.

3. Make the following changes to the default settings in the Display tab of the Customize Profit & Loss Statement window:
   - Report Dates: from: 12/1/97 to: 12/31/97
   - Show: Make sure a checkmark appears in both the Cents in Amounts and Amount as % check boxes.
   - Organization: Supercategory

4. Click the Create button to generate the report. An example is shown in Figure 8–7.

A P&L statement gives you an idea of how much money you've received versus how much you've paid out in job costs and overhead costs. The percentages and timing of the report are key.

Timing

If your company is small and pays its bills as soon as it gets money from a job, then this report will give you a very clear picture of how much income you have generated during the chosen time period. It is a financial picture of all your jobs versus how much it cost you to do those jobs, plus the associated job overhead expenses. Hopefully, the

Figure 8–7

This is a sample of a Profit & Loss Statement you can create in Quicken.

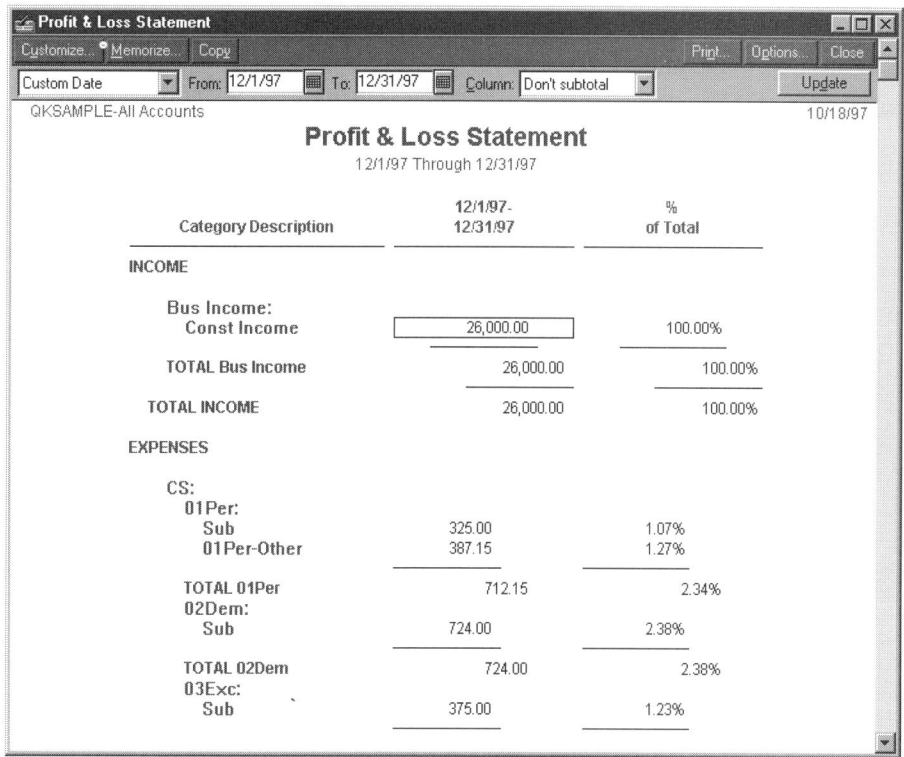

income for the time period covered all the bills for the same period. If it didn't, you'll need to add in all unpaid bills and subtract that amount from the bottom line.

Percentages

Percentages give the reader a quick analysis of the information on the financial statement. Throughout the financial statement, the percentage is calculated by dividing the cost by the total amount of revenue. For example, our P&L statement (see Figure 8–7) shows a Total Income of $26,000. Each line-item job cost and expense is divided by this figure. The important things to look at are the total job-cost percentage and the total expenses percentage. The job-cost percentage gives you an idea of what percent of every dollar was spent on job-related costs. The percent next to Total Expenses and for each expense by category tells you how your overhead percentage is running. This figure is extremely important when comparing your estimated vs. actual expenses. For example, if your goal is 10% for overhead on your estimates but your overhead is truly 15%, you know you have a problem.

Profit & Loss Comparison Report

The Profit & Loss Comparison report is another built-in Quicken report format. It has the same function as the P&L Statement, except that it includes an additional column for comparing one time period to another. The most common use of this report is for comparing this year-to-date versus last year-to-date. The report will clearly show how you are doing this year compared to last year at the same time period.

Comparing Year-to-Date Data

To create a report comparing this year-to-date and last year-to-date:

1. From the menu, select Reports | Business | P&L Comparison.

2. Click the Customize button to display the Create Report window, as shown in Figure 8–8.

3. Make the following customizations in the Display tab:

   ◆ Report Dates: Year to Date from: 1/1/96 to: 12/31/96 (previous year)
   Year to Date from: 1/1/97 to: 12/31/97 (current year)

   ◆ Show: Make sure that Cents in Amounts check box is marked.

   ◆ Organization: Supercategory

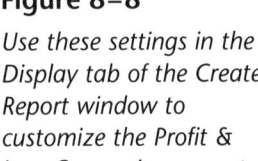

Figure 8–8

Use these settings in the Display tab of the Create Report window to customize the Profit & Loss Comparison report.

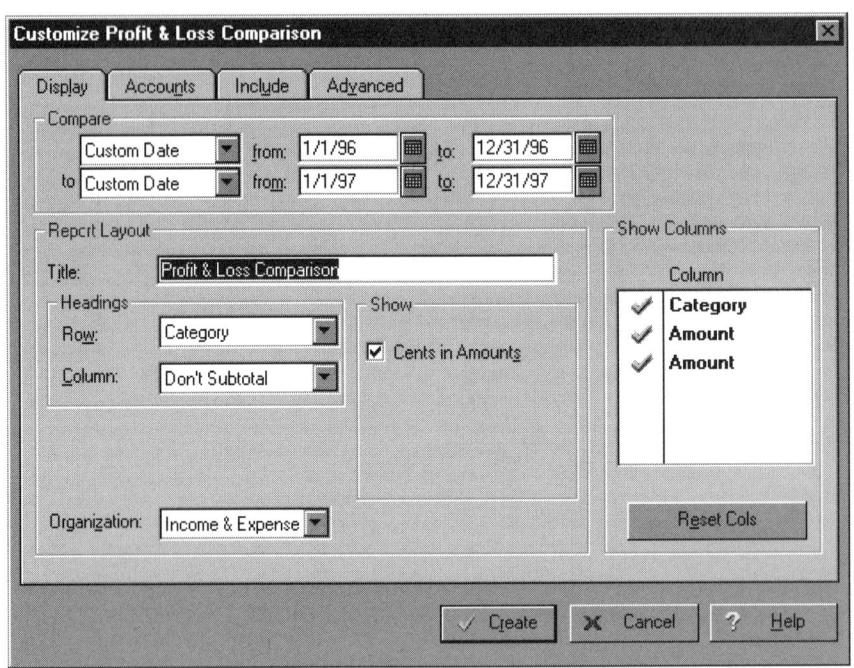

Figure 8–9

This is a sample of a Profit & Loss Comparison report you can create in Quicken.

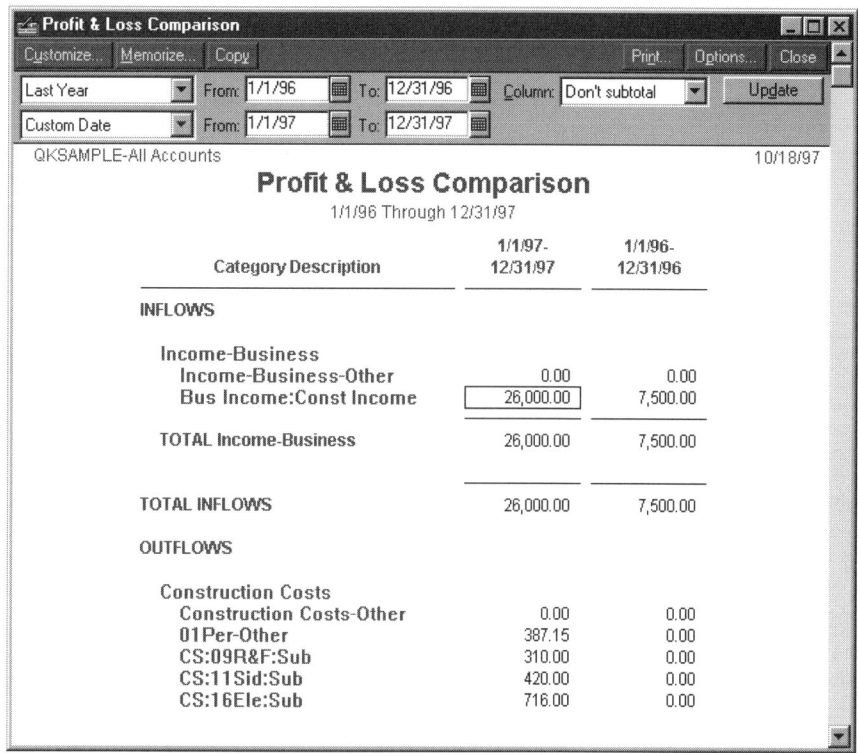

4. Click the Create button to generate the report. An example appears in Figure 8–9.

Comparing Month-to-Date Data

To create a report comparing this month-to-date and this year-to-date:

1. From the menu, select the Reports | Business | P&L Comparison command.

2. Click the Customize button to display the Create Report window.

3. Make the following customizations in the Display tab:

   ◆ Report Dates: Month to Date from: 9/1/97 to: 9/30/97 (current month)
   Year to Date from: 1/1/97 to: 9/30/97 (current accounting year)

   ◆ Show: Make sure the Cents in Amounts check box is marked.

   ◆ Organization: Supercategory

4. Click the Create button to generate the report.

Balance Sheet

The Balance Sheet is a snapshot in time that tells you the dollar value of what you own (your assets) versus the dollar value of what you owe (your liabilities), and the difference (your equity or net worth). The important thing to remember while reading this report is that you want the value of your assets to be considerably higher than the value of your liabilities. If you go to a bank to get a loan, the person reviewing this report will expect to see at least a ratio of 2:1 — meaning that the total value of your assets should be at least two times as much as the total value of your liabilities.

Quicken has a built-in report format to help you review your Balance Sheet. To create a report showing your current Balance Sheet:

1. From the menu, select the Reports | Business | Balance Sheet command.

2. Click the Customize button to display the Create Report window.

3. Make the following customizations in the Display tab:
   - ◆ Report Dates: from: Last day of month being closed
                        to: Last day of month being closed
   - ◆ Show: Make sure the Cents in Amounts option is checked.

4. Click the Create button to generate the report. Figure 8–10 shows a sample Balance Sheet report.

Job-Cost Reports

Job-cost reports aren't necessarily printed at the end of the month, but instead should be printed as needed and given to the project manager. In the Company file on the diskette that accompanies this book, the reports that should be printed *at least* at the end of the project have already been memorized for you. To find the reports, go to the Reports | Memorized Reports menu. The reports that should be printed are the Budget Report-Job____ report, which lists the actual costs to date on the job versus the estimated costs, and the Job Detail Report-Job____ report, which lists all transactions associated with each job-cost division.

For additional information regarding job costing and job-cost reports see Chapter 5.

Armed with these reports, especially the Budget Report-Job____, the project manager can easily see at a glance exactly how the job is

Figure 8–10

This is a sample of a Balance Sheet report that you can create in Quicken.

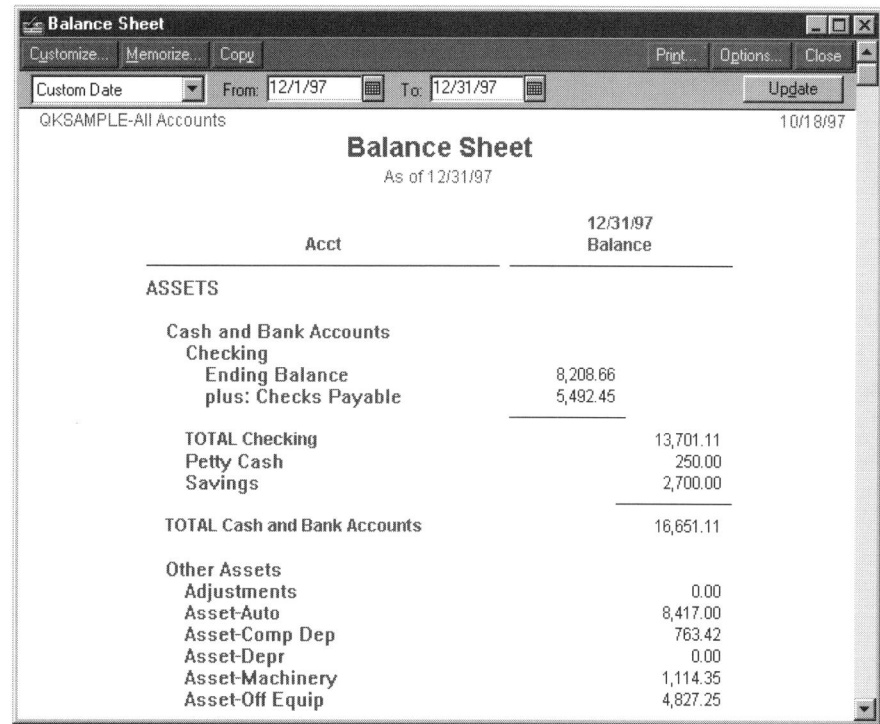

progressing; for instance, whether it is over or under the estimate and by how much.

🏠 Back Up Your Data File

Ideally, you should back up your data after every Quicken session. But at the very least, you should do so at the end of each month. To back up your data file:

1. From the menu, select the File|Exit command. Quicken will prompt you to automatically back up your data, as shown in Figure 8–11. Click the Backup button to display the Select Backup Drive dialog box shown in Figure 8–12.

2. Insert a blank formatted disk into the drive and select the appropriate drive letter to save the backup, usually A or B. Once you have selected the destination drive, click the OK button.

3. When the backup is complete, you'll see a "File backed up successfully" message like the one in Figure 8–13. Click the OK button to exit the program.

Figure 8–11

When you exit Quicken, Quicken's Automatic Backup dialog box is displayed.

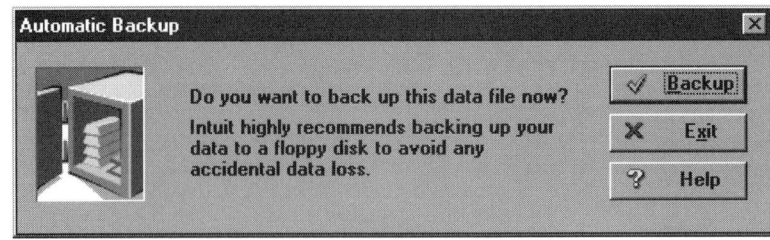

Figure 8–12

Tell Quicken where to save the backup in the Select Backup Drive dialog box.

Figure 8–13

When backup is complete, Quicken displays a screen indicating a successful backup.

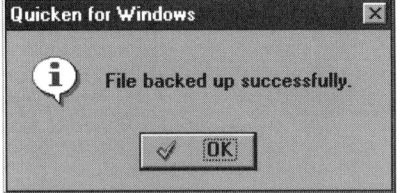

🏠 Working with an Accountant

A key thing to remember about accountants is that they are extremely busy from January 1st through April 15th. The best strategy for getting the most from your accountant is to keep this in mind and set up meetings during your accountant's slow season. Unfortunately, that coincides with the height of your busy season—summer.

If at all possible, you should set up a quarterly review of your company's accounting data with your tax preparer or accountant. If anything is "going wrong," it is better to catch it early rather than when your tax return is being prepared. Plus, it tends to be less expensive to fix errors yourself than to have your accountant shift through your paperwork trying to rectify the mistakes while preparing your return. When your accountant reviews your business finances, ask him or her to highlight trouble spots, as you may be able to find and fix them before the year's end, and learn from your mistakes in the process.

Backing Up
Your Quicken Files

By now we hope you've come to realize that using the computer to do your accounting and job costing is a time- and energy-saving exercise. However, it is easy to become blasé about how simple your bookkeeping is and lose sight of the importance of the digital data that reside on your hard disk. Therefore, you must have a strategy for backing up your Quicken data files.

Quicken makes backing up your files very simple. In practice, Quicken prompts you to back up your current file every time you exit the program. You should make a backup at the end of every Quicken session. In addition, you can back up your data any time you want. Although it is possible to back up to your hard drive, it is much safer to save your backups on floppy disks or some other removable medium, such as a Zip drive. Then, if your hard drive crashes, you will be able to restore your Quicken files from these disks. In addition, it is advisable to keep your backup copies off the premises in case of fire, flood, or theft.

To back up to a floppy disk or other removable medium:

1. Place a formatted disk in the appropriate drive.
2. From the menu, select the File | Backup command. The Select Backup Drive dialog box appears as in Figure 9–1.

Figure 9–1

You designate what drive to use and what file to back up in the Select Backup Drive dialog box.

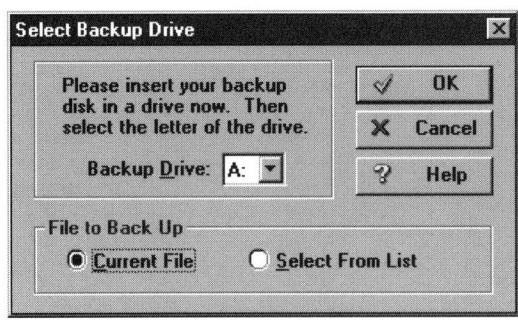

Figure 9–2

When your backup is done, Quicken displays a message indicating that the backup was successful.

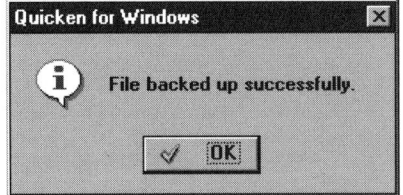

3. Use the drop-down list in the Backup Drive field to select the drive containing the floppy disk or other external medium.

4. In the File to Back Up section of the dialog box, select the Current File option button and then click OK. If the file is larger than the space available on the backup disk, Quicken first fills the backup disk, then asks you to replace the backup disk with another disk. Do so and then click the OK button to continue.

5. When Quicken tells you that the backup has been completed successfully (Figure 9–2), click the OK button and remove the backup disk. Store the disk(s) in a safe place.

Backup Strategies

There are at least two backup strategies that provide security for your data. One is to alternate between two sets of backup disks each time you back up your work. This method makes your two most recent backups available to you, just in case the latest backup disks or files get corrupted.

To use the two-set method, first back up to disk 1 (or a set of disks, if necessary); the next time you back up, use disk 2 (or a second set). Rotate the sequence so neither disk set is more than one backup behind the current data.

Another strategy is to use six sets of backup disks: one for each day of the business week plus a monthly disk.

$ Archiving Your Quicken Files

In addition to making regular backups, at the end of the year you may want to store your data files for safekeeping. Quicken lets you do this in one of two ways. You can either archive transactions earlier than the current year in a separate file, leaving your current file with all its data in it, or create a new file that contains only the data from the current year.

Archiving Data Files

Your first option is to archive copies of all your transactions that are dated earlier than this year and place them in a separate file, leaving your current file untouched. This allows you to continue to use the historical data to create reports and graphs that include several years' worth of information.

To archive a data file:

1. From the menu, select File | File Operations | Year-End Copy. The Year-End Copy dialog box appears as in Figure 9–3.

2. Select the Archive option button and then click OK. The Archive File dialog box appears, as shown in Figure 9–4.

3. In the Archive Old Data to File field, enter a name for the archive file, or use the one that Quicken suggests.

4. Use the Location of Archive File field to specify the location where you want to store the data file. You can store it on your hard drive, on a floppy disk, or (if you have a Zip drive, SyQuest drive, or magneto-optical drive) on removable media.

Figure 9–3

Select a type of end-of-year backup in the Year-End Copy dialog box. The Archive option saves earlier years' data in a separate file, leaving your current file untouched.

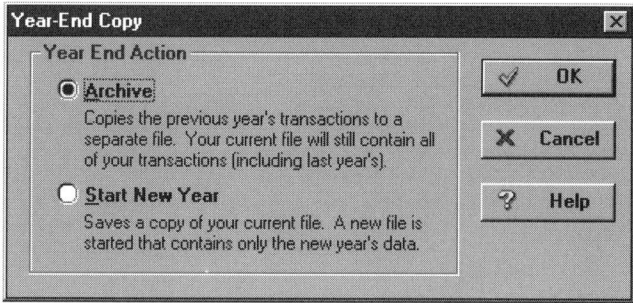

Figure 9–4

You use the Archive File dialog box to specify a name and location for your archive copy.

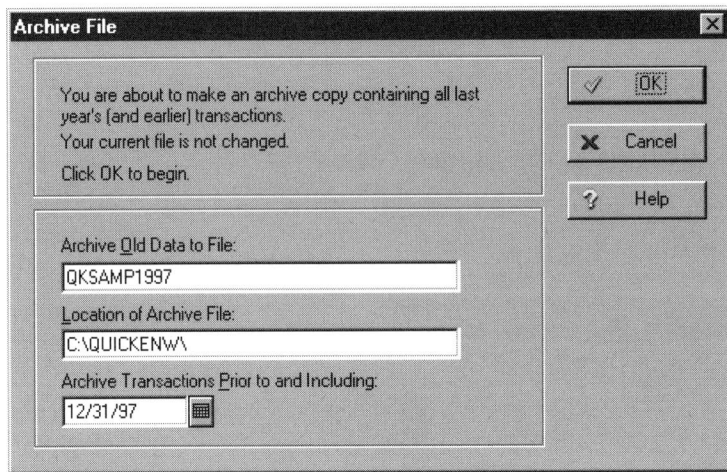

5. In the Archive Transactions Prior to and Including field, specify the last date to include in the archive. Then click the OK button to begin the archive process.

6. When Quicken tells you the archive is complete, click OK.

Starting a New Year

Perhaps you'd rather keep only this year's data in the file you're currently working with, and save previous years' data in a separate file. Quicken lets you do this by starting a new year. This option makes a copy of your current data file and then removes all your historic transactions that are dated earlier than this year. The new data file then contains only transactions dated this year (along with any uncleared transactions and all investment transactions). This method is especially useful if your data files have gotten so large that making regular backups is inconvenient.

To start a new year:

1. From the menu, select File | File Operations | Year-End Copy.

2. In the Year-End Copy dialog box that appears (Figure 9–5), select the Start New Year option button and then click OK.

3. In the Start New Year dialog box that appears (Figure 9–6), use the Copy All Transactions to File field to enter a name for the file where the historical data will be stored. You can also use the file name that Quicken suggests.

4. In the Delete Transactions From Current File Older Than field, specify the date on which you want to start the new year.

Figure 9–5

In the Year-End Copy dialog box, choose the Start New Year option to save a copy of your current file and remove historic transactions from earlier years.

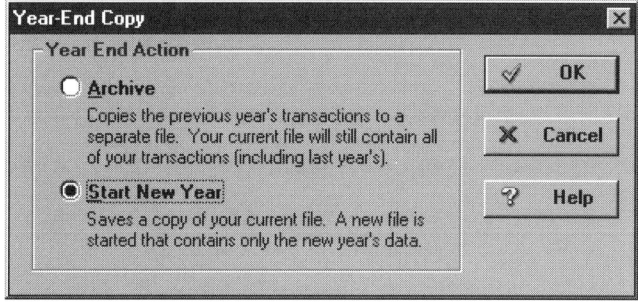

Figure 9–6

You use the Start New Year dialog box to choose the name, location, and dates for the file where historical data will be stored.

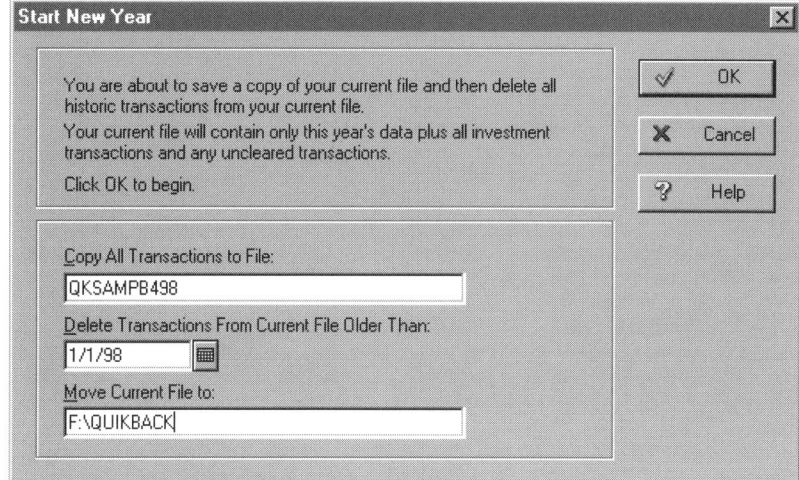

5. If you want to store your data file somewhere other than the default Quicken directory, specify the desired location in the Move Current File to field.

6. Click the OK button to begin the conversion process.

7. When Quicken tells you the process is complete, click the OK button.

Conclusion

Each construction company works in its own unique way—no two are exactly the same. As a corollary, no computer program, whether you stay in Quicken, move up to QuickBooks Pro, or move on to a specialized construction accounting program, is going to give you every invoice, statement, and report you want. It's just impossible to write software that offers everyone everything. The solution is to find an appropriate "workaround." When you come up against a problem, consider moving the data out of Quicken and into a spreadsheet or word processor, then modifying the data to suit your purposes. In most cases, the data you need is already in Quicken. The trick is to manipulate the data into useful information.

If you use our Quicken data files from the accompanying diskette and have followed our suggestions in this book, your business should now be set up with a simple-to-use accounting and job-costing system. The reports you generate should give you a good handle on your job costs, as well as a picture of your financial health.

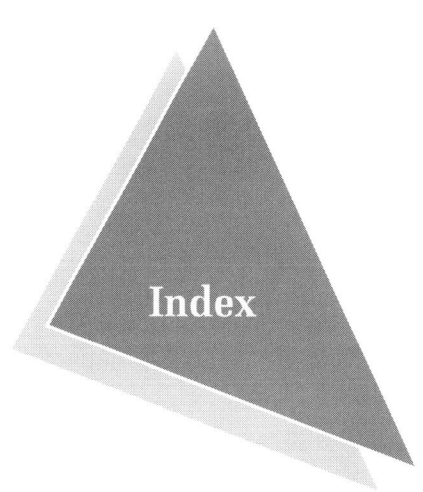

Index

Practical References for Builders

Basic Lumber Engineering for Builders

Beam and lumber requirements for many jobs aren't always clear, especially with changing building codes and lumber products. Most of the time you rely on your own "rules of thumb" when figuring spans or lumber engineering. This book can help you fill the gap between what you can find in the building code span tables and what you need to pay a certified engineer to do. With its large, clear illustrations and examples, this book shows you how to figure stresses for pre-engineered wood or wood structural members, how to calculate loads, and how to design your own girders, joists and beams. Included FREE with the book — an easy-to-use version of NorthBridge Software's *Wood Beam Sizing* program. **272 pages, 8¹/₂ x 11, $38.00**

Bookkeeping for Builders

Shows simple, practical instructions for setting up and keeping accurate records — with a minimum of effort and frustration. Explains the essentials of a record-keeping system: the payment, income, and general journals, and records for fixed assets, accounts receivable, payables and purchases, petty cash, and job costs. Shows how to keep I.R.S. records, and accurate, organized business records for your own use. **208 pages, 8¹/₂ x 11, $19.75**

Illustrated Guide to the 1996 *National Electrical Code*

This fully-illustrated guide offers a quick and easy visual reference for installing electrical systems. Whether you're installing a new system or repairing an old one, you'll appreciate the simple explanations written by a code expert, and the detailed, intricately-drawn and labeled diagrams. A real time-saver when it comes to deciphering the current *NEC*. **384 pages, 8¹/₂ x 11, $34.75**

Contractor's Survival Manual

How to survive hard times and succeed during the up cycles. Shows what to do when the bills can't be paid, finding money and buying time, transferring debt, and all the alternatives to bankruptcy. Explains how to build profits, avoid problems in zoning and permits, taxes, time-keeping, and payroll. Unconventional advice on how to invest in inflation, get high appraisals, trade and postpone income, and stay hip-deep in profitable work. **160 pages, 8¹/₂ x 11, $22.25**

Contractor's Guide to the Building Code Revised

This completely revised edition explains in plain English exactly what the *Uniform Building Code* requires. Based on the newly-expanded 1994 code, it explains many of the changes made. Also covers the *Uniform Mechanical Code* and the *Uniform Plumbing Code*. Shows how to design and construct residential and light commercial buildings that'll pass inspection the first time. Suggests how to work with an inspector to minimize construction costs, what common building shortcuts are likely to be cited, and where exceptions are granted. **384 pages, 8¹/₂ x 11, $39.00**

Estimating Home Building Costs

Estimate every phase of residential construction from site costs to the profit margin you include in your bid. Shows how to keep track of man-hours and make accurate labor cost estimates for footings, foundations, framing and sheathing finishes, electrical, plumbing, and more. Provides and explains sample cost estimate worksheets with complete instructions for each job phase. **320 pages, 5¹/₂ x 8¹/₂, $17.00**

Craftsman's Illustrated Dictionary of Construction Terms

Almost everything you could possibly want to know about any word or technique in construction. Hundreds of up-to-date construction terms, materials, drawings and pictures with detailed, illustrated articles describing equipment and methods. Terms and techniques are explained or illustrated in vivid detail. Use this valuable reference to check spelling, find clear, concise definitions of construction terms used on plans and construction documents, or learn about little-known tools, equipment, tests and methods used in the building industry. It's all here. **416 pages, 8¹/₂ x 11, $36.00**

National Construction Estimator

Current building costs for residential, commercial, and industrial construction. Estimated prices for every common building material. Provides man-hours, recommended crew, and gives the labor cost for installation. Includes a CD-ROM with an electronic version of the book with *National Estimator*, a stand-alone *Windows*™ estimating program, plus an interactive multimedia video that shows how to use the disk to compile construction cost estimates. **560 pages, 8¹/₂ x 11, $47.50. Revised annually**

The Contractor's Legal Kit

Stop "eating" the costs of bad designs, hidden conditions, and job surprises. Set ground rules that assign those costs to the rightful party ahead of time. And it's all in plain English, not "legalese." For less than the cost of an hour with a lawyer you'll learn the exclusions to put in your agreements, why your insurance company may pay for your legal defense, how to avoid liability for injuries to your sub and his employees or damages they cause, how to collect on lawsuits you win, and much more. It also includes a FREE computer disk with contracts and forms you can customize for your own use. **352 pages, 8¹/₂ x 11, $59.95**

Contractor's Year-Round Tax Guide Revised

How to set up and run your construction business to minimize taxes: corporate tax strategy and how to use it to your advantage, and what you should be aware of in contracts with others. Covers tax shelters for builders, write-offs and investments that will reduce your taxes, accounting methods that are best for contractors, and what the I.R.S. allows and what it often questions. **192 pages, 8¹/₂ x 11, $26.50**

Renovating & Restyling Vintage Homes

Any builder can turn a run-down old house into a showcase of perfection — if the customer has unlimited funds to spend. Unfortunately, most customers are on a tight budget. They usually want more improvements than they can afford — and they expect you to deliver. This book shows how to  add economical improvements that can increase the property value by two, five or even ten times the cost of the remodel. Sound impossible? Here you'll find the secrets of a builder who has been putting these techniques to work on Victorian and Craftsman-style houses for twenty years. You'll see what to repair, what to replace and what to leave, so you can remodel or restyle older homes for the least amount of money and the greatest increase in value. **416 pages, 8¹/₂ x 11, $33.50**

National Repair & Remodeling Estimator

The complete pricing guide for dwelling reconstruction costs. Reliable, specific data you can apply on every repair and remodeling job. Up-to-date material costs and labor figures based on thousands of jobs across the country. Provides recommended crew sizes; average production rates; exact material, equipment, and labor costs; a total unit cost and a total price including overhead and profit. Separate listings for high- and low-volume builders, so prices shown are specific for any size business. Estimating tips specific to repair and remodeling work to make your bids complete, realistic, and profitable. Includes a CD-ROM with an electronic version of the book with National Estimator, a stand-alone *Windows*™ estimating program, plus an interactive multi-media video that shows how to use the disk to compile construction cost estimates. **304 pages, 8¹/₂ x 11, $48.50. Revised annually**

National Renovation & Insurance Repair Estimator

Current prices in dollars and cents for hard-to-find items needed on most insurance, repair, remodeling, and renovation jobs. All price items include labor, material, and equipment breakouts, plus special charts that tell you exactly how these costs are calculated. Includes a CD-ROM with an electronic version of the book with *National Estimator*, a stand-alone *Windows*™ estimating program, plus an interactive multimedia video that shows how to use the disk to compile construction cost estimates. **560 pages, 8¹/₂ x 11, $49.50. Revised annually**

Rough Framing Carpentry

If you'd like to make good money working outdoors as a framer, this is the book for you. Here you'll find shortcuts to laying out studs; speed cutting blocks, trimmers and plates by eye; quickly building and blocking rake walls; installing ceiling backing, ceiling joists, and truss joists; cutting and assembling hip trusses and California fills; arches and drop ceilings — all with production line procedures that save you time and help you make more money. Over 100 on-the-job photos of how to do it right and what can go wrong. **304 pages, 8¹/₂ x 11, $26.50**

CD Estimator

If your computer has *Windows*™ and a CD-ROM drive, *CD Estimator* puts at your fingertips 85,000 construction costs for new construction, remodeling, renovation & insurance repair, electrical, plumbing, HVAC and painting. You'll also have the *National Estimator* program — a stand-alone estimating program for *Windows*™ that *Remodeling* magazine called a "computer wiz." Quarterly cost updates are available at no charge on the Internet. To help you create professional-looking estimates, the disk includes over 40 construction estimating and bidding forms in a format that's perfect for nearly any word processing or spreadsheet program for *Windows*™. And to top it off, a 70-minute interactive video teaches you how to use this CD-ROM to estimate construction costs. **CD Estimator is $68.50**

How to Succeed With Your Own Construction Business

Everything you need to start your own construction business: setting up the paperwork, finding the work, advertising, using contracts, dealing with lenders, estimating, scheduling, finding and keeping good employees, keeping the books, and coping with success. If you're considering starting your own construction business, all the knowledge, tips, and blank forms you need are here. **336 pages, 8¹/₂ x 11, $24.25**

Blueprint Reading for the Building Trades

How to read and understand construction documents, blueprints, and schedules. Includes layouts of structural, mechanical, HVAC and electrical drawings. Shows how to interpret sectional views, follow diagrams and schematics, and covers common problems with construction specifications. **192 pages, 5¹/₂ x 8¹/₂, $14.75**

Construction Forms & Contracts

125 forms you can copy and use — or load into your computer (from the FREE disk enclosed). Then you can customize the forms to fit your company, fill them out, and print. Loads into *Word for Windows*, *Lotus 1-2-3*, *WordPerfect*, or *Excel* programs. You'll find forms covering accounting, estimating, fieldwork, contracts, and general office. Each form comes with complete instructions on when to use it and how to fill it out. These forms were designed, tested and used by contractors, and will help keep your business organized, profitable and out of legal, accounting and collection troubles. Includes a 3¹/₂" disk for your PC. For Macintosh disks, add $15. **432 pages, 8¹/₂ x 11, $39.75**

Handbook of Construction Contracting

Volume 1: Everything you need to know to start and run your construction business; the pros and cons of each type of contracting, the records you'll need to keep, and how to read and understand house plans and specs so you find any problems before the actual work begins. All aspects of construction are covered in detail, including all-weather wood foundations, practical math for the job site, and elementary surveying. **416 pages, 8¹/₂ x 11, $28.75**

Volume 2: Everything you need to know to keep your construction business profitable; different methods of estimating, keeping and controlling costs, estimating excavation, concrete, masonry, rough carpentry, roof covering, insulation, doors and windows, exterior finishes, specialty finishes, scheduling work flow, managing workers, advertising and sales, spec building and land development, and selecting the best legal structure for your business. **320 pages, 8¹/₂ x 11, $30.75**

Building Contractor's Exam Preparation Guide

Passing today's contractor's exams can be a major task. This book shows you how to study, how questions are likely to be worded, and the kinds of choices usually given for answers. Includes sample questions from actual state, county, and city examinations, plus a sample exam to practice on. This book isn't a substitute for the study material that your testing board recommends, but it will help prepare you for the types of questions — and their correct answers — that are likely to appear on the actual exam. Knowing how to answer these questions, as well as what to expect from the exam, can greatly increase your chances of passing. **320 pages, 8¹/₂ x 11, $35.00**

Craftsman Book Company
6058 Corte del Cedro
P.O. Box 6500
Carlsbad, CA 92018

☎ **24 hour order line**
1-800-829-8123
Fax (760) 438-0398

Name _____

Company _____

Address _____

City/State/Zip _____
○ This is a residence

Total enclosed _____ (In California add 7.25% tax)

We pay shipping when your check covers your order in full.

In A Hurry?

We accept phone orders charged to your

○ Visa, ○ MasterCard, ○ Discover or ○ American Express

Card# _____

Exp. date _____ Initials _____

Tax Deductible: Treasury regulations make these references tax deductible when used in your work. Save the canceled check or charge card statement as your receipt.

Order online
http://www.craftsman-book.com

10-Day Money Back Guarantee

○ 38.00 Basic Lumber Engineering for Builders
○ 14.75 Blueprint Reading for Building Trades
○ 19.75 Bookkeeping for Builders
○ 35.00 Building Contractor's Exam Preparation Guide
○ 68.50 CD Estimator
○ 39.75 Construction Forms & Contracts with a 3¹/₂" disk. Add $15.00 if you need ○ Macintosh disks.
○ 39.00 Contractor's Guide to Building Code Revised
○ 59.95 Contractor's Legal Kit
○ 22.25 Contractor's Survival Manual
○ 26.50 Contractor's Year-Round Tax Guide Revised
○ 36.00 Craftsman's Illustrated Dictionary of Construction Terms
○ 17.00 Estimating Home Building Costs
○ 28.75 Handbook of Construction Contracting Volume 1
○ 30.75 Handbook of Construction Contracting Volume 2
○ 24.25 How to Succeed w/Your Own Construction Business
○ 34.75 Illustrated Guide to the 1996 *National Electrical Code*
○ 47.50 National Construction Estimator with FREE National Estimator on a CD-ROM
○ 49.50 National Renovation & Insurance Repair Estimator with FREE National Estimator on a CD-ROM.
○ 48.50 National Repair & Remodeling Estimator with FREE National Estimator on a CD-ROM.
○ 33.50 Renovating & Restyling Vintage Homes
○ 26.50 Rough Framing Carpentry
○ 32.50 *Quicken* for Contractors
○ FREE Full Color Catalog

Prices subject to change without notice

QUICKEN AND QUICKBOOKS HELP!

ONLINE ACCOUNTING
can provide:

- ☑ Online analysis
  (see our website @ www.onlineaccounting.com)

- ☑ Telephone support

- ☑ Onsite support

- ☑ Seminars

LET THE QUICKEN CONSTRUCTION
ACCOUNTING PROS WORK WITH YOU TO:

- ☑ Teach you to read and understand your financial job reports

- ☑ Analyze Quicken datafile

- ☑ Identify problem areas

- ☑ Review setup

(650) 327-2765   www.onlineaccounting.com

GC/WORKS
SOFTWARE FOR THE SMART BUILDER

Designed specifically for the small to mid size construction company

Platinum Edition	$750
Standard Edition	$650
Basic Edition	$475
Lite Edition	$375
Developer Edition	$575
Subcontractor Edition	$475

www.synapsesoftware.com

SYNAPSE
SOFTWARE INC.

* Estimating
* Job Costing
* Accounting
* Scheduling
* Purchase Orders
* Change Orders
* Subcontracts
* Options & Extras
* Payroll & Taxes

Powerful
Simple & More
Windows & Mac

Uses Quicken or
QuickBooks Pro
& ClarisWorks

30 Day Money
Back Guarantee

CALL TODAY
800-420-2521

YES—I want to find out more about the hottest
new software tools for the construction industry.
Please rush me all of the details on GC/Works .

Name _____

Company _____

Street _____

City-St-Zip _____

Phone _____   Fax _____

Mail This Card Today
For a Free Full Color Catalog

Over 100 books, audios and estimating software packages at your fingertips with information that can save you time and money. Here you'll find information on carpentry, contracting, estimating, remodeling, electrical work, and plumbing.

All items come with an unconditional 10-day money-back guarantee.
If they don't save you money, mail them back for a full refund.

Name _____

Company _____

Address _____

City/State/Zip _____

Craftsman Book Company / 6058 Corte del Cedro / P.O. Box 6500 / Carlsbad, CA 92018

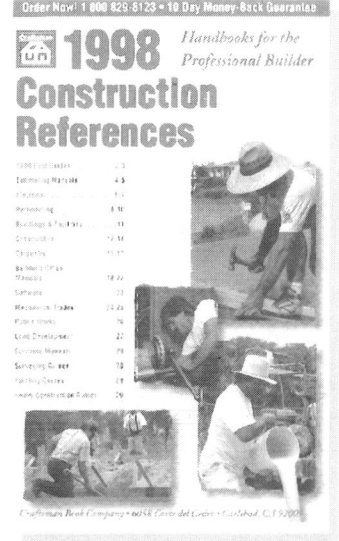

Order Now! 1 800 829-8123 • 10 Day Money-Back Guarantee

1998
**Construction
References**

*Handbooks for the
Professional Builder*

CAN HELP YOU WITH YOUR
CONSTRUCTION ACCOUNTING NEEDS.

CALL US

(650) 327-2765

VISIT OUR WEBSITE

www.onlineaccounting.com

SYNAPSE
SOFTWARE INC
1171 Titus Avenue
Rochester, NY 14617